W9-CKF-812

CORPORATE
GIANTS

Other books by Robert Darden and P. J. Richardson

The Way of an Eagle
Wheels of Thunder

CORPORATE GIANTS

GIANTS

Personal Stories of Faith and Finance

Robert Darden
and P. J. Richardson

Fleming H. Revell
A Division of Baker Book House Co
Grand Rapids, Michigan 49516

Published by Fleming H. Revell
a division of Baker Book House Company
P.O. Box 6287, Grand Rapids, MI 49516-6287

Printed in the United States of America

Library of Congress Cataloging-in-Publication Data

Darden, Bob, 1954–
    Corporate giants : personal stories of faith and finance / Robert Darden and P. J. Richardson.
        p.   cm.
    Includes bibliographical references.
    ISBN 0-8007-1787-2 (cloth)
    1. Businessmen—United Sates—Religious life. 2. Business—Religious aspects—Christianity. I. Richardson, P. J. II. Title
    BV4596.B8 D37 2002
    261.8′5′092273—dc21
                                  2002004899

For current information about all releases from Baker Book House, visit our web site:

http://www.bakerbooks.com.

To Daniel Barkley
May your landings always equal your take-offs.
Robert Darden

To my father, Bill Richardson,
and
my granddaughter, Ashlee Jordan Richardson
P. J. Richardson

Contents

7

Foreword

In the world of business, it's not always easy to see the work of God. Especially in times of economic turmoil or in industries prone to volatility, the dynamics of decision making at the highest levels don't always reflect the Christian values so many of us espouse. In other words, the bottom-line business ethic is not always compatible with "Do unto others . . ." or other biblical teachings. It is often difficult to walk your faith in the marketplace.

It has been said that the next great faith movement in our country is going to be *demonstration*. If Christianity is to have any real meaning in the twenty-first century, besides an eternal life insurance policy, Christians ought to think and behave differently. They ought to be role models for effective leadership. That's why I find it so refreshing that the authors of *Corporate Giants* have chosen business leaders for their third book, chronicling how faith has impacted the lives of some outstanding Christians.

In their first two books, *The Way of an Eagle* and *Wheels of Thunder*, the authors interviewed prominent sports figures— golfers and race car drivers—about the role their faith has played in their careers and lives. Now, in this book, the same questions are put to CEOs and presidents of oil companies, sports franchises, retail businesses, hospitals, and to other major players in the business world. Was your faith always an important part of your life? How would you characterize your relationship with God? How has your faith shaped your career or your business philosophy?

The answers that are given are both enlightening and comforting. These business leaders share with readers their backgrounds, their beliefs, and their philosophies of work and life. They talk about how their faith drives them to succeed not only on a business level but, more important, on a human level every day.

These stories are an inspiration to all of us who toil in the vineyards of faith as well as the boardrooms of business. If you are wondering how to walk your faith in the marketplace, *Corporate Giants* should be a very helpful resource.

Ken Blanchard, coauthor of *The One Minute Manager*,
cofounder, The Center for *FaithWalk* Leadership

Acknowledgments

We would like to thank the following people and organizations for their invaluable input during the preparation of *Corporate Giants:*

Gil Stricklin, Marketplace Ministries

Paul Lantz, Christian Business Men's Committee

Charlie "Tremendous" Jones, Executive Books

Petra Carey, Jerry Colangelo, Meg Cullar, Mary Darden, John Martin, Norm Miller, Tom Newsom, Bill Petty, and Cindy Brinker Simmons

Joan Willoughby for her tireless assistance and patience as the deadline drew near

Carol Hobbs for a book's worth of first-rate transcriptions

Introduction

Joy is the serious business of Heaven.

C. S. Lewis

Do business and religion have anything in common? There is more than you might think. We believe that, instead of being mutually exclusive, the business world and the Christian universe have begun to overlap, to merge, to incorporate. And it hasn't been a hostile takeover.

Our goal with *Corporate Giants* was to interview some of the most successful, most visible Christian business leaders in the United States and ask them to talk about how their faith has influenced their path in life. Each business titan talked candidly about his life and career, and many offered a salient bit of business advice or a tip for budding entrepreneurs and seasoned professionals alike.

We quickly discovered that what excited each interviewee most was not talking about either the bottom line or the top dollar. Instead, it was the chance to share his personal religious testimony, to tell how God had made, and continues to make, a powerful difference in his life.

For these corporate leaders, faith and finance are inseparable. In fact, for a significant number of these giants, participating in this project was a meaningful opportunity to share their testimony with a larger national audience than they had previously experienced. That fulfills our mission as well, and hopefully will offer inspiration to other men and women in the

13

business world that their faith is not only compatible with their profession, it can enhance it.

Is the testimony here relevant? It certainly is. Consider the following facts:

> More than 80 percent of all Americans call themselves "religious."
>
> More than 39 percent of all Americans say they are born-again Christians.
>
> Evangelicals or born-again Christians comprise 43 percent of all U.S. businessmen.
>
> Among leaders of the nation's top one hundred businesses, 65 percent attend church or synagogue regularly.

It's that last little tidbit of information that first caught our eye. In fact, in a recent poll of American elites, sociologists Stanley Rothman and Robert Lerner discovered that—next to military officers—more people in business attend church every week than people in any other profession. Only 13 percent of people in business say they *never* attend church. There are no atheists in foxholes, and apparently there aren't many in corporate boardrooms either!

This, then, was our wish in writing *Corporate Giants:* to find and share the stories of people who found the elusive key to success in the business world, *and* joy in their private lives, by setting out daily to do "the business of heaven."

Joel T. Allison

**President and CEO
Baylor Health Care System**

Founded as a Christian ministry of healing, Baylor Health Care System exists to serve all people through exemplary health care, education, research, and community service.

Baylor Health Care System Mission

Before assuming his current position at Baylor, Joel T. Allison served as president of Methodist Medical Center in St. Joseph, Missouri, CEO of a public hospital in Amarillo, Texas, and president and CEO of Driscoll Children's Hospital in Corpus Christi.

Today he oversees a chain of fourteen owned, leased, or affiliated hospitals that includes 12,800 employees and 2,871 physicians and that saw 85,768 admissions (including 11,390 babies born) in the year 2000. Allison administers Baylor's 1.5 billion dollars in total assets, 6 million dollars in research funds (including a whopping 1 million from the National Institutes of Health alone) and a 320-million-dollar endowment.

Allison's lengthy job title includes operations, development and implementation of system objectives and strategies, and a redesign of the present system into an integrated health-care delivery system. If you really want to see his eyes light up, however, mention the Health Careers Foundation (HCF), an organization that raises funds for students pursuing careers in allied health care. He's the board chair-

15

man of the HCF too, in addition to serving on a fistful of local and state charitable, religious, and professional boards.

Allison explains his calling to health-care administration:

My mother was a very strong Christian. My father might attend church once a year, on Easter. But my mother had a tremendous faith. I was eight years old when I made my profession of faith.

I made a dedication of my life to the ministry in high school. I felt that the Lord was calling me into some type of ministry, and I was actually licensed by my home church as a minister when I was a senior in high school. I went to Baylor University because I felt the Lord was leading me into the ministry. I had a double major in religion and journalism. I always felt that I was being called to some type of service for the Lord, but I wasn't sure whether it was in the pulpit, journalism, or some other endeavor.

My senior year in college, I felt the call to go into health-care administration.

It must have been nice to have had that clear a call that early.

Truly it was the Lord's will. It was his calling and, as I look back on it, he opened doors for me in the ministry of health care that I'd never really envisioned when I was younger. I truly consider what I do today a calling.

How did you know this was the right thing for you?

I was a senior when my wife and I were married. My wife's brother is a physician. At that time he was doing his residency in John Peter Smith Hospital in Fort Worth. We would go up to Fort Worth on weekends to visit with him, and I would follow him on his rounds.

That year I took a journalism course and was required to do a photo essay. I did my essay on my brother-in-law's residency. While working on this project, I began to better understand the

16

hospital environment and gained an appreciation for the challenges and excitement of health care.

One day my brother-in-law and his wife decided to go look at a future practice site in Uvalde, a small town in South Texas. They called us and said, "Would you like to go with us to Uvalde and spend the day?"

I said, "Sure."

We went to Uvalde and met the physicians at the medical clinic my brother-in-law was considering joining. They gave us a tour of the city, the clinic, and then the hospital. While at the hospital, we went by the administrator's office. We were told, "This is our new administrator's office. He is a young man who is looking at going into the ministry. We talked to him about coming here to serve as our administrator and at the same time going to Trinity University to get his graduate degree in health-care administration."

Literally, lights came on and the bells went off. I thought, *I never connected that aspect of hospital and serving.* My wife and I talked about that all the way back home to Waco. I picked up the phone, called Alton Pearson, who was head of the local Baptist hospital, and said, "Tell me about the job you have. Tell me about the ministry side. How do you feel about it?"

Of course, Mr. Pearson is very much a believer that hospital administration is a calling and that it was a ministry for him. He told me, "It's the greatest job in the world."

I told my wife, "I'm going to apply to Trinity. It's the only place I'm going to apply. If it's the Lord's will, then it will happen." I was accepted and, as they say, the rest is history.

Now, as you look back at it, are you happy with the direction your life took at that point?

I loved the hospital environment. It was twenty-four hours a day, seven days a week, but I knew I didn't want to be a clinician. However, the ability to involve business and the ministry and to be a part of a faith-based organization that is mission-driven was just about perfect. Health care in the not-for-profit world is about being mission-driven. I found it to be a fabulous opportunity and a real blessing. I can wholeheartedly say that I've thoroughly enjoyed it. And I feel as though I've been led by God throughout my entire career by trying to follow his will for my life.

You've worked at various hospitals and a number of them are religious oriented. Was that by choice?

Yes. After I went to graduate school and did my on-campus studies, I had to do a residency in a hospital to complete my degree. Because I felt called to this work, I wanted to be with a faith-based organization, preferably Baptist, both because I was Baptist and because of the Christian leaders heading those organizations. I looked at two in particular—Baylor University Medical Center in Dallas, with Boone Powell Sr., and Hendrick Medical Center in Abilene, with Boone Powell Jr. I was feeling very much led by the Lord. I went to Abilene and did my residency, where Boone Powell Jr. served as my preceptor and my mentor. I worked with him until he came to Dallas to be the chief executive officer of Baylor in 1993.

You are one of the few people who work in an organization that makes no bones about the fact that Christian ideals underline what you do.

I think it's very positive. It's something that I feel very strongly about. Our mission statement says that we were founded as a Christian ministry of healing. But our founding statement in 1903, by Dr. George W. Truett, also says that we are to be a place where people "of all faiths and those of none may come with equal confidence."

How does Baylor's mission statement play itself out in the real world?

What I've found, and what I think people appreciate and, I hope, value is the fact that we *are* a faith-based organization and that we *do* have standards and values that will be inherent in all of our dealings, in all of our business dealings and relationships.

It's about *how* we do business. Our business values include integrity, servanthood, quality, innovation, and stewardship, but we also strive to adhere to them in *all* of our relationships—with physicians, patients, vendors, and the community.

In short, I think it indicates to people how we will treat patients and patients' families, how we will treat each other, our employees, and our physician partners. And I think it helps set the tone so that there is no question of how we will perform and what's expected of those who become a part of our organization.

You don't have to be Baptist to be a part of Baylor either. Dr. George W. Truett's statement is as true today as it was in 1903.

How do you go about establishing accountability to that mission on a daily basis?

We create an environment at Baylor that is about taking care of patients in a manner that respects our mission. We communicate our mission and values. This makes people feel we have an environment where they can come and carry out their calling, which is to be of service to people.

Calling yourself a Christian institution holds you up to a heightened scrutiny.

In my association with Baylor, I don't think it has been in any way negative. I think people *do* hold us to a higher standard because of our mission and the commitment to doing the right thing. I think that people *do* look at us differently.

While we have people who are from all different faiths, our mission and values provide a setting where all people can find a way to do the right thing regardless of their beliefs.

How does a family in need, coming in through the doors, know that this is an operation that's founded on Christian principles and is continuing to be run by Christians?

We treat everyone with respect and dignity. I attribute this to our people. It's the way they would treat their own families.

We have employees and physicians from all faiths here and they are valued.

So being from a particular denomination is not a criterion for employment?

It is not a criterion. We're very respectful of all faiths; we want to care for all people—that's part of our mission statement—and do it in an environment where it's okay to be a Christian, where it's okay to have a sense of calling, where it's okay to have a sense of mission about caring for others. Why? Because I think that's part of the differentiation between our institution and others that do not espouse the same mission. Health care is a ministry, serving our fellow human beings and caring for them with safe, quality, compassionate care.

William Bolthouse, who has the largest carrot and lettuce farms in the world in California, wakes up every morning and says, "This is just the best job in the world, because farming and ministry, feeding people and ministry, are the same thing." Sounds like you are coming from the same place.

Exactly! Exactly! I love what I do. There is a passion about it because I have a sense of mission that in some way I'm making a contribution to helping someone. People will care or be cared for and maybe otherwise that would not have happened if it weren't for Baylor.

I am one of a group of twelve thousand employees, plus two thousand physicians, who want to make that contribution. I believe it goes back to our value of servanthood. I love what I do because I serve my fellow human beings.

Jesus did seem to spend a lot of time feeding people and healing people, didn't he?

Yes, he did. It truly is a ministry of healing. We have physicians who pray with our patients. We have a strong chaplaincy program so that if any patient or family member wants the services of a chaplain, they are available.

What advice would you give to a young person thinking about going into some form of direct health care or, like you, overseeing people who give direct health care?

I would ask them, "What is it you have a passion about? What is it that you want to do? What do you feel your calling is, relative to your interests? What are your desires, and what do you feel so strongly about that you would want to do it every day, almost twenty-four hours a day?"

When I talk to young people considering health care, I tell them to be sure they choose a career that is something they enjoy, that it is something they feel follows the will of the Lord. They should be excited and believe they are truly making a contribution. I urge them to choose a job about which they can have positive feelings. I challenge them to know what health care is truly all about. If young people choose health care with all of that in mind, then at the end of the day, regardless of their specific job, they will know they have made a contribution and they truly will have been of service to others. What a wonderful feeling!

James H. Amos Jr.

President and CEO
Mail Boxes Etc.

Alex, catching a motion to his left, turned to see the NVA sweeping over what had been the gun positions for the Gunny and Boston.

So he stood there, this big man, praying, as the soldiers of the 814th and the 813th North Vietnamese Regiments swarmed over the mountaintop of Tam Boi. They took one prisoner alive, a big muscular Marine who was on his knees by the time they reached him. They mistook his position for one of surrender and weakness when, in truth, it was one of victory and faith.

From *The Memorial: A Novel
of the Vietnam War* by James Amos

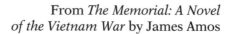

Forget building one of the fastest-growing new corporations in the Free World. That's easy. Dodging bullets in Vietnam—now *that's* hard.

In a few short years, Mail Boxes Etc. has become the world's largest franchisor of postal/shipping, business, and communications services. The distinctive MBE logo is now found in more than 80 countries on more than 4,400 franchise centers located in such diverse sites as college campuses, convention centers, and supermarkets. And the man who has been in charge during MBE's most explosive growth is decorated (12 medals from 2 tours) Marine vet James H. Amos Jr.

Amos, who joined MBE in September 1996, is also the author of two books, *Focus or Failure: America at the Crossroads* and *The*

Memorial: A Novel of the Vietnam War (chosen by the American Library Association as "One of the Best Books of the Year" in 1990 and recently rereleased). The University of Missouri honored Amos as the university's 1998 scholar-in-residence.

Early in 2001 overnight express mail giant UPS purchased Mail Boxes Etc. James Amos remains its president and CEO.

MBE's core values are caring, honesty, fairness, integrity, trust, respect, commitment, and accountability. Although Amos didn't grow up in a Christian home, he learned these values at an early age.

When I was growing up, my folks didn't attend church on a regular basis. When my dad was a boy, I understand, my grandmother used to take him to church frequently. Dad lost both his parents at about fourteen and, perhaps in a rebellious way, just didn't go back into the church. When I left for college, interestingly enough, both of my parents became reinvolved in the church. My dad became a deacon, even leading a men's choir. Both of my parents are very involved today. My mom leads a women's Bible study for the Methodist ladies in south Florida.

But I can't say that I really came from a religious background. I do remember in grade school walking to a Presbyterian summer Bible school class, or vacation Bible school, that one of the neighborhood kids invited me to in Florissant, Missouri. It seemed to have a distinct impact on me, as I recall.

Was there an incident that caused you to come back to the church?

I think watching what was going on with my parents, even though I never moved back home after I went away to college, was important. But frankly, the most significant event that really caused me to turn to God was my Vietnam experience. I graduated from college during the Tet Offensive of 1968. I went straight to Vietnam after I graduated the basic school as a Marine second lieutenant. I carried a little Gideon Bible my dad had given me that I believe he had carried with him in World War II. One particularly vivid experience that took place in the Ashau Valley speaks to the old saw that there are no

23

atheists in foxholes. I tried to explain that in my book *The Memorial.*

Where did you go after your second tour in Vietnam?

I stayed in the Marine Corps for eight more years. I came back to Quantico, Virginia, where I was an instructor at officer's candidate school. While I was at Quantico, I had a specific moment where I asked the Lord to come into my heart. I made a decision sometime after that to leave the Corps, which was the most difficult decision—up to that point—of my life. I went into franchising in 1973 after resigning my commission, and that's really where I've been ever since.

What specifically led you to that moment of decision?

I can go all the way back to that summer vacation Bible school in grade school. As I look back, there was always a pull on my life; spiritual things were attractive for some reason. That is not to say that they were a large part of my life until that moment in the Ashau Valley where I pulled my helmet over my head, lay face down in the mud, and thought I was going to die. I made some promises at that moment—as I'm sure you've heard over and over many times—"God, if you'll just get me out of here, I'll be the right kind of person."

In unexplainable grace, God did allow me to come back. However, I learned that it's one thing to say something like that in the intensity of combat; it's another thing to live it in your life. I really don't think that I dedicated my life at all to the Lord until that moment in 1973, at officer's candidate school, where I was trying to make the decision about staying in the Corps or getting out. In fact every time I have felt committed to the Lord in my life, I have found out later that I only *thought* I was committed. Clearly this journey of growth is lifelong.

Life is a journey, as John Powell says in his extensive writings. It's a process of becoming. I'm very grateful for that journey, and I'm grateful that I've been allowed to live long enough to understand what I now understand. My prayers today are to grow in the Lord, to become closer to the Lord, to do the right thing, to obey, and to understand the joy that comes from obedience in that relationship.

What has being a Christian meant to you as a businessman?

My relationship with Christ is the defining relationship of my life. I'd love to be able to say I've always had that priority in life, but that's not the case. I'd like to say that I've always done the right thing, and that's also not the case. What I understand today is that I am a sinner saved by grace and forgiven every day for the flaws and weaknesses that I possess. We are all flawed and wounded and in need of forgiveness.

What that means to me as I reflect on the position I'm in today as president and CEO of a 1.5-billion-dollar company is that my position, and everything else, is a gift. I know I'm here by God's will; I know it's not by anything that I've done or not done. Everything is a gift that requires a great deal of gratitude and responsibility.

Charlie "Tremendous" Jones, the motivational speaker and author, once said to me, "You know, Jim, if you're fortunate enough in life to have a lot of things, everything you have ought to be another reason to be more humble and more grateful. There should be a greater sense of indebtedness because everything is a gift." I certainly feel that way about my life, my position, and the things that I do. It's not possible to separate these things. The values we embrace are driven by the window that we look through. That perspective makes me who I am as a person and who I am as a leader. Consequently it impacts the culture of every organization that I have been privileged to lead. All organizations are defined by dominant values embraced on a day-to-day basis. Leaders who know who they are, who know where they stand, and who understand themselves to some degree, those are the leaders that drive culture. My faith impacts every area of my life. For me, my faith is the needle on the compass or the anchor in the storm. It is central to everything.

25

Talk about *The Memorial* and *Focus or Failure: America at the Crossroads*.

I wrote *The Memorial* about ten years after Vietnam, and it took six years to complete. It was a project of personal ablution, where I was reflecting on things that happened there. I never intended to publish it.

On the other hand, *Focus or Failure* is a compilation of speeches that I've given through the years on a variety of occasions. That book speaks to the dominant set of values or leadership principles that we were just talking about.

Is it a religious book?

No, it's not, not any more than the terms *family* or *love* are religious terms. I think it reflects who I am as a faith-based individual. I would not define it as a religious book. It's a statement of belief, a statement of faith, and a reflection on a set of transformational or core values that I believe are essential to life and business.

Someone once said that if you took all the messages of salvation out of the Bible, what remains would still be a pretty good business primer.

I think that's absolutely correct. In business we depend a great deal on operating manuals. But the Bible speaks to relationships. I find very little about P&Ls, operating manuals, net present values, and organizational charts in the Bible. But I do find a great deal about people, relationships, leaders, and followers. One of the primary paradigm shifts of this new millennium may well be that business is more about relationships and people and not necessarily about P&Ls, spreadsheets, or organizational charts. Ultimately God creates what is bought and sold and defines the relationships between the buyer and seller. It seems to me our relationship with him is the defining issue.

It's just like love. We are often defined by the people who choose to love us and the people that choose not to love us. Therefore, we're also defined by our choice to either love God or not. We cannot escape the result.

26

Has there been a verse or a passage that has been particularly helpful or instructive or comforting to you as you've walked this part of your life?

I hesitate to go down that path because sometimes people look for some kind of magic in arbitrary verses. However, the Lord's Prayer is very important to me. I try to say that prayer every day. The Twenty-third Psalm also is very important to me. When I am signing one of my books, I will often quote Philippians 4:8: "Whatever is true, whatever is noble, whatever is right, whatever is pure, whatever is lovely, whatever is admirable—if anything is excellent or praiseworthy—think about such things." That is some of the best advice that could ever be given to anyone. Truly our dominant thought patterns and where we choose to focus in life are our destiny. As Spurgeon said, "Within the Bible are words that burn and thoughts that breathe."

What advice would you have for somebody thinking about entering a career in business?

There is a need to define success. In the eyes of some folks, perhaps they think I have enjoyed success because of my position, earnings, or power to make decisions. I don't define success that way. I didn't get here by myself. I'm very grateful for everything, every blessing. My daily journaling reflects that—and my relationship to the Lord. I pray that's where my heart stays.

Executive leaders have two questions to constantly ponder. One is, Who are we? And the second one is, Where are we going—today, tomorrow, and in the future? Those two primary questions never change.

Harry Emerson Fosdick said once that no steam or gas engine can drive anything until it's confined. Or there's no life that ever grows until it's focused or until it's dedicated or until it's disciplined. That is also true about faith and values. It's about deciding who we are, what we represent, what's going to drive our decision making, what drives what we can do and what we can't do. That kind of focus defines the leader, and it defines the organization he leads.

Tied very closely is the only sustainable edge a person has in life or business—his or her character and reputation. Other people can stain your reputation, and I can promise you, if one aspires to any kind of leadership role, it's inevitable. But only the individual himself can stain his character. That's why it's so important to understand we're flawed, to understand that we're weak. Be grateful for forgiveness, pray for faith, and grow in the reflection on the Lord.

Consequently I'd say it's important to realize that in a leadership role, you're no longer your own person. You have a very deep responsibility to those that choose to follow you not to be selfish. You are a role model, whether or not you choose to accept that responsibility.

Bill Bailey

CEO
The Bailey Group

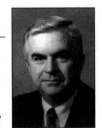

If you say you're going to do something, do it. And if you can't do it, walk up and say, "I can't do it." Don't look for a way out. I think that has given my operating philosophy more strength than any one thing.

Bill Bailey

Bill H. Bailey has enjoyed success in a dizzying array of business ventures, including gasoline distribution, oil, microwave towers in Pakistan, pay phones, and—for now—automated teller machines.

In a few short years, the Bailey Group (cofounded with daughter Beth Bailey Alexander) has become a significant player in the ATM business, establishing thousands of outlets, primarily in the Southwest and West. As with his previous venture—Cherokee Communications—the hallmark of Bailey's new franchised ATM company—the Money Market—has been his single-minded attention to detail.

At a time when others are considering well-deserved retirement, this classic entrepreneur is still going strong: "I've taught Sunday school at different intervals," he says. "I was chairman of the board and handled the finance committee. I guess I've done a little bit of everything in the church."

And don't expect Bill Bailey to slow down anytime soon. His one-hundred-year-old grandfather is still active, visiting friends and doing his own household chores!

Bill talks about his early life in the church:

My beginning years were spent in the country, in a little place called College Mound, just out of Terrell, Texas. My whole existence was in and around a little Methodist church that is still there and is still quite active. I took my naps on a pillow in the front pew as a little kid. I grew up working on a farm with all of those wonderful people.

What came out of all that experience were the relationships I made with people. I learned to network with the people in the church. They depend on you and you depend on them. When you're sick, they come to you. When they're sick, you go to them. When you're hungry, they bring food. It's one of those sharing experiences. I think that setting gave me the base that has ridden with me for all these years. It's a base that goes into the earliest jobs I held.

So it's all about people.

When I got out of high school, I could have been helped to go to college. I looked at the job I had. I could either do that or I could go to college. The one thing that came running through to me was that I enjoyed dealing with people. And I didn't think that any college in the world would give me the ability to deal with people on a daily basis. That's something you just have to learn by doing.

In my upbringing, when we'd go bale hay for the neighbor, he'd then come over and help us bale hay. We'd do the thrashing over at his place, and then he'd come over and do ours. It taught me a work ethic and a people ethic. So I made the decision not to go to college but to stay with the William Cameron Company, a building company, and deal with people. I think that thread has probably run through my forty-odd years of being in business. It's a daily exercise in practicing a faith or a belief. It helps you build an employee base; it helps you build a base of friends.

What else did those friends in that little country church teach you?

One of the things I got out of my early years was if you say you're going to do something, *do it*. And if you can't do it, walk up and say, "I can't do it." Don't look for a way out. I think that has given my operating philosophy more strength than any one thing. People do business with me because, "If Bill says he'll do it, put it in the bank." I call that a Christian faith. I think I got it there. I didn't pick it up in a book somewhere; I didn't read it anywhere. I practiced it, and it works.

It's the same thing we used to do when I was in high school or back in the late '30s and early '40s when things were so tough. We had a two-acre garden. I guess we fed half of Terrell or half of Kaufman. People were hungry. It made you feel good.

I think that still goes into what I do and what I *try* to do every day in my business. For instance, take firing people. I look at firing people as a step toward educating these people. I try to sit them down and make them feel good about being fired.

How do you do that?

You have to spend some time telling them what they did well as well as spend some time telling them what they did wrong. If you show them what they did wrong, they have the chance to correct it in the future or they'll be sitting in the same chair again. I bring them in and counsel with them. And if they just won't do it, then I have to sit them down and explain to them what's going on. But I try never to let somebody go away as an enemy. I don't want anybody thinking that I've taken advantage of them or that I've used them. I've given them every chance in the world to be a long-term employee and to be a part of a good, ongoing operation.

When I've had people working for me that have had major health problems or major family problems, I try to be sensitive to that. It's a sharing experience. I'm just thrilled that I'm able, sometimes, to help a little bit.

You have a strong belief system.

Back in '85 I had a terrible physical problem. I had six months of surgeries. It never occurred to me that everything wasn't

31

going to be all right. It just never bothered me. I had a lot of surgery, a lot of pain, but it just never occurred to me that I wasn't going to recover and get back in the middle of things. When I got back, the company was overdrawn in the bank three million dollars. I'd gone from 210 pounds to 155 pounds. I couldn't drive a car. Of course, people were saying, "What you need to do is take bankruptcy."

I said, "That isn't in my vocabulary. I'm not going to do that. I don't want to do that."

So I got thirty-odd bankers and businesspeople in a room and laid out a plan. I said, "I hope none of you will jump ship on me. Just give me a chance."

And on Christmas Eve of that year, the twenty-fourth of December of '85, at 4:00 in the afternoon, I closed the last deal that cleared the three million dollars. That's from June until December. And it never occurred to me that it wouldn't work. I don't think that there is any way in the world that I could have felt that way—*and* communicated to everyone what I was going to do—unless I had some good strong beliefs and foundation.

You've taken some pretty good risks through the years as you've started new companies and sold companies. How much have you felt the hand of God in what you do in business? Or do you separate the two?

No, no. You can't separate the positive things that happened to you. You can't take credit for any of that. I don't take credit for it. I never have and don't want to start tomorrow. I think that God has blessed all of us in millions of different ways.

It's like the story about the guy sitting on the roof of his house during a flood. A boat came by but he wouldn't get on the boat. "God will save me," he said. The second boat came by, but he didn't get on that boat either. "God will save me," he said. Finally, the water got up so high he drowned. The guy wound up at the Pearly Gates. He said, "God, why didn't you help me?" God said, "Well, I sent two boats by."

That's kind of the way it is with us. We get a lot of opportunities, but we don't always take advantage of them. I've been blessed so many times. I'm not a vocal, real visible Christian kind of fellow. I won't quote you Scripture. But I do know that as I grew up from a one year old to today, I've never gotten away from him. I've never let something jerk me out into left field.

How have you experienced God's presence in your life?

One Saturday night years ago, as a young kid of maybe fifteen, I was sitting on the square in Kaufman, Texas. One of my best friends had just gotten in the car and he wanted to go to Dallas to see the wrestling matches. It was 9:30. I always told mom what time I was going to be home. That was a cardinal rule—and you were there at that time. Bubba said, "Come on, let's go."

I said, "No, I told mom I'd be home at 10:00."

He said, "Oh, my gosh!" He went on to Dallas with a couple of other boys. They had a wreck coming back that killed two of them.

You say, "What caused you to do that?" It was the love of my mother and father, the love they had shown me, the caring comfort they've shown me. Be it religious, be it what—I don't know. But it's an atmosphere and an attitude, and I try to instill that in my own kids and I try to do the same thing with my people.

Someone might come walking in and say, "We've got a deal down in Bryan where we owe eight hundred dollars in commissions, but we're going to have to pull the machine. We can just dodge the commission."

I say, "No. You owe the eight hundred dollars, don't you?"

"Yes."

"Pay it!"

You don't want those people to think that you're a chiseler. That's not how we conduct our business. I don't want to look back and start trying to separate that kind of stuff from the way I do business. I want a heads-up business, I want an honest business, and I want a good reputation.

It's like I've told so many of my people, the day they put you in the box and the day people are looking down on you for the last time, they need to be able to say, "He was a great person.

He had an excellent reputation. I never knew him to do bad things." You can't put money in that box—you can't put *anything* in that box—but that reputation. They can put that word on you and it'll go with you.

Is there a Bible verse that's particularly meaningful to you?

I would guess it's just the plain old simple one: "Do unto others as you would have them do unto you." I don't know how you could get any more direct than that. There are a whole bunch of them that have strong meanings, of course, but in dealing with people—99.9 percent of my time is dealing with people—that's number one. I tell my folks, "Let me tell you what, guys. Our business starts on the street with our customer. I don't care whether the machine makes money or not. You make sure that our customer loves us and our machine will make money. You'll make money if you take care of your people."

For a young person who's thinking about going into business, what kind of advice would you have?

I bump into some of these kids and I tell them there are two or three things that you must understand are going to happen. Number one, your rewards are going to be very, very low. But be prepared to accept them at whatever level they come at you. Number two, the workload is going to be huge. Because the more you put in it, the more is going to come out. The third is always, always be fair with every deal you make. Be fair and up-front about it. Don't try to make a quick buck off of anybody. Be methodical in your approach but understand that the real reward you're going to get out of it may very well be—for the first few years or the first few months—only the fact that you're an entrepreneur and you're in business for yourself. You can look across to the other pasture and some old boy is making fifty thousand dollars a year and you're sitting over here making ten thousand. Make up your mind. Do you want to pay the price to be in business for yourself and be your own boss? Make that decision up front. But don't think that you're going to go in business for yourself and hit a home run from day one. It doesn't work that way. That's kind of the way I try to talk to them.

How does that advice go over with people?

It turns a lot of kids off. I tell some others, "You may be best served to work for someone else and learn more about your trade." If money is critical to you, then you probably need to say, "I'll work for whatever period of time. I'll lay aside a little bit of money along the way, so that when I do go in business for myself, I'm not going cold turkey."

I've made a plan. I think it has worked at times. You've got a lot of kids that feel like they're a lot smarter than you are. I tell them, "I've got a Ph.D. in making mistakes. I don't like to see people make the same mistake I've made."

Several years ago, I met Bill McRae, who is a very good friend of mine now. He came to town and brought with him a little money and a lot of energy. He bought the Ford dealership and did well. One day I was driving down the street and I saw him standing out in front of five rental houses. At the time, I didn't even know the guy. But I went out to the Ford place the next day and met him for the first time. I said, "Bill, I saw you at those rental houses over there."

He said, "Yes, I'm going to buy them."

I said, "Are you going to remodel them?"

He said, "Yes, I'm going to use so and so."

I took a chance. I said, "Bill, don't do it."

He said, "Why?"

I said, "The guy that you're going to use has a terrible reputation. It'll cost you dearly to go with him. Don't take a chance on him." And I left.

He didn't do the deal. Every once in a while, he'll come by and say, "Thank you." I didn't know him, but I wasn't going to let him get hurt. I didn't owe him anything, but I wasn't going to let him get hurt. And I'd be the same way to you or anybody.

If it will work, I'll tell you what to do. If it won't work, I'll tell you that too.

I think that's that sharing thing that goes back to my beginnings, to that little town with the little church, to that little nest of real fine Christian people.

By the way, that little church is still there. The second and third generations of the people I knew still go there. We still go up there once a year to Decoration Day at the cemetery. It's got two or three generations of my family buried there. My great grandmother is there. My grandfather and grandmother are buried there as well. On Decoration Day, we decorate the graves, cut the grass, have a picnic on the grounds, and talk about how it was and how we hope it will be. We raise a little money and keep the church going. The little church right now is just bursting at the seams. And that makes me feel awfully good.

John F. Baugh

**Founder and Senior Chairman
of the Board
SYSCO Corporation**

*Many speak of John Baugh with reverence, say-
ing this enterprise succeeded largely due to his
integrity, intelligence, and dogged perseverance, as
well as the example he set of fairness to suppliers,
customers, and employees.*

*We salute a gentleman who set the standard for
SYSCO, raised it higher and continues to uphold it
in every facet of life.*

From a tribute to John F. Baugh in 1998

It began in a single room with three employees—only one of whom
was paid. ("We started out with no money, no capital and no mer-
chandise.") But in the days following World War II, John F. Baugh had
an idea: Working families are going to want to eat out more.

Today SYSCO (Systems and Services Company) is the world's
largest food service distributor. Founder John F. Baugh—who was *not*
the paid employee—now presides over an empire that includes:

- nearly 50,000 employees
- service to 356,000 restaurants, schools, hotels, and health-care
  institutions
- 122 facilities throughout North America
- more than 275,000 products
- sales last year in excess of 20 billion dollars

In 1976 Baugh was the first person inducted into the Institutional Food Services in America Hall of Fame. His extraordinary resume includes the Texas Business Hall of Fame, the Bank of Houston (director), Houston Baptist University (founding trustee), Baylor University (regent emeritus), and twenty-five years with the Baptist Foundation of Texas (including a stint as chairman).

But you'd never know that SYSCO was one of America's one hundred largest corporations to talk to Baugh and his wife of sixty-five years, Eula Mae Tharp (the other original unpaid employee). "We were driven by the desire to avoid what we'd experienced in the Depression," he says modestly.

He continues to give most of the credit for SYSCO's astonishing success to his employees: "We have the greatest number of honorable people I've seen assembled at this company. That's the reason I still like to come to work."

Self-effacing, genuinely funny, and deeply religious, Baugh is a wonderful role model for aspiring Christian businesspeople everywhere. His character was forged early in his home and church.

I was sixteen years old when I was baptized. I had had an experience that for me was very interesting and compelling. Mr. Buford Glenn was my Sunday school teacher when I was about twelve to thirteen years of age. I sat on the front row in the classroom because I wanted to be very certain that he understood that I was going to play third base in every game of the baseball team's season.

One day in a discussion, he and a kid were exchanging some thoughts and comments. At one point, the young man said, "Mr. Glenn, I would say the very same thing if Jesus Christ were standing in the back of this room right now."

And Mr. Glenn said, "Well, son, I don't know whether you know this or not, but Jesus Christ *is* with us in this room at this time."

I stood up, turned around, and looked. It was such a shocking thing. Then it finally dawned on me what he meant. It was a great experience for me. I haven't necessarily tried, but I haven't been able to shake Jesus from being around me since that time. It was a remarkable experience.

Could you give us a short recap of your business career?

When I was a kid in Waco, Texas, I had an executive position with A & P food stores. I was a "teller." I would *tell* the people to please move so I could mop the floor. I started working when my father died when I was twelve. I learned a lot about human nature. I worked until I finished high school in 1932. I was to have enrolled in Baylor University, but I couldn't do it. We didn't have the money. By that time it was the middle of the Depression.

There had been seven A & P stores in town at the time and one after the other they all closed until there was just one left. It was staffed by former managers, and one day there wasn't a job for me. But the A & P food stores superintendent in the Dallas area was a very nice man. He called the superintendent in Houston and said, "This is a good boy and he really wants to stay with the company." So Mr. Terry in Houston passed the word along that if I were to come to Houston by a given date, he would have a job for me. So, after walking most of three days and two nights, I arrived in Houston and had a job at an A & P food store.

And you probably felt lucky to get it.

I certainly was. We had some very strange experiences. My boss in Houston, the A & P superintendent, was a Mr. H. J. Martin, now deceased. Wonderful Christian guy. There were literally thousands of men without work in 1932. Even so, Mr. Martin was very nice to me. He asked me to come to the warehouse office on Thursday nights to interview men. There were no jobs, but there would be a line sometimes four blocks long. Mr. Martin would sit there and weep and listen and try to encourage every man that stayed. He also ordered, from the Dallas bakery, boxes that contained twenty loaves of bread each. They were stacked up behind his desk. I was the kid who was helping him. He would ask a man, "How many people are there in your family?" They would tell him, and he would give them bread. It was all he could do.

People would also come in my store very hungry. I could feed a man for a nickel because bread was two loaves for a nickel, pork and beans was two cans for a nickel, and potted meat was two cans for a nickel. So for that five cents, I could give a man a loaf of bread and his choice of one of the others. We had so many destitute people.

One day a man came in and he said that he wanted to work or do anything for food. I told him the standard thing—there were no jobs. But I did tell him about what he could get for a nickel—a loaf of bread and something else. He said, "I really don't know what my wife would like to have."

I said, "So you're married?"

He said, "Yes. We have two children." And then, rather wistfully, he said, "My children haven't had anything to eat for two days."

So I went to the store manager, a man named Holland Ramey—still alive and still a good friend—and I said, "Mr. Ramey, I would like to borrow some money."

He said, "For what?" And I told him about this family. He said, "I know how you feel. Still, you loan people money and you hope they're going to pay you someday and they don't. But if you want to borrow some money, I'll loan you some. But you can't do that forever, you know."

So, in a day when strawberry preserves in a four-pound jar was twenty-nine cents, this man and I loaded up two dollars' worth of food that he carried home to his family. It was enough to last them for a long time. The next day he came in with his wife. She stood there very demurely and thanked me for the food for her children. Tears ran down her face and then she reached over and touched me on the cheek. That's something else I'll never forget.

Later on that man became the president of a Houston company and, as long as he lived, we were friends. It was an absolutely incredible time.

How long did you stay with A & P?

Until the end of World War II. When the war was over, my wife and I started the business that became SYSCO Corporation. I tell the story that she began the business with only one other illiterate man and me, and that's how we started our little food distribution business. The office was in the back bedroom of our house and my wife, Eula Mae, didn't leave that office in the daytime. Not that she was answering the phone that much, but I suspect that she was praying that it *would* ring.

After a couple of years, she was able to go back to being full-time homemaker for our kids. My sweet wife and I have been married for sixty-five years, incidentally. I'm one of the luckiest people in this world.

When my wife left to be at home with the kids, though, it cost the business because then I had to pay somebody at the office. My administrative expenses skyrocketed! But we persevered, and in 1969 SYSCO was formed by the simultaneous merger with several other companies scattered about the nation—West Coast, Midwest, Northeast, Southeast, Southwest. Today we have 122 distribution centers in the United States and Canada, along with a lot of overseas business.

Why has SYSCO been so successful?

SYSCO has been very fortunate. We've had two advantages. One is that we have a very favorable market to pursue. Most women would like to mothball their kitchens—if they haven't already done it—and our customers are those who provide food to be served away from home: restaurants, hospitals, airlines, steamships, schools, and other places where "away from home" food is served.

The other advantage is that we've had absolutely wonderful people. Before we started this public company, I spent an aggregate of about six months' time in New York interviewing investment banking firms. They provided some case studies for me as regards major companies that have done well—and some that *haven't* done so well. That tended to support some of the feelings that I had already gained from earlier experiences. Some of those feelings are very simple: *Attempt to do that which is right in the sight of God.*

For instance, unethical shortcuts usually generate long-term penalties. You can learn that as a kid when you lie to your mother. So in our company, that now has almost fifty thousand employees, elitism is not a way of life, nor is arrogance. We have an environment in which we have been successful in the

41

desire *not* to go outside the company family to engage the services of an officer. We have more than thirteen hundred officers and all are homegrown. We try to match them up to different positions as to their desires and capabilities. At the same time, the positions we've matched for them are designed to add to their responsibilities the eight or nine basic disciplines required to manage one of our operating companies. So we've been fortunate with good people.

You mentioned the guiding principles of ethical behavior and lack of arrogance with which you operate the company. These sound like they come as an outgrowth of your Christian faith.

Some were from instances of erroneous management that I had observed, and some were from experiences in which I participated. I have seen men who would arrogantly proclaim that they were the boss and, "You do as I tell you." Of course, anyone in an organization knows who the boss is. But if the one who is the chief executive or has other major responsibilities can discipline himself or herself to be courteous to everyone, to guarantee the dignity of anyone, that's a tremendous encouragement in the building of a sound organization. On the other hand, discourtesy, impatience, the weakness to embarrass a colleague, just because you have the power to do it and can get by with it, is a ludicrous waste of everyone's time and energies.

Those feelings came out of my experiences as a kid in an A & P and the other experiences that I've had as our business has progressed. Incidentally I don't have a very good memory, so I have to speak truthfully, because if I told a lie, I couldn't remember what I originally said!

As a Christian do you manage SYSCO differently now that it is so big that you no longer can know every employee by name?

Up to about seven or eight thousand employees, I think I knew them all. But after that, it got out of hand. Of course, when I said I knew them all, it was just absolutely thrilling to walk into a warehouse, such as in Grand Rapids, Michigan, and for a burly Hollander in coveralls to come up to me and say, "Gee whiz, ain't we runnin' this company good?" We were buddies. Or in a delivery room, the same thing.

Some people look on delivery persons as being low on the totem pole. But from my perspective, there are only three people that our customers know. That's the sales representative, the telephone voice, and the delivery personnel. The more that all three are enthused about what they're doing and the greater encouragement they have to bring forth their creativity by making suggestions, the better off we're going to be. It's just worked out that way—as it *should* work out that way.

Do you run a business of seven thousand employees differently than you do a business of fifty thousand employees?

We try not to. There is a disease that I dread called "big company-itis." Everybody in this company is aware of my universal fear of "big company-itis." Not only is it conducive to business failures, or a business not gaining the advantages that it could, but it isn't very much fun.

How do you avoid it?

Just by being insistent. We're now under the guidance of a fourth chief executive officer. As you can imagine, this company is run by younger and smarter people. This chief executive is one of those people who started out as a young man in a very low-level position. For instance, we have one operating company chief executive officer who started out as a deliveryman, David Dekoch. His boss was a very fine man who believed in the principles to which we attempt to adhere. He was treated as a friend and respected as a deliveryman. Now that David has been the chief executive for several years, he hasn't forgotten those things. He recalls the advantages of personal enjoyment that he gained and therefore can enjoy the success of others as well as that of the business.

Technology is whirling at a dizzying pace, but it has been for fifty years. We have to learn to make certain procedural changes in how we manage our business or some segments of our business. We're aware of the changes within our professional disciplines. But how people treat one another hasn't changed yet. I am convinced that, without any question, if we can develop the right relationships with our colleagues—and that is by speaking truthfully, being fair and being honest, being as kind and considerate as we would like for them to be to us—then we can get through these technological changes more easily. And we can think more clearly about any operational procedure or modifications that will improve the business and, indeed, prepare our own people to perform all of the professional disciplines. And it's more fun that way!

How does being a Christian affect the way you interact with your employees?

Let me say this. Almost everyone in the company knows I am a Christian. They know what kind of a Christian I am and the church of which I am a member. They know that, but they didn't learn it from me. I don't impose Christianity on anybody in this building. But I am not unwilling for them to know that I believe that Christian principles are practical and will work and will be rewarding—not necessarily in dollars and cents but will be rewarding in relationships. So we don't impose Christianity on anyone.

I don't walk around with a big red Bible under my arm. But you need not do that. I would be no more comfortable attempting to lead someone to look on Christianity with favor than I would be trying to coerce someone to change to a technique with which he or she isn't comfortable. I know of one man who bankrupted three different companies, major publicly owned companies. He is the most pompous person I've ever known.

It was that pomposity that alienated him from his staff and other people.

The reality of any relationship, as you are well aware, is that not only is it sensitive, it's fragile. I have the same challenges with my children, my grandchildren, and now my great grandchildren. I can be their encourager, and they will be open to some guidance if it's presented in the right way. But I'm not able to dominate anyone by threats or coercion and still be effective and of any assistance to them.

Speaking of young people, if someone is thinking about a career in business, what advice do you have?

I would advise them first to try to avoid ever placing themselves in an embarrassing position relating to a moral or ethical situation. I would suggest that they consider very carefully the advantages they can accrue for themselves if they can avoid ever placing themselves in an immoral or unethical position. That's sort of a negative suggestion isn't it?

But if you want people to be open with you, to be cooperative with you, and to aspire to follow your leadership, then you have to pay a price. That price not only is related to ethical and moral situations, it's related to courtesy and respect for the dignity of other people. There are great numbers of people who don't believe that or haven't thought about it or haven't tried to make that kind of an approach in dealing with others effective for themselves.

Finally, I would also say that, depending on the kind of profession or business they're in, no one can ever capture all of the business that is available. But you can identify a certain segment of the business and do it better than anyone else. That's worth aspiring to do. Our company now has annual revenues in excess of twenty billion dollars. We're very comfortable and our job is to contribute to the success of our customers. We don't try to do business with all customers, just those who we can be sure will try to play fair with us as we with them. That's the kind of customer we want. We provide almost all the food that's served at Baylor University through our customer Aramark. We cannot always respond to every request made by customers, but we can look them straight in the eye, state precisely what we can do for them, and then keep our word on a timely basis.

And you can sleep easy at night.

Yes. And I don't have to try to remember which lie I told!

Doug Bawel

President
Jasper Engines and Transmissions

I've made money and lost money. We have been blessed beyond belief with our company and family and all of those things are simply gifts from God. They're not ours; we're just here to take care of them; we are the caretakers.

Doug Bawel

The experienced world traveler can't go anywhere without encountering Jasper Engines and Transmissions. In fact, in many countries, you can't go anywhere period without either a Jasper engine or a transmission. That's because Jasper is the world's largest mass remanufacturer of a diverse line of drivetrain components. Jasper's 1,500 employees produce 80,000 gas engines, 50,000 transmissions, 5,500 diesel engines, 3,000 differentials and real axle assemblies, and 1,200 stern drives *annually.*

Since Doug Bawel assumed the helm of the sixty-year-old Indiana company, it has achieved an even higher profile. Today it is the sponsor and supplier of the popular Jasper Engines and Transmissions/Federal-Mogul #77 NASCAR Winston Cup Thunderbird. Jasper also sponsors teams in the NHRA and Busch divisions and sponsors the Jasper Engines and Transmissions National Modified Tour and the JASPER/American Tractor-Pullers Association Series.

Bawel himself is active in the National Heritage Foundation and many regional, state, and local charitable and religious organizations. He received the Entrepreneur of the Year Award for Manufacturing in 1997. And when he's not checking on things at

47

Jasper's 250,000-square-foot manufacturing plant in mostly rural Crawford County, Indiana, or at the shop of the #77 outside Charlotte, North Carolina, you can find him at home with his wife, Kathy, and their seven children.

Despite the stress of juggling those multiple roles, Bawel still manages to epitomize Jasper's mission statement: Do it right and have fun! This doesn't mean, however, that he doesn't take his work and his Christian life very seriously.

I grew up in a Christian home and later in life, when I returned home, I joined the same church that my parents were members of. I even became an adult Sunday school teacher. But my faith really became important to me in 1991. In March I attended the Christian renewal weekend Walk to Emmaus. Although I had been raised in the church, and although I'd even been a Sunday school teacher, I don't think I ever really realized the personal commitment that the Lord was asking of me. He wanted that personal relationship that comes from fellowship.

What was it about Walk to Emmaus that spurred that change?

I can tell you exactly what it was. I was sitting in a chapel during one of the breaks. I looked up at the cross, and just below the cross they had a small poster where the name of Jesus was reversed out of the background, but I couldn't see it.

It was an optical illusion.

Yes. And I tried to close one eye, then the other. Nothing. So I just happened to open up the Bible, not looking for anything specific, and there Jesus was talking about the lady who had committed adultery: "If any one of you is without sin, let him be the first to throw a stone at her" (John 8:7). I then realized that I'd just gone through a divorce and was carrying that burden. I said, "Lord, this is too great to handle." At that time, all my children were living with me. I looked up again, and I could see "Jesus" plain as day. So, doubting Thomas that I am, I closed one eye. I

48

could see it with that eye. I closed the other eye and I could still see it. It was just then that I realized, he was really talking to me. He had died for me. I knew that, but it had never sunk in before. He died for me. He was there just waiting for me.

They say when you return from either a Walk to Emmaus or Cursillo, the Catholic version, that you're not supposed to talk about it. The big thing that they said was, "Don't be out singing from the mountaintops. Show them in your actions." Over the next two or three months, my entire executive committee started seeing changes. We had always started shareholders meetings with prayer, but now we were starting executive sessions with prayer. We were starting our advisory committee meetings with prayer. We were starting board meetings with prayer. And then some people said, "Doug, you've changed."

I wrote letters to my ex-wife, I went back to her and said, "Hey, is there any way we could maybe work this out?" She said that she'd moved on. And I said, "That's fine, but I want you to know that I want to be your friend and work at raising our kids together." We have remained friends. Although she's moved away, and the kids have lived with me, they've always been there for her.

Then finally I made the statement, starting with the executive team, "Guys, this is my deal. I want you to go on either a Walk to Emmaus or a Cursillo. You pick. And here's the deal. If you don't think it was the best time you've ever had, and you think you know something better, I want you to do it. I'll pay for it." No one has ever asked for that second trip. I think it has bonded us together as a team.

I understand you've made a similar offer to your children.

What I told my children was, when they reach age sixteen, if they'd go on the Walk for teenagers and if afterward they could tell me they didn't get anything out of the weekend, I'd give them five hundred dollars. I'll never forget, my daughter Kelly, when she got out at the end, she said with tears of joy, "I wanted that money so bad." Now she's gone into the ministry. She's helping young people.

Your daughter Lori once lost her sight but miraculously regained it. How is she doing?

She is doing great; she just called yesterday. She's going to be a senior in college. She worked at a camp last year for challenged children coming from challenged homes and challenged backgrounds. At the end of the camp, she wrote a pretty strong letter to the camp directors and said, "Hey, we can do so much with these kids if we just do this, this, and this." So they've now approached her to be the director of the camp this coming summer. She's accepted. I'm proud of every one of my children, but that young lady has battled some serious problems and just loves helping others.

Talk about your time at Jasper.

I started in 1976 as a sales trainee. As a sales trainee, I spent seven months on the shop floor disassembling engines and did virtually every task for the company. Then they moved me into the advertising department, for six or seven months. After that, they asked if I would take an outside sales position. From there, I went into sales management and in 1987 became president of the company.

You were a nominal Christian during all that time?

Very nominal!

And then in '91, after the Walk to Emmaus, things changed.

I think the big thing was that I began trying—emphasize the word *trying*—to have more patience and also to change my style of communication. I always would tell people, "I don't pay anybody to take a cussing and I don't pay anybody to give one." But some of those words would slip into conversations. I was really trying to change that.

As for our giving practices as a company, we had always been a giver to universities and hospitals. Now we take a more active role giving to churches. Last year, during Christmastime, we asked our advisory committee, a committee of associates on the floor, to make the decision on year-end giving. They sent checks to 350 churches in a five-county area. Every church received the same amount. All we asked was that they spend the money on something that wasn't budgeted, either to help somebody, to buy something new for the church, or whatever. In fact the company as a whole just increased their whole level of giving. We have built two Habitat for Humanity homes and most recently funded a Christian home for adult mentally challenged people.

How has your newfound walk with the Lord changed how you deal with employees?

When we did our vision statement, we took a stand. Paragraph four of our corporate statement of principles says, "We want to be known as a Good Corporate Christian Citizen." When I teach our culture class, which is to every new associate, we share that with them. We explain that if that's not their belief structure, we respect them for that. But that is our belief structure here.

For instance, we have a greater-than-life-sized nativity set that we set up each and every year right after Thanksgiving. We pay for the materials, but the associates donate the time. We have over ten prayer groups that meet in our building, before work, at lunchtime, or after work. We have a community room downstairs that various Christian organizations can use, free of charge, either during work hours or after work hours.

And, as I mentioned, we strongly encourage our people to attend a Walk to Emmaus, a Cursillo, or whatever. We even pay them for the day they are gone, although we do not tell them until they're at the Walk.

Finally, we as a company have a prayer line that our people feel free to call. There are several different people in the company who take these calls. The callers say, "Hey, would you put me on the prayer line today?" Those are things we never did prior to 1991.

How have your corporate relations with your suppliers and sponsors changed since your faith became a dominant theme in your life?

Over the last two years, we have provided everyone a minimum of eight hours of training on [Steven Covey's] *Seven Habits of Highly Effective People*. Supervisors and above receive a three-day course. We've sent people to Steven Covey's school. I've been there too and have helped teach. From that, we try to explain to our suppliers that we want a partnership. This is not something where we say one thing and then go back and beat you up and work on pricing only. If you don't make it a win-win situation, they or you aren't going to be around. I've got a piece of cut glass on the conference table in my office. It's from one of our partners. It says, "Like a bridge that spans both time and distance, a supportive partnership is a bond to be celebrated."

Has there been a situation where holding firm to your Christian principles has been a handicap in your business dealings?

No. I don't think it's been a tremendous handicap, because we're very up-front about it. And, therefore, we probably walk away from certain deals, or they walk away from us. I think the hardest thing for me personally is that, since I've committed myself to the Lord, things are not easier, they're harder. That's because certain things that you used to sort of overlook, now you say, "That's not right."

I'll give you a specific. In licensing software for computers, when you buy a computer they normally have the current software. But as you update your computers or add new stations, you take that license and put it in another computer. One day one of my compliance people came in from our Management and Information Services group and said, "Mr. Bawel, we're out of compliance on our software licenses. We don't think we'll ever get caught, but it's going to cost us $127,000 to get in compliance. What should we do?" Well, if you're going to walk the talk, you've got to say, "That's what we've got to do." So I've had more of those decisions, where in the past I would have said, "Well, let's not worry about it until we get caught." You can't say one thing and do something else.

As a Christian who happens to be a businessman, what advice do you have for those interested in a career in business?

Number one is, don't sell your belief structure short, and don't sell your personal relationship with God short. I've made money and lost money. We have been blessed beyond belief with our company and family, and all of those things are simply gifts from God. They're not ours; we're just here to take care of them. We are the caretakers. And if all those are gone tomorrow, if you still have that personal relationship with God, then you can look back and say, "I did it the right way." You've got to believe it will work itself out in the end.

I heard a song the other day, about the young lady who was killed at the Columbine tragedy. When the gunmen pointed their guns at her and asked, "Do you believe in Jesus Christ?" she said, "Yes." It made me firmly realize that's what we're all called to do, whether it's in business or whatever. But if you sell your soul and give in, well, there are all kinds of sharks out there that would love for you to do those kinds of things. You've got to stand tall and stand proud.

In my office there is a picture of Christ talking to a businessman. It sits at the end of the table, so I can see it. It's there to remind me how I should act and react. Value your relationship with Christ. He valued his with you by his life.

John D. Beckett

President
R. W. Beckett Corporation

John Beckett is one of the most remarkable men I know, whose life demonstrates the beautiful balance between spiritual maturity and business acumen.

Bill Bright, Campus Crusade for Christ

R. W. Beckett is built on a platform of three core values: integrity, excellence and profound respect for the individual. Beckett works to nurture relationships daily: with our employees by creating a work environment that fosters their growth and well-being; with our customers by providing them with a product that is well-made and priced as a cost-value to them; and with our suppliers and others with whom we conduct business by treating them with respect and fairness. We strive to serve others, helping meet human needs in the community and beyond.

Guiding Principles of the R. W. Beckett
Corporation
(from the R. W. Beckett Corporation handbook)

John D. Beckett is an unusual CEO. First, he's written a best-selling book—*Loving Monday: Succeeding in Business without Selling Your Soul.* Second, he heads up the highly successful R. W. Beckett Corporation, the nation's premier manufacturer of oil-heat burners. And third, he's been featured on national television in a segment on faith and business for *ABC News,* hosted by Peter Jennings.

The Beckett Corporation was founded in 1937 by R. W. Beckett and Stanton Fitzgerald. John Beckett assumed the mantle of leadership when his father died in 1965. At the time, the company had about 3 percent of the U.S. market in oil-heat burners. Today there are three Beckett companies in a variety of diversified services, five hundred employees, more than one hundred million dollars in annual sales, and about 80 percent of the U.S. market.

Beckett's attractive office and manufacturing complex in Elyria, Ohio, has won numerous awards, as have the company's employee programs.

John Beckett talks about the relationship between business and faith:

The remarkable thing to me is that there really is much more of an intersection between faith and business today. In earlier times, I think people had so totally disconnected their walk of faith from their walk in the workplace that there was no intersection. It is happening more now because people want to have their whole lives integrated. They do not want to be one person in one phase of their life and another person in another phase of their life.

You own your own company. What would you hope to do if you were in a publicly held company?

I don't think I would do things a great deal differently. There is, of course, the issue of the outside shareholder, the analyst, and yet I know that some of the people you have already interviewed are working in that context and they've decided to be who they are. Unquestionably, it is a different arena. I know business leaders who are walking in a holistic way who have not had to compromise what they believe because they have outside shareholders. But they do need to go to extra measures to inform the outside shareholders of the basis on which they are leading the company.

A person who comes to mind is Ralph Larson at Johnson and Johnson. He's been pretty transparent about the high ethical standards he expects in that large, publicly held company. Ethically based decisions may result in an impact on earnings on a short-term basis, but he's saying, "I'm in this for the long term. And I believe there has to be consistency in the way that I conduct my affairs."

As a Christian, you have to make the same employee-related decisions everyone else makes. I believe that regardless of whether someone is a person of faith or not, there have to be judgments made on a business basis. That could mean laying off or terminating a believer, a brother or a sister in the Lord. Where it is appropriate, I would encourage the person who is being terminated to see God's hand in the process and to be in faith that if God is closing one door, he's going to open another that will, in the long run, be to their benefit.

Ten years ago I had to terminate a young man, recently married, shortly after he began working with us because he failed a drug test. Quite recently I was chatting with his wife—actually, she was the dental technician who was working on my teeth. Out of the blue, she said, "I want to thank you, because when you terminated my husband, you said to him that he had a choice. He could either go on in his current lifestyle and ruin his life, or he could come to grips with it and lead a whole and productive life. That so impacted him that he really changed his lifestyle. He abandoned his drug habit. Today he has a very responsible position and is a good father and a good husband."

So ten years later, she's thanking me that I didn't just terminate him but gave him some guidance in a way that redirected his life—and probably saved their marriage. Incidentally, I thought it was very good of the Lord to give *me* that encouragement. It made the trip to the dentist much more pleasant!

How much does the Bible influence your daily business life?

I would say it has a considerable impact. In fact I'm really trying to attune myself on a daily basis to know what the Bible is saying and look for ways in which a biblical insight might apply during the day. When I do this, I find there is almost always some application of Scripture that relates to a business issue I am facing.

I was with a senior business leader just a few days ago in Boston. Over lunch, he began sharing some personal struggles he's been going through. It was just amazing because I was able to encourage him through the scriptural ideas that had emerged from my Bible reading a few hours earlier.

How many employees does Beckett have?

We have about 550 employees.

Is it possible to know every one of them?

We're in three separate divisions. The division that I'm most directly involved with has about 200 employees. The answer there is yes. With the other divisions that I'm not directly involved in, I do not know everyone in the same way. But I think with 150 to 200 people, it is definitely possible to know them on a first-name basis and have a good relationship with them.

What happens as it gets bigger? How do you keep that sense of what Beckett is with the larger community of employees?

That's an enormous challenge, but if it's something important, then there are ways to do it. A starting point is to anchor in the company's core values first of all with other leaders—that must be there—and then to reinforce those values with larger groups of people.

I just met Don Soderquist, recently retired as the senior vice chairman of Wal-Mart stores. There are 1.2 million employees in that organization. He related how they have taken their three core values and so integrated them at employee training sessions, orientation programs, and in follow-up programs that he really believes there is a strong buy-in. If you're really committed to establishing a value-based corporate culture, then it can work.

Another example is Gen. Chuck Krulak, who until recently was the commandant of the Marine Corps. Krulak impacted the whole Corps with a strong set of values. Did everybody fully walk them out? Probably not. But they were all very clear where the Marine Corps stood. And, by the way, the Marine Corps is *the* most successful of all the military branches in recruiting. People *want* to believe in something that draws out their best.

A young person comes to you and says, "I'm thinking about business as a career." What advice do you have?

First of all, I would encourage them to get prepared educationally. I think that they need to have a broad background in the basic aspects of business as well as developing some specialized skills.

If they're a person of faith and asking that question, I would encourage them to make the choice of a career a matter of prayer—and to look for a dimension of calling in their choices so that their life direction is not just their own impulses or their own desires. Instead, they would seek a sense that God is leading them into their work.

Beyond that, I would encourage them to find a mentor, someone they can model themselves after. I would encourage them to read broadly, expanding their minds in areas of good business literature.

Can you suggest some good business literature that meant something to you?

This may be more for a person of faith, but the most valuable book that I have read is *Secular Work Is Full-Time Service* by Larry Peabody.

How was that book helpful to you?

It's a study of the life of Daniel. Daniel was an extremely able young man, who was called into public service. We see him working for several very secular kings in positions of senior administrative responsibility, yet without compromising his faith. His story, to me, is a tremendous example of how it is possible to follow the Lord in a secular environment and still have a broad impact.

William J. Bolthouse

President
William Bolthouse Farms, Inc.

The purpose of this Company is to glorify God through our business transactions, our work, and our relationships. It is further our desire to bring honor and glory to the Name of Jesus Christ by following God's Word in all of our dealings with employees, suppliers, and customers. God's Word as contained in His inspired Scriptures will be the final authority in all Corporate matters concerning direction, decision, and disputes.

Corporate Philosophy

We are a market-driven, fully integrated produce company. We are innovative in agricultural and packing technology. Within the parameters of our Corporate Philosophy, our focus is to offer quality products at the lowest possible cost through a "state of the art" plant, quality raw materials and maintain trust and credibility with our customers, growers and employees.

Corporate Mission Statement

The numbers are little short of mind-boggling. William Bolthouse Farms is the world's leading producer of carrots. The farm's 2,400 full-time employees process and ship 35,000 tons of carrot products *each month*—or about one pound per month for every family in the United States. Accomplishing that prodigious feat takes 25,000 football-

fields-worth of carrots each year. Five plants run day and night, five
or six days a week, 52 weeks a year.

William Bolthouse is the third-generation Bolthouse to run the family business, which began in Michigan in 1915. It was Bolthouse
Farms that modernized the carrot business, cropping the green tops
and bagging whole carrots in cellophane. (In fact grocers still call
whole bagged carrots "cellos" today.)

William H. Bolthouse, son of the founder, moved the family farms
to Bakersfield, California, in 1972 to meet America's year-round
demand for carrots. And it was his son, William J. Bolthouse, who introduced the cut, peeled, and cleaned Shortcuts in 1990—necessitat-
ing, in short order, three new processing plants. Since then, the fourth
generation of Bolthouse children have joined the family business.

But perhaps the most fascinating statistic of all is that all four generations of the Bolthouse family have made Jesus Christ—not profit—
the center of their business. Today William J. Bolthouse is an eloquent
spokesman for the faith, happily coming to work each day to be a part
of what he believes is a holy calling—feeding hungry people.

I was saved when I was eight and rededicated my life at age
thirteen. I guess I was destined to go into the family business.
Right out of the womb, my father said, "There's my successor."
And at age nine, I was given one acre to grow onions on. I've
been farming ever since.

Was your faith a part of what you were doing, even with your first jobs on your dad's farms?

I think somewhat so early on, but not a real total commitment. Probably the total commitment came when I heard Bruce
Wilkinson at FCCI [Fellowship of Companies for Christ Inter-
national] challenge us to use the company as a platform ministry. I can't even tell you the year, but it would have been probably twelve years ago.

What changed with Bill Bolthouse after that message?

I think it was more of a proactive thing. We always ran our
business under Christian principles. We paid our bills, treated
our employees the way we would want to be treated, and ran

a good quality business. We basically tried to hire Christian people, so we had kind of a culture, a Christian culture here. Therefore, it didn't necessitate trying to integrate or to use our company as a platform.

But when this encounter with Bruce happened, I was challenged to use our company as a platform of ministry. We had more and more people involved in the business because it was growing. We just became more proactive. We started putting Bibles in the lobby; we started talking about our faith more openly. It was more of a proactive effort rather than, Well, everybody knows I'm a Christian because I don't drink, I don't steal, and I don't do all the don'ts. And God started blessing us and that was really a challenging thing—for good—for us.

What changed in your interactions with your customers and suppliers?

I've had two or three supplier appreciation dinners since then where I bring in people and challenge them both spiritually and other ways. About five or six years ago, we had Walt Wiley in for various luncheons. His ministry is in Charlotte and it is called Winning with Encouragement. Walt's a motivational speaker, but he also can put a Christian twist on it. We had about three people accept the Lord at those luncheons.

We've had employees accept the Lord through employee appreciation dinners when we bring in speakers. In fact Bruce Wilkinson spoke one time and some people accepted the Lord there too.

In short, I think the changes are that we became more proactive. It's not just because everybody knows we're a Christian company because we hire mostly Christian management, but people know we're a Christian company because we integrate our faith into our business *and* because we're more open, more proactive in our dealings with others. It's not a Goody Two-shoes kind of thing. We still do business the hard-nosed way. But people know that when they cut a deal, we're going to follow it. They know we're not going to bail out on them.

Have you felt the need to put Bolthouse's beliefs in written form?

Yes, we have a full-page mission statement. It's a pretty strong mission statement too. We basically did this at a management planning meeting a long time ago. Our management people said it was important that we have a corporate philosophy and a mission statement. So we had one of those strategic thinking gurus come in to facilitate our strategic planning meeting. I've been a president for sixteen years, so it was probably fifteen years ago. This is what we came up with. We've basically never changed it. It probably needs to be modified, but it works.

Is it included with the new employee packets or is it posted?

It depends on the level of the people that we're hiring. In management, it's one of the first things I show them. I say, "I'd like you to read this; it's pretty strong. What would you think of working for a company that has something like that? Because that's the first thing you need to know." Most of the people already know it, so that's fine—they love it. But if they don't, why, that's fine too. We don't have to waste each other's time—*because that's who we are*. We're a little bit different than most companies.

There's something spiritual about providing food for the world.

Absolutely. You're in a service with goods and labor that are very wholesome. It isn't even marginally good; it's good. Most of the chain stores are good, but then they may sell some magazines that you really wouldn't want to buy or show your kids. Or you might be working for other companies that are mostly wholesome but there is a piece of it that you wonder about. All of us have those issues. Our business is pretty wholesome all the way through. We don't have anything that anybody could say, "I don't agree with what you're doing."

You don't see many stories in the paper about people with a carrot addiction.

No, other than some environmentalists who say we're using too much water or that we're doing something that is not environmentally correct. But even there we use all the latest technology to farm in an environmentally correct way. We have our own fertilizer plant and we do a lot of prescription blending and different things. And we're getting more and more into organics to please even those people. Anybody can criticize somebody for something.

If you're working in this company as an employee, you can feel proud of what you're doing at the end of the day because you are helping society by feeding people. And even in the food business, there are some foods that aren't any good. It's not healthy, it's not low fat, or something. Even like the best national fast-food chain, as good an outfit as they are, the stuff they sell isn't that good for you.

What advice would you give to a young person who is thinking about going into business?

Patience. Most kids today want it all right now. That's the way the world works. If you are a Christian and God's given you some brains to use, give your employer 100 percent. Give your employer 110 percent. Sooner or later, somebody is going to notice you. But you've got to have patience. That's where most kids fall down. They want too much too quick. You've got to learn to work hard, you've got to learn to give it 110 percent, and you've got to learn that if the reward isn't there this year, just wait. God will take care of you.

If you are working for a company that, because of one reason or another, doesn't promote you, it could be any one of several reasons. One of them is that there's no place to go. The other thing is that maybe you're not quite as smart as you think you are. And finally maybe you haven't been noticed yet. If that last one is the case, if you have enough patience, you will be noticed. Management *does* see quality and they *do* see a good work ethic. That's what makes businesses. It's people, people,

people. It's like in the real estate business—it's location, location, location. In the business world, it's people.

There are businesses that have certain things like trade secrets or patents to protect them so that they can have basically incompetent people running them. They can make mistakes. They can recover because they've got some sort of protection there. But in the commodity business like we're in, or a lot of other businesses people are in, most of us can be eclipsed pretty easily. There are good people that want to work, that want to serve, that want to put out a good product, and you do it day after day and stay excited about it. You want to serve your customer. It's just what so many companies don't do, and that's why they go down.

What other factors have contributed to the success of Bolthouse Farms?

I think that God has given our family and our management a strategic vision. And we have been willing to take risks. We have tried to stay one step ahead of the curve, wherever the curve is. Just twenty minutes ago I was talking to one of my managers about some ideas for the future. These are ideas that—if we do them, which we might not—it would be at least four years out before we'd ever be able to get to it because we've got so much on our plates now. We have to deal with the day-to-day, but a good part of our time is thinking strategically. You have to ask yourself daily, *What are our strengths? What are our weaknesses? What are the opportunities out there, and how will we stay one step ahead of everybody else?*

Actually, I don't think that we're big risk takers. I don't think that we're crazy like some companies. We're pretty conservative and the stuff we do is pretty well thought out. A risk analysis is taken of every new venture.

Does being a Christian impact your long-term decision-making process?

I don't think so. Strategic decisions are just that. A non-Christian could make the same decision. I don't know if that really has anything to do with being a Christian. It's totally strategic.

Still, I think how you implement that vision, *then* you get into the Christian aspect. For instance, we looked at a *maquilladora* [manufacturing plant just south of the U.S.-Mexico border] down in Mexico years ago. There's where your Christian worldview comes into play. Because as much as we looked, and as much as we tried to figure it out, we came to the conclusion that there was no way to do business in Mexico without *mordidia*—which is "feathering somebody's palm," bribes. We came to the conclusion that—our mission statement—there's no way this company can operate there. Why? Because you can't operate without paying people off and that is not the way we operate. And in our business, we're not looking at getting into anything that's questionable. We're not making wine and alcohol.

So don't look for Bolthouse Farms Sparkling Carrot Wine in the near future?

No, don't. You won't find it. You might find some pretty good carrot juice, though.

Edwin V. Bonneau

Founder
The Bonneau Company

Honor God in all that we do. Colossians 3:23: "Whatever you do, work at it with all your heart, as working for the Lord, not for men."

Meet the needs of our people (physically, spiritually, professionally). Romans 12:13: "Share with God's people who are in need. Practice hospitality."

Serve our customers (honestly, fairly, diligently). Romans 12:7: "If it is serving, let him serve; if it is teaching, let him teach."

Grow profitably. Matthew 25:22–23: "The man with the two talents also came. 'Master,' he said, 'you entrusted me with two talents; see, I have two more.' His master replied, 'Well done, good and faithful servant! You have been faithful with few things; I will put you in charge of many things. Come and share your master's happiness.'"

My commitment to all people that this company touches (suppliers, employees, customers, outsiders) is that we will base our objectives, policies, and actions upon these values and beliefs.

The Bonneau Company Statement
of Values and Beliefs

Ed Bonneau doesn't fit the stereotype of a successful entrepreneur. Tall, thin, soft-spoken, and humble, Bonneau nonetheless dominated the sunglasses industry in the United States for years.

But the "Sunglasses King" began his venture with just his wife, Barbara, in a rented office and an old car. As a salesman, Bonneau had noticed that most retailers sold sunglasses only during the summer. He transformed the industry by making it year-round and by applying the same marketing and wholesaling techniques that were commonplace in other industries.

Along the way he spotted several well-known, but suffering, national brands caught between the cracks after multiple corporate takeovers. In time, Bonneau purchased ninety-eight-year-old Pennsylvania Optical (with its patents and contracts with Wal-Mart, Kmart, and Woolworth) and industry giant Foster Grant (with its patents and manufacturing divisions). Bonneau also struck deals with Disney and Spalding to distribute brand products.

At its peak, the Bonneau Company was generating more than seventy-five million dollars in sales and created a whole new market for sunglasses. But a couple of years ago, Ed and Barbara sold the company while they were still young enough to enjoy the fruits of their investment. Since then, Ed has committed his time to his burgeoning family and his church, recognizing how important they are in his life.

I was born in the church. I am sure the first trip I ever made was to the church. My dad was a preacher and the church was the center of our lives. My public confession of faith was when I was baptized at age thirteen.

How did you get into the sunglasses business?

When I filled out my application at the employment agency, I wrote, "I do not want any sales job." But the agency set me up with a sales interview anyway. After I heard their pitch, I remember asking, "Do you mean you'll hire me *and* you'll pay me this amount whether I sell anything or not?" They said, "Yes!" I didn't have much faith in that, but I took the job. And it went pretty well. The job was outside sales for a cosmetic company. I was there six years. It was also a good learning experience. Although we were mostly based in the Southwest, I got to travel to places like New York. The first time I went there for a sales meeting was my first time on an airplane.

After this job, I decided to get rich in the food business. I opened a restaurant, and it took a full year to lose all the money

I had borrowed. Afterward, I went for another job interview in Dallas. The interviewer told me that he had a job for a sunglasses salesman and I took it. That was in the early '60s. I took those sunglasses and headed down the road. I knew a lot of the merchants because I'd been selling cosmetics out that way before.

It was a great job—zero benefits, zero expenses, zero anything—you just worked your tail off selling sunglasses. Best job I ever had. One hundred percent commission sales.

But eventually you quit that job, and you and your wife started your own business instead.

I got fired first—*then* I decided to start my own company. We found an old retail space in a shopping center that was eighty feet long and eleven feet wide. We paid eighty dollars a month for that thing. Then I got in the car and drove to New York City to buy sunglasses from wholesalers. Two months later, I was in the market selling my own brand of sunglasses. Of course, we didn't have any money to pay for good store placement or product brochures. And cash flow was zero because it would be another 60, or 90, or 120 days before we collected any money. We were going broke in a hurry.

I'd borrowed from a little hometown bank down in west Texas. The guy in this bank came to Dallas and personally signed my note at a bank here for another twenty-five thousand dollars—and that pulled us through.

When it was all said and done, you had two hundred people working for you in Dallas, another one hundred to three hundred at the Pennsylvania Optical manufacturing plant, and many more besides. How do you choose your employees?

I look for a person who has a spiritual base. I look for people who put God and family *before* their job. That was strange to some employees to hear that you want to be third in their lives—not first, but third. If you've got somebody like that, then you've got a person that already knows things in life like "do unto others." That's good business. When you hire a person with God/family/job priorities, you end up getting a lot more value for your company. They already have direction in life.

So one of the philosophies of the company was to bring like-minded people aboard, people who have that same kind of philosophy, people who have their priorities of life straight.

The second thing I look for is the ability to build relationships. Any business depends on relationships. You may think it depends on your accounting guy or your legal guy, but it always comes down to a matter of trust. The commandments "Love God and love your neighbor" summarize all of the laws in the Bible. They are both relationship laws. They deal with your relationship with God, your relationship with your neighbor, and your relationships within your family.

Once you start using that principle to build relationships with others, you build trust, trust with your employees, trust with your clients, trust with your suppliers. You build relationships in business. You can hire somebody that will get your accounting right. You can hire somebody that will make sure you're not violating any laws. But getting somebody that can create and maintain relationships, now *that's* a talent.

Is it possible to remain a person of faith in the business world?

Absolutely!

What do you have to do?

In some respects—certainly in my own case—it's easier to stay a person of faith in the cutthroat world of business because the inner strength that allows you to overcome all kinds of situations in life—including business reversals and whatever mistreatment you might have at somebody else's hand in the marketplace—comes from your faith. Disappointing things happen in life, plans go awry, and goals that were once so sweet end up in the trash because, for whatever reason, they could not be met, they could never be achieved. But having a faith means you *know* that the most important thing is there, regardless of whatever else you're doing. That helps a lot.

The Bible is the most practical success book ever written. It contains principles that work. If you apply these principles in your business, they work because they are universal. It addresses things like enthusiasm, work ethic, striving for excellence, doing first things first, giving people more than they expect. These principles are straight out of the Bible. If you take these principles and apply them in the business world, hey, they work!

As you go through your business life, you need to keep your faith and family healthy. There will be plenty of times in business when you are tempted to abandon your faith principles. And I'm not saying I haven't been tempted. But when you get older, you will see that it's easier with faith than it is without faith. Otherwise, when you get to be sixty and look back over your life, if all you have is the number one company in your industry and a pot of money, it won't be enough. You will feel empty and unfulfilled. Take your faith and your family with you on your business journey.

How did that play out as a Christian businessman dealing with employees, customers, and vendors?

When you honor God in what you do, it is beneficial to all three parties. That is the first statement of values and beliefs of our company—*honor God in all we do*. My postscript on the bottom of that page says, "My commitment to all people that this company touches, suppliers, employees, customers and outsiders, is that we will base our objectives, policies, and actions upon these values and beliefs."

When you think about honoring God, you're talking about the simple things of honesty, openness, and truthfulness. How does that work with customers? It works very well. How does that work with employees? It works very well. How does it work with enemies? It absolutely dumbfounds them. They don't know what to do. A simple, basic thing like honesty is very powerful.

70

If you apply the Golden Rule and treat your customers like you would want to be treated, they respond positively. Love your customers. We're told by famous marriage counselors that you need to love your wife before somebody else does. Well, in the business world, you need to love your customer before somebody else does. Taking a customer's point of view when you're serving him will not go unnoticed.

What about giving an extra measure? If an employee's job calls for him to work eight hours but he decides to work nine hours every day, there is no way he can hide that from his supervisor, from his peers, or from his boss. That person will absolutely be seen because he is giving something extra. If you commit to work for eight hours and you work them and you get paid, nobody owes anybody anything. But if you work nine hours for eight hours' pay, somebody is going to notice. They know that you're giving more.

If we do that for our customers, it works that way too. Those principles work in the marketplace. Those are simple loving facts; giving more than what's demanded makes a difference. You can do that with customers in many, many ways.

How does making money fit into your Christian view of business?

One of the values that we have that is strange to some people is to grow profitably. I think growing profitably is a biblical principle. If you don't grow profitably, sooner or later your company shuts down. How have you taken care of your employees then? You haven't taken care of them at all. How have you taken care of your customers? You haven't taken care of them at all.

Where do we get the money to build the schools and hospitals? Where does the money come from that funds the social agencies? Only from people that are making money. You can't get it from the people that don't have any. You support all those institutions by growing profitably. Your tax dollars are a blessing to others. Everybody loses if you don't grow profitably.

Is there a verse or passage in the Bible that has been particularly meaningful to you in your business life in recent years?

The central theme of Christianity is belief, having faith. One of Jesus' statements is, "All things are possible to him that believes." That's a statement that has depth beyond what most people understand.

I was really influenced by Napoleon Hill, who wrote *Think and Grow Rich*. It was based on a biblical principle, although he never mentions it. His statement is, "Anything the mind of man can conceive and believe, it can achieve."

Jesus' statement is, "All things are possible to him that believes." I believe that statement—but the key is to *believe*. First, you have to be able to think of it. I don't know how our minds work exactly, but the makeup of a person's mind is such that if they can think of something and believe it, it's possible to achieve it. I'm not saying they *will* achieve it every time, but it is possible.

I made that statement one time to someone and they said, "Okay, why don't you just jump over the house?" I said, "I don't *believe* I can jump over the house." You've got to be able to believe. My mind won't let me believe I can jump over the house. We are limited by our belief.

Keeping that thought in mind, human beings were created by God with such incredible potential. Most human beings never touch 95 percent of their potential. We scratch about 5 percent of it. One of the reasons we limit our potential is that we do not believe.

When you and your wife set up in a little eight-hundred-square-foot warehouse and office all those years ago, did you believe at that time that you would end up with Foster Grant?

No. I couldn't see that far. But I believed I might make a living if I put my heart and soul into it. I believed I could market sunglasses because I'd been in the marketplace doing similar things for ten years.

Any good business is the sum of all the little things done right. I started the first year doing the things we had to do to stay alive. The second year we built on the first year's foundation. The third year we built on the second year's foundation. After twenty-five consecutive years of doing that, we ended up with a substantial company. There is no way in the beginning I could have foreseen what the company would grow to be. Looking back on it, I am still amazed.

Did you start out with a mission statement that reflected your Christian commitment?

I didn't start out in my company with a well-formulated statement of values and beliefs. I didn't start out with the intention of my company conforming to all of those things. I had a keen sense of right and wrong when I started—and I wanted to do right. And I wanted other people in our company to treat people right. My statement of values and beliefs came later. It was a process in getting there. It wasn't actually put on paper until after I'd been in business maybe ten years. I was moving toward that day. *Then* I put the statement out to show people in our company what we wanted to be. And to show our customers what we were.

When I started the company, I had some strong beliefs, but I wasn't really tying the spiritual and the business endeavors together at that point. I had a strong faith in God, but I was not yet focused on this statement of values and beliefs. That process came in time.

I speak of it today in the perspective of somebody who has been through the whole gamut of business, has retired, and is looking back. I wish I'd had it earlier. I encourage young people today, when they start businesses, to get a statement of principles down first.

Would you agree that living by Christian principles is a process? It is not something you perfect.

We are never perfect in living our Christian principles. Along the way, I violated every one of those statements of values and

73

beliefs. I didn't live up to those things 100 percent, but it was good for me to have them hung on the wall as a reminder to focus, knowing my employees would look at it as well. It was placed inside their sales book so that when they opened their book in front of every customer, it was there. The customer could see it; the salesperson could see it. That set the tone for us to do business. It helped us focus on what we wanted to be. And when we missed, it was the standard we came back to.

A good statement of faith and principles can carry you through some tough times.

You need to write it down and stick it on your mirror because you need the reminder. This will help you build a culture that thinks about those things first. And it's good to focus on it, particularly in times when things are not going so well, and to ask, *What are we trying to do here, anyway?* We became a better company because of our statement of values and beliefs.

Bob Buford
Chairman of the Board
The Buford Foundation

None of us knows when we will die. But any one of us, if we wish, may select our own epitaph. I have chosen mine. It is, I should confess, a somewhat haunting thing to think about your gravestone while you are vitally alive. Yet there it is, a vivid image in my mind and heart, standing as both a glorious inspiration and an epic challenge to me: 100X.

It means one hundred times. I have taken it for myself from the parable of the sower in Matthew 13. I'm an entrepreneur, and I want to be remembered as the seed that was planted in good soil and multiplied a hundredfold. It is how I wish to live. It is how I attempt to express my passions and my core commitments. It is how I envision my own legacy. I want to be a symbol of higher yield, in life and in death.

From *Half Time: Changing Your Game Plan from Success to Significance* by Bob Buford

---

Bob Buford had it all. As chairman of the board and CEO of Buford Television, Inc., he had seen the family-owned business grow from a single small-town network affiliate into a powerful network of cable systems across the United States.

But in 1995 Buford wrote *Halftime,* which chronicled his search to find meaning and fulfillment in the second half of his life. Four years later, he sold his share in the business to establish a series of groundbreaking Christian initiatives as part of the Buford Foundation, including:

Leadership Network—This is a resource broker that supplies information to and connects leaders of innovative churches. Leadership Network serves the leadership teams of large churches, as well as leaders in the areas of lay mobilization, denominational leadership at the middle and regional level, and the next generation of emerging young leaders.

Leadership Training Network—The organization's purpose is to identify, train, and provide an ongoing peer-coaching network for leaders of lay mobilization in local congregations.

The Peter F. Drucker Foundation for Nonprofit Management and the Drucker Archives and Institute—In 1988 Dick Schubert, Frances Hesselbein, and Bob Buford convinced Peter Drucker to lend his name, his great mind, and occasionally his presence to a foundation with the purpose of "leading social sector organizations toward excellence in performance." Through its conferences, publications, and partnerships, the Drucker Foundation is designed to help social sector organizations focus on their mission, achieve true accountability, leverage innovation, and develop productive partnerships.

Halftime—This ministry was established to inspire business and professional leaders to embrace God's calling and move from success to significance. Buford has launched "My Halftime Coach" at www .halftime.org to assist those who have read his book and have additional questions.

Buford has also played active roles in the Young Presidents' Organization and World Presidents' Organization and serves on the board of the Hauser Center for Nonprofit Organizations at Harvard. Since the publication of his first book, Buford has written *Game Plan* (1997) and *Stuck in Halftime: Reinvesting Your One and Only Life* (2001).

The foundation for Bob Buford's life and success is his strong faith in God.

I was given the gift of faith as a child and I literally accepted Christ as a child, just exactly the way it says in the New Testament. For whatever reason, I never struggled with the question of whether God exists or whether Christ is really who he said he is. The question I've struggled with for a whole lifetime is not what to believe, but what to do about what I believe, what the implications of belief are.

76

Could you give us a short capsule of your business career to this point?

Let me begin with what I just said: The two pulls on my life when I was a child were would I follow a religious direction or a business direction, because I was also drawn to business.

I can't tell you the exact day and hour of my religious conversion, but I can tell you the exact day and hour of the time I decided *not* to become a minister, that the implication of my faith in Christ was not to be in the full-time ministry. I was in the ninth grade, Ms. Minnie Marsh's English class at Hogg Junior High School in Tyler, left-hand row, second seat back. I thought, *You're not going to be a minister; you're probably going to go into the television business.*

My mother was a pioneer in the radio and television businesses. She received the license for a television station in Tyler in 1954, when television stations were first going on the air around the country. So I felt I would go into television, and that's what I did.

But the call of Christ was always, for me, kind of like a cable car in San Francisco. If you think about cable cars, the cable moves all the time, and the car moves when it's attached to the cable and then stops moving when it isn't. So this religious side of me was always moving under the ground. Every now and then I would attach myself to it, certainly by church attendance and a good deal by Bible study. And then for quite a long while, maybe twenty to twenty-five years, I taught the Bible, which had the effect on me that I learned the Bible. Whether or not anybody else learned anything is a different question! But in a way I was teaching myself. I received through that experience a very deep sense of Scripture, almost as good a grasp of the Scripture as I would have had if I'd been professionally trained in that discipline.

So, did your faith enter into your career choice?

I graduated from the University of Texas, determined not to be the boss's son. That was a big issue. Instead, I worked my way through a variety of positions at a television station in Tyler and became the general manager of the television station in 1970.

My mother, who was the pioneer and chief owner of the company, died in October 1971, which made me the senior family member in this company. I was determined to grow the company at a rate of at least 10 or 15 percent a year. The way we set out to do that was to acquire one additional television station, buy it, develop it, sell it, and grow my net worth and the company's net worth.

For me, the faith part was always a parallel track, like it seems to be for most people. It was about church; it was about Bible study; it was about all those things, and business was about business. I think the key question for many people seems to be—and this comes as an implication or a result of their faith—the question is what *not* to do. You don't want to have affairs; you don't want to lie, cheat, or steal. And I'd say I've done a pretty good job of that. I haven't had affairs and, for the most part, I'm pretty near the top of the class in not lying, cheating, or stealing. I'd say the main implication of faith for me, in my leadership role in the television and the cable television business, was more the way I treated other human beings. My witness was not one of propaganda but of relationship.

Was there a time when they did finally intersect?

If you're in the media business, specifically in the television business, there are all kinds of content issues to deal with. If you ever said, "I want to be in the television business, but I don't want to show any objectionable content," it's like trying to get the salt out of the sea. It just can't be done at the network television level. If you just think of the content of television talk shows or soap operas or prime time violence, any of those sorts of issues, you're either in that business or you're not.

It's hard to be in cable television without having a pay movie channel—HBO, Showtime, Movie Channel, and Cinemax. Half or more of the basic content of movie channels is R-rated movies. So I think you simply have to decide whether your ministry, so to speak, is going to be against those things or your ministry is

78

going to be what mine turned out to be, which is to say, *What can I contribute and what can I do to be useful?* The road I always seemed to go down was the latter of those two, rather than standing against the tide. I kept asking, *What can I contribute?*

Is that question part of what prompted your career change?

Yes. I think that people's lives are seasonal. What works for one season doesn't work for the next season of your life. And a good deal of the challenge in any life is adaptation to the next season. The way I picture it in the book *Halftime* is a series of overlapping sigmoid or S-curves. Anytime you embark on a new season or a new enterprise of any sort, you have the kind of downward part of the S-curve where it's just ugly for a while. You really don't have a set of relationships; you don't have a network; you don't know what you're doing altogether. You're amateurish and kind of all thumbs.

Or maybe you've chosen the wrong path anyway. If you're going to play football, you're going to throw some interceptions, fumble some, and make some touchdowns, but you try to eliminate the errors. But if something begins to work, you're kind of up the strong slope of the S-curve and then, as the bumper sticker says, "Stuff happens"—usually a vein plays out.

You spoke of adaptations. What adaptations have you had to make?

For me, those adaptations have been several. In my early twenties, it was an adaptation from being a student to being a father, primarily, and learning how to do business, how to function within the business world.

In my mid-thirties, the adaptation became more one of achieving balance in my life, not being so driven in my business involvement. The question I asked myself in my mid-thirties was, *What am I going to lose in the process of all this gaining?*

I wrote down six goals or directions for my life, which basically influenced the future course of my life. They were to serve

God by serving others, which I knew was the desire of God and the command of the Scripture because I'd been teaching it. I didn't altogether know what that meant for me, but I knew that was it. Second, to grow my company at a certain rate, I wrote 10 percent a year down, meant 25 percent, and achieved the latter. Third, to stay married to the person I was married to originally and for that to be a vital, robust experience and not "armed neutrality" as you sometimes see. Fourth was for my son to have high self-esteem, which is how I measured myself as a parent. Fifth was to grow culturally and intellectually, to be a lifelong student—not to quit being a student when I quit going to college and started being a businessperson and just kind of going brain dead. And the sixth was to invest the money I would make in the greatest cause I could conceive when it came time to do that.

In my early forties, I came to this period I call "halftime." The subtitle of the book *Halftime* is *Changing Your Game Plan from Success to Significance*. People usually begin to have a feeling that they've had enough of business during their early forties if they've been successful.

We live in a time that is made extraordinary by the fact that many people are successful, at least in the middle class sense. They're successful academics or doctors or entrepreneurs or big company executives or whatever. If you're reasonably bright and you're diligent and you're willing to be focused and apply yourself, you will be successful in the United States today. You have to do all those things, but those are things that ordinary human beings can do.

So the experience of many people right now is that they are finding themselves successful in midlife and saying, "Is this all there is?" There are seventy-eight million baby boomers who currently find themselves at or about fifty years old and wondering those kinds of things.

What happened to you at midlife?

I began to wonder those kinds of things pretty seriously in my early forties. The effect of that was that I began a parallel track in ministry. I really didn't feel like I could do those things within the context of the television business. I think, as it relates to business, what I would say is, You can change the game, but you can't change the rules of the game.

If you're going to be in cable television, you're going to show MTV on some of your systems. We've never put it on where we built the system, but we would buy a system with MTV on and you've got contractual obligations to carry it, plus people rise up in protest if you take *anything* away from them these days. You're going to show R-rated movies, you're going to do a lot of things that would be embarrassing in the context of a Sunday morning service.

So my witness in a business sense was not to lie, cheat, or steal, not to do the most egregious things that one might do— show pornography or things of that nature—not to put MTV on when I had the realistic option not to. But that left plenty of sin that needed to be covered by grace.

I think that's true of any business. If you're in the hotel business, are you going to allow people to stay together who aren't married? If you're Bill Marriott for example, who is a good devout Mormon, are you going to carry SpectraVision or whatever? Of course, 80 percent of the profits of SpectraVision are from adult movies. There are similar ethical conflicts in every business, none of which I think anybody solves to the level of 100 percent purity.

How did you handle this conflict?

What I did was begin a very robust ministry as a parallel career to what I was doing in television. I went to the people who ran my company. First, I went to my two brothers, who own two-thirds of my company. I owned the other third. I said, "I feel called to do something different. I'd like, over a period of time, to reallocate myself from 80 percent business, 20 percent ministry, to 80 percent ministry, 20 percent business. And I'm not going to let this business fail, but it may not grow."

I had to face the fact that I was in a business that had grown at 28 percent a year compound for a dozen years and I was the goose that laid the golden egg. I was the person who set strategy and did the deals and so on.

The conversation I had with myself, and to some degree with my co-owners was, *What if this business grows at 5 percent a year instead of 28 percent a year?* The answer to that involves a loss of multiple millions of dollars. I mean, a *lot* of money.

My brothers were kind enough, wise enough, forgiving enough to say, "If you feel called to do that, we'll go along with you."

I then went to the nonfamily executives in my company and said, "I feel like we have one of two forks in the road to take here because I feel so strongly called to do the things that I've embarked on. We can talk about that, but for the moment just leave that aside. I think either we ought to sell this company, just liquidate it and each go our own way, or I want you, the nonfamily executives, to present me with a plan where I recapture most of my time to do these other things and you run the company." And that's what they did.

That was in about 1984. We ultimately did sell the company in July of 1999, but that's fifteen years in which I became the chairman of the board, set the basic policy, picked the executives, set the standards, and more or less answered the questions in cooperation with others: What business are we in? What are our values? But in terms of day-to-day running the business, they did.

Are you happy with the decision you made?

Looking back on it, in that period of time, the business grew at a rate of 9 percent a year compound. So I have to ask in retrospect, *Was I willing to earn a good deal less net worth for myself and my brothers and the nonfamily executives than I might have?* Who knows? I might have done worse than that, in order to do the things I felt God was calling me to do. But you don't know. Still, I had some regrets about that because that's a quantifiable number.

I once had a conversation with Peter Drucker about that, wherein I was expressing some regret. He said, "Yes, that's true.

But you wouldn't have had your life in those fifteen years. And there wouldn't have been a Leadership Network, which focuses on large churches, the Leadership Training Network, the Halftime organization, the foundation conferences, the Peter Drucker Foundation for nonprofit management, and *Halftime, Game Plan,* and *Stuck in Halftime.*"

Explain your concept of halftime.

What I feel happens to most people in midlife is that they have this halftime experience. The metaphor I use in the book is a game with three periods. A very intense first period, which for most of us is preoccupied with questions of success; a halftime is the period when your options open up a bit. As a result of your success you have choices to make about what to do with the rest of your life. And then a second half where you have at least the option now of reallocating yourself.

With little or no advertising support, *Halftime* now has 170,000 copies out circulating around, so it must be that a lot of people are asking these kinds of questions. And I've concluded that 80 or 90 percent of people are what I call "stuck in halftime." They kind of, at some level, long for significance. At some level, they absorb biblical truth. They go to a good church. They have biblical ideas circulating around in them.

I feel everybody has a calling. It's just part of the spiritual DNA that God wires into people. Look at Ephesians 2:10 as a scriptural reference, but there are plenty of others. In Ephesians 4:1 [NASB], Paul says, "Walk in a manner worthy of [your] calling," after three chapters of fairly intense doctrine.

But I think 80 or 90 percent of people, for the most part, ghettoize their religious experience and say, "Well, that's about church" and don't really make this transition from success to significance.

How do we integrate our religious beliefs into our business life?

It's really hard. I think there are three choices when you come to halftime. The first is more success. The rationale for that is,

It's who I am. It's what I know. It makes me lots of money. I get lots of recognition. And I'm a star in the field. I mean, I've been in this field for whatever it is, twenty to twenty-five years. They basically retreat to success.

The second choice is that they increasingly allocate themselves to significance, however they might define that. Whether it's building homes in Mexico or, in my case, developing effectiveness in large churches, which is how I would define what Leadership Network's focus has been for seventeen years.

I think the third choice is leisure world, retirement of one sort or another—even if it's retirement on the job. Most people, I think, in their forties or fifties can more or less coast on their old lecture notes, if you want to use the academic equivalent of that. But the business equivalent of their old lecture notes is that they're now experts in a certain way and they can continue to be experts. They can do their job with 50 percent of their energy and kind of bluff their way through things. I think a lot of people do that.

What about retirement and leisure? Should a Christian retire?

A lot of people retire to leisure. My opinion of leisure is that I'm very much challenged by the parable of the talents. On October 10, 1988, I wrote "Goals for Life," my goals for myself, for my life—which were pretty balanced. Then I did a study ten years ago of the parables, which have influenced me a lot. The two main parables that influence me are the parable of the sower and the parable of the talents.

I think we're all given a life to invest, and at the end of our life—if we look at life in terms of eternity—this life we're now living is just a scratch on the whole line that is eternity. People have to say, *To what degree am I willing to live in the light of eternal reality versus being captured by the scratch?* If we're living in the light of eternal reality, all of us must know at some level, and certainly if we're biblical, that we'll be held accountable for our lives.

84

I visualize, when we come to the end of our lives and face our Maker, that there will be a final exam with two basic questions. I think the first question is, "What did you do about Jesus?" And I think the second question is, "What did you do with what I gave you to work with, with the life I gave you to work with, not the life I gave Billy Graham to work with or Mother Teresa, but the life I gave Bob to work with?"

My point of view on retirement is that retirement is like the pe"rson who is given one talent and basically buries it, who chooses not to invest himself or herself in the work of serving others, which is so clearly described and commanded in the Scriptures. Or they allocate small portions of themselves to church attendance or modest giving. The normal giving pattern is maybe 2 percent of income. People aren't going to suffer very much pain doing that, so it's a choice that people make.

In terms of my choice for me, I'm influenced by the parable of the sower. I recall the four soils, the hard soil and the superficial soil. Where I think most people are is the third soil in that parable, where the plant which is the life of Christ in the believer is well planted and has taken root but is choked, as Jesus says, "By the cares and concerns of the world." In that parable Jesus says, "The plant therefore becomes unfruitful."

In many ways, the American experience is a Christian experience still, not unlike Europe. But it has a lot of unfruitful "plants" that live busy, busy, busy lives or lives that are preoccupied with money. Jesus always uses the word *deceitful* to describe money, meaning that it promises to deliver something that it doesn't. It's deceptive; it appears to be something that it isn't in reality.

Then Jesus describes the fourth soil, which is for kingdom purposes. I think every human being has the capacity to multiply their lives thirtyfold, sixtyfold, or one hundredfold. For me, I want to be the soil the seed fell in that multiplies one hundredfold.

In order to do that, in my early forties, I reallocated 70 to 80 percent of myself to that end. And when I was sixty-one, I sold my company and allocated more or less 100 percent of myself to that end. In the next season of my life, I basically intend to invest myself and—after setting aside a provision for myself and my family—my money so that by the time I'm seventy-five years old, I want to die broke.

Andrew Carnegie said that it's a sin to die rich.

Carnegie has been a big influence. When you've got the majority of the people in South America and Africa living on a dollar a day or less, you don't have to look far back in history to see what an exceptional situation we have here. And it's not just for rich people. I'm talking about in a middle class sense, which is the situation of a good part of the American population just now and compared to any other time in history. Carnegie said if you have more money than you need, you can do three things with it. You can leave it to your kids, which he thinks is a dubious proposition beyond a certain level, because you'll distance your kids from having a life of their own. Second, you can leave it to your lawyer or whomever you choose as your executor, but nonetheless, you're going to leave it to someone to disperse (someone who, by the way, doesn't have the same calling you do). I don't think God calls lawyers to execute our calling particularly after we're deceased. Or third, you can put the money to work in good works while you're alive, using whatever aptitudes and abilities God has blessed you with. I don't know any other choices beyond those three.

I guess you can default to the government of course, and that is the default position. The tax laws, in my view, somewhat appropriately, make social provision for procrastination and unwillingness of well-off people to make their own voluntary choices to allocate themselves to the good of the greater culture.

Fifteen years ago, I changed the primary loyalty in my life from making more money to serving Christ. But it didn't mean that I got out of business. It simply meant that I allocated less of myself to business. Finally, at age sixty-one, I said, "I want to be fully allocated to good works or to serving God. And I can't be fully allocated if I own a minority interest in stock in a closely held company." So I turned that into money, which I can allocate to kingdom purposes. And I turned my life into doing that.

What advice do you have for a young Christian person thinking of a career in business?

The advice that I'd have is to simply acknowledge that life is seasonal, that the first season in your life is likely to be this very intense period of forming a marriage, raising children, and making your mark in the world. The important job, by the way, in that season of your life is more likely to be your third job than your first job. Because it may be that your first two jobs are how you really sort out who you are and how you work. You may hit your stride on your third job.

But at some point all of us are going to say, *Is that all there is? Where's the finish line in this game?* And we're either going to move the finish line forward or we're just going to stay in business and continue to let that preoccupy us. We're going to reallocate ourselves as I've done, or we're going to reallocate ourselves fully as I've done in my sixties.

The success stories I see are the stories of people who actually make this transition of success to significance. I really believe the second half of one's life should be devoted to issues of significance, rather than issues of running up the score in a game where you've long ago passed the finish line. I think that's the midlife question.

It leads you to another question, which is to say, *What can I do to be useful to others?* Not to simply live a life of accumulation but to live a life of service, at least in part. The people I see that are successful develop a parallel career in their midlife where they don't say, *Someday when I'm too old to do what I'm doing now, when I'm put out to pasture, when I'm reallocated out by the system itself,* then *I'm going to serve others.* Mostly they don't. I find very few people who say "someday" and actually get around to it.

So my advice would be: Life is about more than success. It's certainly about success—it was for me—but it's about a good deal more than that and, for most people, that's going to be seasonal.

So simply acknowledge that's what is in your future and don't wait until you are sixty-five years old to reallocate yourself.

Herman Cain

Founder, T.H.E., Inc.
Former President, Godfather's Pizza

When I get up, I don't take my beliefs off. That's like coming to work with one shoe. Some people think prayer is separate from business, but I don't.

Herman Cain, on speaking to secular audiences

Herman Cain is the prototypical renaissance man. He crunched numbers for the U.S. Navy. He resurrects faltering corporations. He's a much-in-demand motivational speaker. He's a published—and popular—author. Oh, yes. He's also an accomplished gospel singer.

Cain joined the Pillsbury Company in 1977 at age twenty-nine. Within five years, he was vice president of corporate systems and services. He left Pillsbury and started from scratch at Burger King. Nine months later, he was managing four hundred Burger King units in the Philadelphia region. Within three years, his region was the top producer in the chain.

Cain rejoined Pillsbury in 1986 to assume the presidency of the struggling Godfather's Pizza chain. Two years later he led his executive team in a buyout of the now financially lucrative company.

Herman Cain held some other interesting positions along the way, including a slot on the Economic Growth and Tax Reform Commission and a stint as senior advisor to the 1996 Dole-Kemp campaign for the presidency. In 1996 he left Godfather's (now with 550 restaurants and more than a thousand employees in the United States and Canada) to become the president and CEO of the National Restaurant Association. In 1999 he became the CEO of Retail DNA, a provider of technology marketing solutions.

Cain is also the founder of T.H.E., Inc., a leadership consulting company that manages his motivational keynote speaking engage- ments, promotes his books (Leadership Is Common Sense, Speak as a Leader, and CEO of SELF), inspirational video and audio tapes (Save the "Frog," Leadership Is Three Plus Three, Happy Customers, and Success Is a Journey), and gospel CDs (Herman Cain's Sunday Morning).

Sound like too much for one person? Cain's father worked three concurrent jobs—chauffeur, barber, and janitor—to see his family through the tough times. "We were put here to make a difference," says Cain. "We don't have forever to make that difference."

Cain's Christian family had a big impact on his life.

The Scriptures say, "Bring a child up in the way they should go, and when they depart from you, they will not stray from it." Well, that was us. You were expected to do it. If you didn't go to church, you'd be in trouble. And we didn't want to be in trou- ble. So we would go and participate in church activities and youth activities, such as the youth choir, Easter programs, and plays. We did enjoy it, but obviously when you're a little kid, you don't fully appreciate the spiritual side of Christianity.

After I graduated from college, my first professional job was working for the Department of the Navy. I was away from home for the first time, living with a friend of mine in an apartment. I wasn't married; we were bachelors, enjoying life. I woke up that first Sunday morning and said to myself, *I don't have to go to church if I don't want to. I'm a grown man; I'm working; nobody's here to bug me. I'm going to stay home and watch a football game.*

I did this for one Sunday.

The next Sunday, I woke up and I felt like that expression, "fire set up in my bones." I had a very definite feeling: *Some- thing's wrong here.* I guess it was so ingrained in me, or maybe it was the Spirit saying, "No, you're not going to get into this routine," that I got up out of that bed and drove to a little church nearby.

As you went from position to position in your life, how were you able to manifest your beliefs?

A related question that I have been asked over the years is, "Did you ever have to compromise your beliefs in order to succeed?" The answer is, "Absolutely not." I have *never* compromised my faith, my morals, or my beliefs in order to succeed. Young people have the misperception that, in order to get ahead in the corporate business world, it's necessarily cutthroat and ruthless. But I relay to them that you *always* have a choice. You always have the choice to walk away, the choice to change jobs without compromising either your beliefs or your morals.

When I was at Pillsbury, I treated people the way I wanted to be treated. That comes from my faith and it always ultimately paid off in the end. There were times when I knew some people did not like me because I had been selected for a particular job. But this did not cause me to treat them the same way that they treated me or even view them the same way that they viewed me.

I joined the Burger King Corporation as part of its Fast-Track Program. I had been a successful executive at Pillsbury and I'd worked at Coca Cola. When I went to Burger King, I started at the bottom in a restaurant to learn the business from the bottom up.

One of the things closing managers do is tie out the register receipts with the actual cash on hand. You'd then balance it out, take a certain amount to the bank, and keep enough of it to start the business the next day. I'd been at this particular restaurant about a month or two when one night, I came up fifty dollars short. Normally the closing manager would close the restaurant at 11 o'clock, and it takes about two hours to finish closing duties. I would normally leave around 1 A.M. I stayed there all night trying to find that fifty dollars and figure out what was wrong.

I was there until four in the morning, counting and recounting and recounting, trying to find that missing fifty dollars. *Am I doing something wrong? Are all the record tapes correct?* It drove me nuts! I'd never had that happen before. I finally gave up on it when the opening manager came in at five o'clock. When something like that happens, it would be put in your file that you were more than twenty-five dollars off. My report said, "Fifty dollars short." Then I went home.

I was supposed to close the following night and when I did, guess what happened? It was fifty dollars over! I thought, *I don't understand this.*

After a while I became manager of that restaurant despite the report. The store ultimately ended up outperforming a lot of other restaurants in the region, simply because, quite frankly, of the attitude I created in the restaurant.

I was promoted to regional vice president out of that restaurant. I went around and said good-bye to everybody. One of my assistant managers asked if we could go out and have a little celebratory beverage.

"Sure," I said, "but why don't we invite the other assistant managers to go with us?"

He said, "No, no. I just want it to be the two of us."

As we were having coffee together, he confessed to taking the missing fifty dollars out on purpose—and that he had purposely put it back. He was crying as he told me.

"Why?" I asked.

He said, "When you came into the region, the regional vice president told everybody to put you—and he didn't say you, he used an offensive expletive—through the wringer. This was a test to see that, if you were fifty short, whether you were going to put the money in the cash register to make it balance or whether or not you were going to report it."

Through his tears, he asked me if I would forgive him. He said that while I had been there, he had developed such a high level of respect for the way I dealt with people and the way I had treated him that he could not continue to feel good about himself if he did not confess. And now that I was leaving, he regretted that he had taken it.

I said, "I forgive you." Let's call him Kevin. And then Kevin and I started to talk. He asked me about my career. "How did you end up here? How did you end up becoming a vice president at Pillsbury and now with Burger King?" He was just amazed at all the things that had happened to me. And so, over coffee, I told him about some of my dreams and plans. Then we started talking about his dreams and plans. He really didn't want to be in the restaurant business. He wanted to be a stockbroker.

I asked him, "Why haven't you pursued that?"

He said, "I don't know. I just have never taken that first step."

I said, "Kevin, you're a young man. Now is the time for you to take that first step or you're never going to truly be happy."

After I left and went on with my career, Kevin did leave and did pursue a career as a stockbroker. He called me about five years ago and said, thanks to me, that he had gone into the brokerage business. He was not only a stockbroker, but he was running a big office for his company.

Now, I was using my faith. I could have very easily been angry with Kevin and held that against him because of what he did. It was ill-spirited and ill-motivated. But by remaining true to my faith, by remaining true to myself, I could forgive him. But it was also important that I go beyond that too—as Kevin was reaching out in his own way—to try to find out how he could be happier in his life.

That's a long answer. Let me give you another more general answer to your question. I have made a lot of moves, more than most people. In every instance, I made those moves totally confident and totally believing that I was going to succeed at whatever it was that I was trying to do. And it always started with my faith in God and in my belief in myself. I always believed that if I worked a little harder, worked a little longer, then I *could* get it done. I was also motivated by a dream or goal that I was attempting to reach. I never looked back. When I made the decision to switch from one company to the other or made the career change from computer technology over to the restaurant business or to go run the National Restaurant Association, once I felt it in my heart, that meant that I had prayed about it.

You pray about each career decision?

Absolutely! I prayed a lot about each one. I talked each move over a lot with my wife, who's also a believer. It's best to have someone who is also in touch with God who can give you feedback when you're making these kinds of decisions. I listened to my wife as to what the Spirit may be saying to her as well. So that way I went into these positions never looking back, with total faith and total confidence that it was going to work out. And if there were going to be detours or bumps in the road, so be it. But I remembered to always keep my eye on the prize. Generally speaking, my life's choices have always been with a feeling inside that *this* was the direction that God wanted me to go.

Once you reached positions of authority, did you put into place any kind of written or spoken principles? Or did you lead more by example?

I always led by example. I was the director of management information systems at Pillsbury and had a staff of about fifty people. It was a major move because previously I had been in charge of about fifteen people in an analysis group. Less than a year later, we merged with Green Giant and I was selected to head up the organization that had doubled in size. All of a sudden, I'm up to a hundred people.

I talked with the group at large and talked with the people reporting directly to me. Treating people the way you want to be treated was the fundamental rule that I used for *any* organization that I ran. Even if we had to fire someone, we could do it with compassion and consideration, which is what we did.

That approach told people more about the type of person I was than anything that I could have written down. It was by example, it was by actions that people could clearly see, and it was by encouraging people, talking with them about being as productive as we can by making sure that we all do as good a job as we can. It's about communication.

Is that level of communication possible even in bigger companies like Godfather's Pizza?

Yes. I talked to the people reporting directly to me about not only how we needed to be successful as a company but about how to be successful in life. This included the vice presidents and, at the next level, the area managers and, at the next level, the district managers. I would also attend restaurant manager meetings in the regions at the request of my area managers. I may not have touched all of them one-on-one, but I made it a point—even at Godfather's, an organization of twelve thousand people—to try. When I would speak at conventions, I would never talk just about how we were to succeed as a company. I always talked about what we needed to do in order to succeed as human beings, what we needed to do to be happy. I talked about the need for balance between your personal life and your professional life. I was not a stay-in-the-office president of the company or CEO. I was a get-out-in-the-field CEO, an interact-with-people CEO. I met them in the restaurants and talked with them in the restaurants. My goal was to create that kind of rapport. *That's* how you do it: You do it by creating that kind of relationship with the ones you *do* come in contact with, so that it will spread and be contagious throughout the organization.

Now that doesn't mean that there weren't some times when some people didn't get it or they didn't want to get it. I had to deal with those situations. That's part of leadership. I was never hesitant to deal firmly with those situations that were clearly out of order or out of the culture that I was trying to create.

With a multinational public corporation like Godfather's, you dealt with people of many different faiths. How do you handle that?

I believe that all of the major religions have a common spiritual connection, regardless of what words you use to describe it. If I say *God* in a speech, which I do sometimes, I will qualify it by saying, "In my religion, I believe in God. Your religion is your religion. Whoever that Higher Power is in your religion, that is an individual choice." You diffuse it right away by letting people know you're not trying to get them to use *your* words, *your* terminology, *your* practices, or *your* religion. I think that comes through because I don't have to carry myself in a preachy manner. They see it by the way I treat people, the way I am, the way I talk.

I give a lot of keynote speeches, so I speak to a lot of audiences with every different faith represented. I even speak to some international audiences. For example, when I spoke in Egypt recently, I didn't dare go off on some religious tangent. Still, I believe this: Most religions have more in common than they don't have in common.

I never evaluate people by how they practice before their Almighty, as long as they don't evaluate me based on how I practice before my Almighty. At the same time, in a lot of keynote speeches, if I feel so inspired, I'll say, "I've often been asked the key to my success. The key to my success starts with my belief in God. Second is my belief in myself. And third is my belief that you must always have your eye on the dream."

Has moving from Godfather's to a smaller organization changed anything?

Here again, you live by example. In this small group, T.H.E., Incorporated, I have four employees, including myself, my wife (who shares Christian beliefs), my chief operating officer (she's a Christian but I'm not exactly sure which denomination), and my executive assistant, who is Jewish. We have Christian/Jewish discussions all the time, just very matter-of-factly. We do this so we can better understand what those differences are.

Truett Cathey, the gentleman who founded Chick-Fil-A, said, "We will not be open on Sunday." To this day, Chick-Fil-A is closed on Sundays. Why? To allow his employees and their families to pursue their own individual religious beliefs on Sunday. He's not dictating, but he incorporated his belief in remembering the Sabbath so that his people could make their own choices.

I don't think you have to dictate it. I think that's probably the *wrong* way to go. You can encourage people to seek out their own set of beliefs. If they ask me, and they often do, that's when I share with them and give my personal testimony. You wait for those opportunities.

96

Jesus taught that when the opportunity was there, deliver a lesson. A situation would arise and he would deliver a lesson or a parable. A lot of those passages begin with somebody else saying, "Rabbi, what do you think about . . . ?"

And in that same spirit, whether running a company or any organization, you don't have to mandate it. There are certain principles of ethics that I've always insisted on in any organization I was affiliated with *without* having to explicitly talk about or mandate any sort of religious practices.

What advice would you have for a young Christian person thinking of going into business?

First, always remain true to your Almighty. Second, believe in yourself. And third, believe that your God wants you to be all that you can possibly be, as Dr. Schuller would say. That means dreaming and pursuing those dreams, looking for those things in life that not only will provide a livelihood, but also will provide you happiness and satisfaction. Happiness is not money; success alone is not just riches. It is what you do to make a difference in the lives of other people along the way.

In *CEO of SELF*, I go into more detail on the personal decisions and choices that I had to make at all of these different stages. But the essence is the same: Just remain true to your faith and remain true to yourself—but have dreams. And as you achieve those dreams, *have more dreams.*

Wesley E. Cantrell

President and CEO
Lanier Worldwide, Inc.

Customer Vision means seeing our business through our customers', employees', and shareholders' eyes, responding to their needs, and exceeding their expectations.

Lanier's Customer Vision

In the fiercely competitive world of copiers, dictation equipment, fax machines, and printers, Atlanta-based Lanier Worldwide, Inc., successfully slugs it out daily with the likes of Xerox, IKON, and Canon. Lanier's 2,600 employees generated 1.325 billion dollars in sales last year. Now a subsidiary of Japanese office machine manufacturer Ricoh, more than 40 percent of Lanier's sales come from outside the United States.

For the past highly successful decade, Lanier has been led by Wesley E. Cantrell, a gentleman's gentleman in this highly competitive market—and a wonderful Christian witness.

Cantrell began as a field engineer in Lanier's customer service department in Atlanta in 1958. The years that followed saw his impressive climb up the corporate ladder:

1962—District manager, Baton Rouge, Louisiana

1967—Vice president and sales manager for Dictating Machine Products, Atlanta

1972—Executive vice president and national sales manager for all Lanier dictation products and 3M copiers

1974—Board of directors of Oxford Industries (formerly Lanier's parent company)

1977—President of Lanier Business Products, Inc.

1983—Lanier was acquired by the Harris Corporation; Cantrell remains president

1987—President and CEO of Harris/3M Document Products, Inc.

1989—President and CEO of Lanier Worldwide, an officer in the Harris Corporation

1999—Lanier spins off from Harris Corporation; Cantrell becomes chairman and CEO of Lanier Worldwide, Inc.

Perhaps the most important date is March 2000 when Cantrell successfully overcame his toughest challenge of all—cancer. Like all of the tasks he's overcome in the past, Wes Cantrell has somehow managed to use his battle to bring glory to God.

As soon as I was diagnosed, I called my senior staff together and explained to them what was going on. For a period of time there we had an unusual period of closeness and prayer support. The support going on in the organization was really heartwarming. The guys were really pulling for me in every way.

Did you come from a religious background?

Yes, I did. My father was a preacher and I grew up in a Christian home. I had a strong Christian foundation and background. My father's life was very true to his preaching, which was a great advantage because, being a preacher's kid, it's a big problem when your dad is not consistent in his behavior. My father was totally consistent in his behavior. This made me believe all the things that he thought because that was the way he lived.

Still I had a kind of inconsistent life. I was saved when I was eleven years old, but somewhere along the line, at about the age of fifteen or sixteen, I became discouraged about the Christian faith. A lot of it related to my father's work in his church. When I was fifteen years old, the church kicked him out. Some churches do that. When that happened, I went through a thought process that would say, *If the church would do this to my father, and my father is the best man I've ever known, then I don't want to have anything to do with the church.* I wrote the church off. And for a period of time through high school and into college it had very little effect on my life.

Fortunately, I married a good Christian woman. I don't know if Bernadine was in the same position as I was, but she was definitely born again. She definitely looked at herself as a Christian. Shortly after we got married, we decided that we wanted to put our lives back on track, so we joined a church.

When our first child was born, it was a wake-up call to me. When I looked at that sweet little girl, I said to myself, *Here is a person I'm responsible for. In the eyes of God, Bernadine and I are responsible for her upbringing and her guidance.* That made a major change in my life. That was an important step. I call it the "birth of maturity," or something like that.

You have been with Lanier most of your adult life.

That's right. It was my first job out of college. I went to work for Lanier June 13, 1955, and I've been here ever since. The ownership of Lanier has changed, but I've always been with Lanier.

When was your daughter born?

My daughter was born in June 1958.

So pretty much the entire time of your business life, you've had a reasonably consistent walk with the Lord.

Yes. I would say that's true.

You were transferred a lot during your early days with Lanier. Talk about what your faith meant to you during those days.

The first church we got into that really had a big impact on my life was when we moved to Augusta in about 1959. We went to a little church there that had a good preacher and it really began to penetrate. The fact that we now had two children by the time we got to Augusta was bearing heavily on me. We got very active in church in Augusta. In fact I taught a Sunday school class there for the first time. I was ordained as a deacon there. We were pretty serious about it. It definitely had an impact on my life.

How did your faith affect your life in the business world?

In terms of my diligence, my commitment to customers and to employees, all were impacted by that. I believe that if you profess to be a Christian, your walk should agree with that. During that period of time, I had some habits in my life that I gave up.

One of my bosses, the big boss in Atlanta, had a meeting with me during that period of time, about 1959 to 1960. He said, "Wes, I understand that you won't even so much as take a social drink anymore."

I said, "That's true, Gene."

He said, "You realize that you'll never make it in this company if you won't have a social drink? If you invited me over to your house and you didn't offer me a drink, I'd be insulted."

I said, "Gene, I guess I'll just have to be the best salesman you've got in Augusta, Georgia, for the rest of my life then."

Not more than a year or so after that, he called me up to Atlanta and offered me a promotion to move back to Baton Rouge as district manager. For some reason, my performance and my character outweighed whether or not I would take a drink. You've got to understand that drinking was extremely important to him.

The interesting thing is, even though he told me I'd never make it, he gave me that promotion. And then, about four years later, I moved back to Atlanta as general manager of the dictating business. In 1977 I was invited to a meeting where it was announced that we were spinning off from the then–parent company and going public on the New York Stock Exchange. They also announced at this meeting that I'd been made president and chief operating officer of the company. It was all totally surprising, partly because one of the founder's descendants was there. He was the man that I thought would get that job. And when the chips were down, they did not give it to him; they gave it to me.

How do you account for how you have moved up in the company?

Years later, I came across Psalm 75, verses 5–7 [KJV]. It says, "Lift not up your own horn on high: speak not with a stiff neck. For promotion cometh neither from the east, nor from the west, nor from the south. But God is the judge: he putteth down one, and setteth up another." In short, don't toot your own horn. All promotion is from the Lord. The Lord lifts up one and he puts down another. So I came to realize that God really determines all promotions, including that promotion, although I'm sure Gene and the board thought that *they* had decided to give me that promotion. But that promotion was really driven by the Lord.

In the tenth verse of Psalm 75, it says, "All the horns of the wicked also will I cut off; but the horns of the righteous shall be exalted." The Lord cuts off the horn of the ungodly, but he lifts up the horn of the godly and faithful. That's a very interesting passage of Scripture. It said two things to me. First, it made me understand that I didn't really need to politic for a job; and second, that I shouldn't take credit for having gotten the job because it was of the Lord. Since then I've used that Scripture a lot in teaching young men to say that ambition is a wonderful thing, but it needs to be in submission, total submission, to the Lord.

I once had a student in my Sunday school class who wanted to know why I didn't drink, so I wrote him a list of five reasons. I told him I have many reasons. Some of these reasons were practical, while two of them were based on Scripture. One of the practical reasons was that if you don't drink, there is absolutely no chance of becoming an alcoholic! But I was really concerned about my influence on my children. If you really wanted to get down to why I don't drink, that's what it was.

Later on, I became concerned about the many others under my sphere of influence.

For a number of years now, you have been a Christian who has been a head of a company, but not a Christian company. What has that meant from a practical standpoint?

There are a number of things from a Christian perspective that are treasured by bosses of all stripes, whether they are Christian or non-Christian. Those are things like truthfulness, honesty, integrity, trust, and the ability to generate trust, which are treasured by everyone. In my business career, I never attributed those things necessarily to my being a Christian, but obviously, that was the basis. Those are behaviors that are expected in the normal practice of business to generate trust with your employees, with your bosses, with all those who report to you. These are things that you *should* do, but they are becoming uncommon in business today.

One of the key things that came out of this was a verse that became really meaningful to me early in my career. It was Proverbs 22:1 [KJV]: "A good name is rather to be chosen than great riches." That became a governing force in my life about all the decisions that I made in business.

First of all, you would choose to have a good name with your wife and family. That was most important to me. I've been married to the same woman for forty-four years. The development of inappropriate relationships is common in the marketplace today. I do not understand how you can expect your employees to trust you when they realize your wife doesn't trust you. That is inconsistent behavior.

In addition, I would say that my commitment to Proverbs 22:1 resulted in the company's commitment to customer satisfaction. In all of the TQM—total quality management—studies, the first item was focus on the customer. It dawned on me that we are obligated to put the customer first, making sure we exceed the customer's expectations. We do everything we can for the customer to get everything they've paid for, plus a little extra. We use the old Tom Peters phrase: "underpromise and overdeliver." I think that this "good name" principle is really translated into that. Because even before we put in a TQM process as such, we already had very good customer satisfaction, but we were able to improve it quite a bit with the TQM process.

Do you have a company philosophy or motto?

We do. We have a vision/mission statement and a statement of principles, all of which reflect some of the values that we're talking about. Ten years ago I realized there needed to be a written values statement. When I was no longer around, I wanted these values to live on.

Since I always worked for public companies and had a board of directors who were not necessarily all Christian, we just worded it in a way that we didn't put a scriptural reference to it. Certainly they knew where I was coming from. In fact our statement of principles is really based on the Ten Commandments, but you won't recognize the Ten Commandments in it. You have to do a little philosophical analysis of the intent of the Ten Commandments and apply them to business. But you'll see the strong family values, the respect for the individual, and all those kinds of things that come from the Ten Commandments.

You've recently come through a serious health problem.

Actually in August 1996 I was diagnosed with prostate cancer. For a few days, I went through the "Woe is me" and "Why me, Lord?" struggles.

I worked my way through that and I found a Scripture, Job 5:25–27, which basically says your offspring shall be as the grass of the earth. I have twenty-one grandchildren, so that's already happened. Then it says you shall live to a rich and full life, like a shock of corn not being harvested until its season is full. I took that as a personal message from the Lord for me.

You've heard the concept of getting a word from the Lord or a *rhema?* The Greek word *rhema* means a word from the Lord at a special time and place to respond to a special need at that time. When you pray and you ask the Lord to reveal something to you and you search the Scriptures, he will give you that word. That's the process I was going through when I found those verses in Job. My special word was that I was not going to die until the Lord was ready for me to die. I guess I already knew that anyway, but with or without prostate cancer, I was going to live the full life that he had planned for me.

The final thing that those verses said is to be assured that this is for your good. I began to see the good things that were coming out of my diagnosis in terms of focusing my attention on the brevity of life and trying to do some things that count during the remainder of my life. As a result of that diagnosis, I did a lot of study and research and went on a pure vegetarian diet. Ultimately, we were able to control the growth of the cancer. It didn't grow at all. In fact it went backward for about the next three years.

In 1999 Lanier was spun off from Harris. Harris gave us a boatload of debt, and the industry was turning south. It created immense stress for me. And, as you know, stress is counterproductive in terms of building your immune system. So my PSA went up. It had been down in the low threes and it went up to 3.7 and then rose to 4.7 in just a short period of time, and then to 5.7. I got very concerned since it was rising so quickly that the indication would be that the tumor was growing fast.

How did you respond to this negative news about the growth of your cancer?

My good friend Larry Burkett connected me with some people at Emory he knew and trusted. We met and I went to San Francisco and had a special spectroscopic MRI made at the University of California in San Francisco. That picture revealed that the cancer was larger than everybody thought. The MRIs also revealed that it was pushing against the capsule that surrounds the prostate gland. You don't want to let it get outside of that container. We came right back and we scheduled surgery here in Atlanta with Dr. Marshall at Emory. Dr. Marshall is a marvelous, gifted physician. He did the surgery and did a wonderful job. Since that time, I've had no serious side effects from the surgery. My PSA has been a zero ever since I had the surgery. I'm feeling really, really good about that.

I think that the word from the Lord was the most important thing that came out of that incident. It also prompted a sense of urgency on my part to be willing to give of my time to other men who have cancer, specifically prostate cancer. I've felt an urgency and willingness to give my testimony whenever it would be important, particularly men's groups. And through it all, to really make sure that I've discovered what God's purpose is in this and be sure that I fit into that purpose, both from a personal and a corporate level.

If someone is thinking about business as a career choice, what advice would you have for them?

For one thing, the ideal thing for a Christian young person is to own their own business because then you can chart your own course as a Christian business. Of course, not every young person is going to have that opportunity.

Perhaps the second best thing is a career in sales. With a career in sales, if you're productive in terms of generating sales, you have a lot of freedom. Additionally, people don't always try to fit you into some secular mold that they've created for the company, so you still have that same kind of freedom. I always encourage young people to examine selling as a career. I've spent a lot of time in selling and I've found a lot of freedom.

There is another interesting thing about selling and that is, if the Lord chooses to reward you financially, it's real easy. This is a strange way to say it, so let's just put it this way. The Lord can easily bless you in a selling career because he just gives you a lot of business. You make a lot of money—and then he wants you to demonstrate the proper principles in how you use that money. What *do* you do with that money? Do you tithe that money? Do you use it for his work? Do you view him as the owner of all the money, and are you just the steward? What's your view of these dollars? I think selling is a wonderful career in that regard.

Another thing we need to understand as Christian young men and women going to work in a secular world is that the world still tremendously respects keeping your word, being on time, and being courteous. Those things are still highly regarded. They're becoming less and less obvious in the world today. Just having good manners is looked on with great favor because so many people don't have good manners anymore.

This is the kind of advice I would give a young person going into business.

Philip A. Clemens

Chairman and CEO
Clemens Family Corporation

Hatfield will continue to honor the values of its past and provide quality products to our customers produced by our greatest asset, our employees, and we will strive to operate in a way that will honor the Lord Jesus Christ.

Mission Statement

1. *Produce approved quality products with maximum efficiency, to sell them at reasonable prices, to meet our customer's needs through service and product value, and to realize a reasonable return on our investment.*
2. *Provide our employees good working conditions with modern equipment to perform their jobs efficiently, fair wages for work performed, adequate benefits, and a share of the company profits.*
3. *Maintain and apply Christian principles in all our customer, employee, and vendor relationships.*
4. *Support our community through financial contributions, environmental concerns and extend a helping hand whenever possible.*

Philosophy of Business

The Clemens Family Corporation (formerly Hatfield Quality Meats) was founded in 1895 by a Christian family and has become the fifth largest pork processor in the United States. The company's amazing twelve hundred products include such well-known brand names as Hatfield, Beaver Falls Quality Meats, Medford Deli, Prima Porta, and others, all overseen by chairman and CEO Philip A. Clemens.

Clemens's other legacy is equally prestigious. He's a direct descendant of Samuel Langhorne Clemens, a writer better known by his pen name—Mark Twain. For some, twin legacies like these would be overwhelming or at least intimidating. But Philip A. Clemens relishes the challenges that have come with his name.

Today Clemens stays busy on numerous boards, ranging from multinational corporate food producers and the American Meat Institute to the United Way in northern Pennsylvania. He's active in his local church, a ten-year volunteer for the American Red Cross, and—along with wife, Linda—doting dad to three children.

Along the way, Clemens has built a reputation for honest dealing and plain talking. Or, to quote his illustrious ancestor: "Always do right. This will gratify some people and astonish the rest" (from a speech by Samuel L. Clemens, delivered to the Young People's Society, Greenpoint Presbyterian Church, Brooklyn, New York, February 16, 1901). Philip Clemens attributes to his Christian roots the qualities that have helped him in the business world.

I was very fortunate to come from a Christian family. Both my father and mother were raised in Christian homes. Their parents on both sides were Mennonite. Soon after my parents were married, they joined with a small group of evangelical Christians that started a church that had both an outreach and a missions emphasis. As part of growing up, we were expected to be in church whenever the doors were open. As a result of what I heard and saw from both a home and church view, I accepted Christ as my personal Savior at the age of five in our home.

My faith grew and was challenged. As a teen, I rededicated my life to Christ. Being raised in a Christian home and working in the family business gives you choices. Do I choose to accept what my parents believe about Jesus Christ and do I want to follow their steps into the family business? Fortunately they set the model that was one that I wanted to follow. First and foremost, their walk with Jesus was one that I saw as genuine and a faith that I desired. My dad clearly put his walk with Christ before the business and set an example for me to follow.

When did you get involved in the family business?

I had the privilege of growing up right in the business. When I was ten, my parents gave my two other brothers and me the chance to work in the business or do more chores around the house. I chose working in the business with no pay. We could not go on the payroll until age twelve. I continued to work part-time at the business until I graduated from high school. For several summers I did work as a volunteer at a Bible camp. In addition, I worked some other part-time jobs until I took a full-time position at Hatfield. I worked a full-time schedule—up to sixty hours per week—while attending college full-time.

When I graduated from college, I chose to look for other employment and also interviewed with Hatfield. After reviewing my choices, I chose the most difficult, in my estimation, and went to work in the family business. They immediately sent me back to school to learn what was then called data processing to program our first computer.

Shortly after I moved from our data processing department to start our personnel department, I was offered a full-time ministry position to operate a Christian camp. After much prayer, I felt that God confirmed my being in the family business. Since then, I have had other offers, but God has always confirmed that this is the place I am to be at this point, even up until today.

As I sit here today, I am convinced that this is where God wants me to be. If he gave me a call tomorrow, I would be willing to move where he would have me to be. A good friend of mine, George Murray, currently president of Columbia International University, challenges people: "Are you ready to go, but willing to stay?" I am willing to go where God wants me to be, but I am also willing to stay here if that is what he wants.

Your web site says that Hatfield, Inc., was founded by a Christian family in 1895. How has that made Hatfield different?

The Clemens Family Corporation, the owners of Hatfield Quality Meats, states its mission this way: "It is the Clemens Family Corporation's goal to own profitable diversified enterprises that honor the Lord Jesus Christ. We are committed to be a Clemens Family controlled corporation. We will be good stewards of all God has given us, including our assets, employees, the environment in which we work and the neighborhoods in which we live."

This statement goes back to our foundation. We believe that God *does* own our business and will hold us as a family, and me in particular as the chairman and CEO, accountable for what we did with what he has given us. We try to operate our businesses with this in mind. As a result, we tithe our profits. We have profit sharing and share one-third of our profits with our employees. We strive to uphold all laws and regulations—knowing we are the second most-regulated industry in the United States, next to nuclear power—and we even go well beyond many minimum regulations.

How does operating as a Christian company affect your business?

At times our honesty and the way we do business *do* lower our profits. For example, we have a complete waste treatment facility and could discharge our wastes into the local streams. However, we intentionally send our treated water to the local sewer plant because we believe it is a better way to do business. That is just one example of how we go beyond what we could do to be good community citizens. Sharing one-third of our profits with employees is just another example.

I believe operating our business according to our mission statement has some advantages and disadvantages. Most of the advantages come when non-Christians come into our businesses. They often comment on our mission statement and how unique it is. Most say that they appreciate that we are willing to say where we stand. It does open the door to share what we believe and how we see this business.

Some of the disadvantages come from fellow Christians. The only critical statements that I have received on our mission statement are from fellow believers. They are critical of the use of the name of Jesus Christ in our statement. Also they sometimes look at decisions we have made and say that we are harming the name of Christ by what we have done. At times they may be correct. Then we are encouraged to relook at how we do business in his name.

Has your personal faith had an impact on your decisions since you joined Hatfield?

It certainly *does* have an impact on how I do business. Let me give one clear example. A few years ago, we were considering acquiring another business. After doing some of our due diligence work, we saw this was not a business for us. The person I was dealing with on the other side was telling his boss that this was a done deal. When he told his boss that we were walking away from the deal, his boss got very upset—rightfully so, since he was not being told the truth all along. We were threatened with a suit because we "had led them to believe a deal was to be signed and just got cold feet." His boss was going to enforce the contract, saying we had continually lied to them.

My response was that it was not true. I could show what had been clearly communicated all along. However, even though our communications were clear, if he really felt I had misled him, we would buy the business and close it down. Our reputation of our word was more important than the dollars. When his boss heard this, he immediately withdrew his threat and said his employee had confessed his wrongs, and he commented he rarely does business with individuals that are as honest and are willing to "put their money where their mouth is" by making sure they were not misunderstood. It was a test on my part. I would have liked to take him to the cleaners for his lies, but as a Christian, I couldn't do that.

One of the things we do on a regular basis at our companies is to open all management meetings in prayer. Our chaplains, through Marketplace Ministries, help lead employee prayer groups and Bible studies. In addition, we take every opportunity possible to convey our faith—especially at special times like Christmas and Easter.

How does God work through the fifth largest fully integrated pork processor in the country? Does Hatfield as a corporation operate by a set of principles?

The one that is used is the one that most all can understand—"Do unto others as you would have them do unto you." We attempt to practice that in all relationships—employee, customer, and vendor. One way this was expressed was just several years ago. The hog market across the U.S. fell to record low prices. A farmer normally has a break-even price of about 40 cents per live pound. Grain prices fell; thus their costs fell and farmers overproduced. The price fell to 8 cents per pound. Farmers were losing their shirts; some of them were losing their farms. We initiated a minimum payment of 25 cents with that low market. We paid out significantly more money than our competition—and realize we process more than 7,000 hogs per day at an average live weight in excess of 250 pounds. It was the right thing to do. A few other packers followed our lead and set minimums of 15 cents per pound. The Secretary of Agriculture of the U.S. called me and personally thanked us for what we were doing for hog farmers in the United States. We did not do it for the publicity. It was the fair and right thing to do.

One principle we use—certainly not biblical, but from a famous relative of ours—Mark Twain. He said, "When you're green, you grow; when you are ripe, you rot." We attempt to be always growing in our Christian walk and talk. We don't want to ever convey to our employees, customers, or vendors that we have arrived and have it all together. We will make mistakes. We want to be known as much for *how* we do business as we are known for correcting it when we have blown it. We never want to be "ripe" in our Christian walk, because we will be rotting.

113

Do you have any advice for someone about to enter the workplace?

Each individual clearly must make the choice of allowing God to rule every area of life. Too often those who profess Christ on Sunday never bring him to the workplace on Monday. God has called us to live for him in every aspect of life, including work.

However, I have a very strong feeling about sharing Christ on the job. If sharing Christ on the job requires me to steal from my employer's time, it is wrong. I believe we are called to let our lights so shine before men that they would see Christ. There is a time to share, but not on company time.

I believe it is also wrong to use your position to give you a captive audience. I could have employees come into my office and I could force them to listen to a gospel presentation. That would be wrong. I need to be sensitive to the leading of the Holy Spirit about when to cross that line. My position should never be used as a weapon to beat them over the head with the gospel. It violates all scriptural principles. Yet if someone comes to my office, or I observe someone that is hurting, I need to reach out with Christian compassion and love.

Do you have any advice for Christians in the market-place?

If you are going to start a business venture, don't put Jesus Christ in your mission statement or what you are doing unless you know the costs. It is better to operate as a purely secular business than to try to be a halfhearted Christian businessperson. Too often Christian businesspeople are seen as no different than any other businessperson. That's a shame. We need to be the salt and light God has called us to be. We will be held accountable for how we have conducted his business.

Jerry Colangelo

Chairman and CEO
Phoenix Suns, Arizona Diamondbacks,
WNBA's Phoenix Mercury, Arena Football
League's Arizona Rattlers

If you have strong beliefs about how you conduct
your own life, then deciding whom you wish to be
associated with in business and how you want to go
about making your business decisions doesn't have
to be a dichotomy. Matter of fact, if you stick to your
principles and conduct yourself accordingly, it does
more than mix. It's the way it should be. It's what is
expected of you as a Christian.

Jerry Colangelo

Today Jerry Colangelo is one of the most powerful men in Arizona. The PBS series *Imaging America* recently did a feature on the "poor kid from Chicago [who] now manages or owns every major sports franchise in Phoenix." To be precise, he has 36 percent ownership of the Phoenix Suns, worth about 200 million dollars[1]; 1 percent ownership of the world champion Arizona Diamond-backs, worth about 350 million dollars[2]; 36 percent of the Phoenix Mercury license, worth about 25 million dollars[3]; and 25 percent ownership of the Arizona Rattlers, worth about 50 million dollars. He's also on the board of directors of virtually every civic, com-mercial, and arts-oriented organization in Phoenix. He's been the most visible, most convincing force behind a number of civic pro-jects, including arenas, ballparks, and public funding initiatives.

---

1. Colangelo controls the management group that owns 36 percent of the team.
2. Colangelo management group holds options to purchase up to 25 percent of the team.
3. Colangelo controls the management group that owns 36 percent of the team.

But yesterday he was just another skinny kid scrabbling the mean streets of Chicago's famed Hungry Hill neighborhood looking for yet another pickup game of basketball or one last disorganized, informal game of stickball in the streets.

What's the common thread between yesterday and today? A deep and abiding faith in Jesus Christ. Jerry Colangelo was raised in a large and happy Catholic home in Chicago Heights, an informal village of working-class Catholic families.

Family extended beyond the four walls. Family was the neighborhood. You could walk into anyone's home and be welcome. Growing up in Chicago Heights on Hungry Hill gave me the basics for a work ethic. You're in a neighborhood where people go to work every day with a lunch pail. There is an appreciation for putting in a hard day's work. I was very blessed to have that kind of upbringing. I learned early on you have to work, and the most important things in life are faith, family, and friends.

What were some of your early jobs?

I had four daily paper routes and a regular caddie job at Flossmoor's Idlewild Country Club. And I spent a lot of time playing baseball and basketball. In time, sports consumed all of my time. I grew up following the Chicago White Sox and Chicago Cubs and was a pretty good pitcher, so when the University of Illinois offered me a scholarship, I jumped at the chance. While at Illinois, I met my wife-to-be, Joan. At that point, church was the farthest thing from my mind.

How did you become more committed to serving Christ?

I certainly, at the time, thought I was committed, having been raised a Christian. But it was not until I met my wife-to-be that I really started to understand that there was something different about her. And what I came to find out was that she was a born-again Christian. I learned a great deal from meeting her and being exposed to Christianity at that time. But that was only the first tentative step in my faith journey.

116

A sore left arm ended my pitching career, but I excelled as a point guard in basketball and was named captain of the University of Illinois Illini and was an All-Big Ten selection.

Did you think you were on your way to playing professional ball?

Yes. But in pro basketball at the time when the league was only nine teams, they were drafting just a few players out of college and maybe one player a team made it. I wasn't one of the nine.

Reality began to set in and so I had to go to work. What I decided to do was go home, go back to my hometown. I went into private business. I was playing in a semi-pro league and we were having children.

Meanwhile, Joan was very patient with me. It was a gradual thing—watching her, week after week, go to church. Finally, I became interested enough to discover for myself just *where* Joan's apparently endless reserves of love and patience originated. I came to find out that the minister at the particular church she was going to had a lot in common with me. He was from an Italian family, was raised in a Catholic situation, and had converted to American Baptist. And so I was somewhat intrigued.

John Nastari was the minister of the Morgan Park Baptist Church in South Chicago, and we really hit it off. When they opened a satellite church in Homewood, Illinois, in a small church in a grade school building, that's when we began attending.

It was through the efforts of my wife, as I mention first and foremost, and then being exposed to John, that I made a commitment in my life to Jesus Christ and became a Christian. It was attending that church and listening to that man that I saw the light of day and made a commitment to the Lord to change a lot of things in my life. It was the beginning of a process for me that changed my life forever. That was back in 1963.

What was happening in your career at this time?

I was playing semi-pro basketball, but my primary income came from operating a tuxedo-rental business. It was during this period that I discovered I enjoyed selling as much as shooting and rebounding.

In 1965 I met a fellow named Dick Klein, who was in the incentive merchandising business in Chicago. A few weeks after he'd hired me, he informed me that he had this dream of getting a National Basketball Association franchise for the city of Chicago. Klein quickly lined up enough investors to pay the NBA's 1.25-million-dollar franchise fee.

Six months later, Dick's dream became a reality, and I had the fortune to be involved with the Bulls' start-up. In January of 1966, when the franchise was awarded, Dick asked me to be part of that organization, and that's how it all began.

What was your job with the Bulls?

I was named head scout and director of merchandising and marketing. It was a small mom-and-pop operation back then, but even in those pre–Michael Jordan years, the Bulls were a popular success.

Two years later, I became the first general manager of the NBA's expansion Phoenix Suns. I was twenty-eight and the youngest general manager in all of professional sports.

The franchise flourished from the beginning and, by the 1976–77 season, the young Suns met and eventually lost to the mighty Boston Celtics in the NBA championship series.

We had absentee ownership with the franchise, and I've probably had as much autonomy over the years as anyone in that capacity. I even coached the team on a couple of occasions early in those years, and with some success, but got *that* out of my system. As interim coach, I was able to lead the Suns to a 24–20 record during their second season and the team's first playoff berth. Players like Alvan Adams, Dennis Johnson, Larry Nance, Connie Hawkins, Truck Robinson, Dick Van Arsdale, Paul Silas, and Gar Heard were heroes in Phoenix. In 1980–81 I was honored to be named the NBA's executive of the year.

And you would receive that honor an unprecedented four times. Did your Christian faith influence the way you managed the team?

From the beginning, my goal was to operate the Suns by Christian principles. I remember reading a Billy Graham column in the local newspaper some years ago, and the title of that particular article that day was "Business and Jesus Christ Do Mix." Of course, there was certain Scripture quoted in the article. It hit home with me that if you have strong beliefs about how you conduct your own life, then deciding whom you wish to be associated with in business and how you want to go about making your business decisions doesn't have to be a dichotomy. Matter of fact, if you stick to your principles and conduct yourself accordingly, it does more than mix. It's the way it *should* be. It's what is expected of you as a Christian.

And I think over the years, although we've all had our slips—and those who've had the opportunity to talk about it would admit that we've all had our slips and our failures—you keep persevering. You start with trying to prioritize your values. The relationship with our Creator should be number one. And our family comes number two and our business comes number three. We should be consulting the Lord in *all* decisions. Most often when we make our own decisions, we come to wonder why we made them in the first place. It's a continual battle, living in this world with all of the pulls and tugs and pitfalls. We have to keep a focus on what really is important.

In 1986–87, the Suns were struck by a drug scandal. How did you handle that?

That blow rocked me and the fans of Phoenix's only professional sports franchise. We felt a cloud of oppression settle over the city. Suddenly, amid the darkness, a once-in-a-lifetime opportunity shone through. I had the chance to purchase the Suns.

I had spent a lot of years with this franchise and I felt like it was mine from day one. And so in 1987, when the purchase was made, it just took things to a different level because I didn't have to negotiate with partners. Even with the autonomy, there was still always someone to report to. With the ownership change, I started to react more instinctively. What my gut told me is what I would do.

Your instincts have proved sound time and time again. The franchise has evolved into one of the sport's show-cases. *Sports Illustrated* calls Phoenix a "fantasy land" under your leadership.

We're thankful that the Suns are a perennial contender, even taking the Chicago Bulls to six games before we bowed out in the NBA finals in 1992–93. Popular players like Kevin Johnson, Tom Chambers, Dan Majerle, Jeff Hornacek, Charles Barkley, A. C. Green, Jason Kidd, and Danny Ainge have called Phoenix home. I think because players knew I would be fair, several marquee athletes have accepted much less than their market value to play in Phoenix.

No less an authority than the *New York Times Magazine* has had this to say about you: "He is experienced in sports, has marketing expertise, and has an impeccable reputation in the business field."

It's been an unbelievable run over the past twenty-plus years. As I think back on my life in terms of the old neighborhood that I came from, people didn't have anything to speak of, and yet they were happy. People shared whatever they had. I've often told the story that I knew about roots before *Roots* became popular. I still keep a picture of my boyhood home at 156 E. 22d Street in Chicago on my desk. As I think about all those things that have taken place in my life, and as much as I have to be grateful for, you can't help but wonder, as I did at one time, why me? Why did this happen to me? Why not someone else?

Does your strong religious foundation provide the answers to those questions?

Yes. You come to believe that it's not by happenstance. We are who we are, and we do what we do because that's part of God's plan. So, for whatever reason, to be put in a high-profile position in a community, and to have spent the thirty years that I have here in Phoenix, there *is* a responsibility and accountability. I believe I have to set an example because of my personal beliefs and what I stand for. It entails just about everything you do as a human being—what your priorities are, the people you choose to associate with, the people you hire, the players you have in your uniforms, your involvement in the community, your giving to the community, your commitment to making life better for those around you. I think it's all part of the plan for me.

So how did you move on to acquire other teams?

In time the success of the Phoenix Suns (they have the second longest consecutive sold-out streak in NBA history, second only to the Bulls) has enabled me to branch out. In the early 1990s, I led the drive to build what would become America West Arena in downtown Phoenix. When it opened in 1992, it became the new home of the Suns and the site of dozens of other sports and entertainment events.

In the following years, I turned my attention to bringing major league baseball to the Valley of the Sun. I led the investment group that raised the whopping 150-million-dollar franchise fee needed to found the Arizona Diamondbacks, along with another 50 million dollars in start-up costs and 100 million dollars for the state-of-the-art Bank One ballpark.

We were also able to lure the Winnipeg Jets National Hockey League team (now the Phoenix Coyotes) to Arizona, as well as women's professional basketball and arena football to town.

It's well-known that your outspoken faith has meant that top free agents with similar values, including Travis Lee, Matt Williams, and Jay Bell, have chosen the Diamondbacks over equal or larger offers.

Since the Suns' debacle in 1987, I have tried to acquire athletes who are both talented *and* solid citizens. Once you make a commitment and you come out of the closet and the world knows that you are a Christian, you quickly realize there is a responsibility that goes along with that. When it comes to athletes and the perception of them and the reality of what some of them represent, I'm a little dismayed at the ills of society today—the permissiveness that exists, the breakdown of the family unit, the anything-goes attitude. Obviously, as it relates to athletes, a system that allows young people who are gifted to get through—be it high school or even college—and not be equipped to deal with the real world is flawed. There's something wrong with that. That system needs to be addressed. I've been a very strong proponent of that.

The bottom line is, in basketball, at least, we get a finished product when players come to us. So, what we try to do, as best we can, is investigate. We get to know them as people; we learn about their backgrounds and, sometimes, we see red flags. We need to be aware going in about potential problems. Since we are not in the rehabilitation business, it's important to be very, very selective in the selection process.

I'm a strong proponent of basketball emulating baseball's minor league system. Athletes that come into baseball usually have signed as seventeen- or eighteen-year-old kids, and they've paid their dues in the minor leagues. They've ridden on the buses and they've played for four hundred or five hundred bucks a month. When they get to the big leagues, it's kind of a different attitude—they're so happy to be there. That may not apply to all, but to many. I think because they've paid their dues, they have more of an appreciation. Not so in basketball.

I wholeheartedly disagree with those who believe that they're *not* role models, because I think if you're gifted with talent, you're expected to conduct yourself as a good human being and have your priorities correct—knowing that people are looking to you as a role model.

When athletes come to Phoenix, do they already know that your religious faith is paramount both in your daily life and in your business operations?

When Paul Westphal was coaching the Suns, we had Scripture up in the locker room because Paul was a strong Christian. I look at the locker room as belonging to the coach and his assistant coaches and the players but, in the end, the head coach is responsible for what he chooses to be in that room. I do not step over the line. It really depends on the beliefs and the personalities of the people who are working for you at any particular time. I think it's important to lead by example, so that's where I try to keep my focus.

What advice do you give to someone interested in succeeding in business?

First and foremost, in terms of principles, every individual needs to have a solid foundation. You have to live by those principles; you can't just talk them. It's how you conduct your life.

Number two, it's important for every individual to be positive, to look forward, to be willing to fail. Too often people are so concerned about failing that they're not willing to move forward to make a decision, to take a calculated risk. Again, if you have the foundation, if you believe in your Savior—who promised us an awful lot in terms of looking to him for guidance and support—and if you share with him in the decision-making process, there's no reason to fear going forward and making those decisions. If it's meant to be that you don't make it, that there is a failure involved, that's quite all right, because that's the way it was meant to be. That's something that I've always truly believed in.

Too many people are so concerned about lack of opportunity that they fail to see opportunities walk right by. You've got to keep your eyes and ears open and be willing and content to go forward and make the decisions without fear of failure.

I'm going to qualify all of this by saying it does need to be a *calculated risk*. It's not blind risk. You need to be prepared; you need to know the facts. And if you're prepared, you go forward and don't look back—because they may be gaining on you!

Finally, you don't have to take the shortcut; you don't have to make an under-the-table deal. There are ways to do it that are aboveboard, that have honesty, that have integrity. It's something you must work on daily because Satan's always out there tempting you to take that shortcut. It's an ongoing contest, one that I'm very cognizant of as I conduct my business daily.

Charles L. Collings

**Past President
Raley's Superstores**

Learn about the community, explore the opportunities and give time a chance. Be ready for those God-interfering times when you find yourself in the right place at the right time, and be loyal to the people you work for.

Charles L. Collings

I also made a commitment that any business decisions I made would be based on his Word. I desired to be a Christian who happened to be a businessman, not a businessman who happened to be a Christian.

God will show you how to work successfully with people. I follow the scriptural admonition of thinking more highly of others than I do of myself. So many people have followed books like Winning through Intimidation and Looking Out for #1, which are utterly destructive. You don't build a successful team through intimidation; you get people to work together because they want to, and because they trust you.

Excerpts from "A No-Lose Proposition"
by Chuck Collings

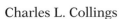

When Tom Raley built his first market in California's Gold Country in 1935, he proudly proclaimed it "the nation's first drive-in market."

Charles L. Collings—known by CEO and stockboy alike as Chuck—joined the chain in 1956. Today there are more than 150 Raley's, with more than 18,000 employees. Annual sales are now edging past the 3-billion-dollar mark.

Raley's has been voted the number one supermarket chain several years running by *Consumer Reports* magazine. And one of the things its customers appreciate is its commitment to community, including Food for Families, a nonprofit organization that has contributed more than 10 million dollars to feed hungry people. When earthquakes ravaged San Francisco and wildfires scorched Los Alamos, Raley's was there first, distributing more than 500,000 pounds of food and necessities. It pioneered recycling and pesticide testing in grocery stores. And the list goes on.

Don Beaver, past president of the California Grocers Association, had this to say of Collings: "I consider him one of the top CEOs in the grocery industry today and that's because of the innovations he has brought to the industry."

Michael J. Teel, Thomas P. Raley's grandson and now Raley's president and CEO, credits Collings with much of Raley's success. When Teel joined the company, he said that Collings served as his mentor: "Typically he concentrated first on the spiritual. 'I'm praying for you, Mike,' he said. I didn't know then how much I needed it. But he did. And that's been his pattern ever since. He prays first. Then he guides, directs, instructs, and encourages."

Collings values the opportunities he's had at Raley's.

I came to work with Raley's in 1956. The founder of the company, Thomas P. Raley, had eight small stores doing approximately 8 million dollars a year, with two hundred employees. When I retired from Raley's in 1998—although I am still involved—we were at 2.4 billion dollars, with more than 100 stores and about 14 or 15,000 employees. Since that time, I've been involved on the board of directors. We're now at more than 3 billion dollars annually and around 19,000 employees. And we're still a privately owned company.

Did you come from a religious family?

Yes. My folks reaffirmed their Christian faith when I was about nine or ten years old, and I accepted Christ at the age of ten. I was the oldest of seven boys in a very poor Oklahoma family. We attended church on a regular basis, and I made the commitment to Christ in the summer of my tenth year.

Of course, every family member was a consumer, and since we were very poor, every family member had to be a producer. I did odd jobs around stores. My dad introduced me to a local grocery man, and soon I was cleaning sidewalks, cleaning the interior of the store, and doing whatever the odd jobs were.

The Christian faith, the real impact of it, didn't come until shortly after I was married. When I was married, I began to realize that I had some responsibilities. My wife, Frances, was a believer and more strongly committed at that time than I. Our fifty-fourth wedding anniversary was June 28, 2001. As our two daughters came along, we immediately began to realize that we had to have a commitment to Christ. We realized that they needed to be raised in a Christian atmosphere, in a Christian commitment. So I started teaching Sunday school, getting time in the Word, spending time in prayer, and soon I began to see my faith become meaningful.

Did you have other jobs before you started work at Raley's in '56?

Yes, I did. In that first grocery store, as World War II came along, my responsibilities began to increase. I became a store manager when I was sixteen in Ada, Oklahoma. I was actually born in Wewoka, but my folks moved to Ada when I was about two years old, so I was raised there. Anyway, I was running the store, going to school, trying to do the things that were necessary to put food on the table. Oklahoma was not blessed with any of the defense plants, and my dad was out of a job part of the time, so actually the income for the family, many times, was the money that I brought in. In fact I had even convinced the teachers at my high school to let me accelerate my junior year in school so I didn't have to go the last half of the year and I could work full-time.

When I graduated from high school in 1943, I had already signed up to go in the Navy. I was in the Navy for three years, came home, and went to work for a meatpacking company in Madera, California. It was a small, family-owned, wholesale meat plant or slaughterhouse. It later became a processing facility as well. I did very well with them. By the time I was twenty-six or twenty-seven years old, I was corporate secretary and assistant to the president. Then I found myself training two of his sons-in-law in a very small company and I realized I wasn't going anywhere there. So I left that job.

I went to work for two years in Oakland, California, in the accounting and accounts payable departments, for Montgomery Ward's mail-order house. My education had been along the financial area, and I was interested in accounting and finance. In my two years there, I took that mail-order house from number nine out of nine in the country to number one. They were going to reward me by sending me to Chicago. I had been there and had no interest in Chicago. So I started looking around again.

It was about then that I met the president of Blue Chip Stamp Company, which was a new organization that would later become very, very successful. Mr. Raley was one of the shareholders for Blue Chip and he had been looking for a financially oriented person. I actually responded to a blind ad. The gentleman at Blue Chip got my response, called Tom Raley, and said, "I think there is a man in Oakland you ought to talk to." So Tom came down and hired me in 1956. I became president of Raley's in 1969.

Did you bring any changes once you became president?

I think the main thing that I am fairly well-known for is my commitment. When I give my word, it means something. I had determined that the decisions that I would make would be based on biblical principles. I determined that I would not say or do anything that would dishonor the Lord. The man that I worked for originally was not a believer but was very open. He allowed me to espouse my faith. I was able to do that and I was still able to gain credibility with the people that were very important to us—our suppliers, our bankers—people that realized that whatever we said, we would do. That became very important to us.

There was a time in the late '60s, along about '66 or '67, when Mr. Raley got involved in some investments outside of the supermarket business that almost broke the company. He got involved in the hotel business and in a couple of large discount stores that were about ten years ahead of the industry at that time. We actually went before the Board of Trade. Had it not been for the banks' faith in my commitment, had they not believed what I told them—the fact that I had figured a way out, that I had sold some of the properties that he'd gotten involved in, including the hotels—we would have been taken over. From that point on, Raley's really took off.

It was based on trust. When I retired, I got a letter from an attorney who told me that one of the things that he had always told people he was dealing with was, "If Chuck Collings gives you his word, you don't need a big legal document. He'll deliver on it." That faith is really what saved us. Then we watched the company grow by leaps and bounds.

It was about then that you produced a small tract that you'd give away.

It's called "A No-Lose Proposition." And when I'd give out my business card, I'd give out that little sheet and say, "This tells about my life's purpose, and if you're interested, call me."

It came about because my wife and I had been involved for about twenty-some-odd years on the board of directors of an organization called Pro-Athletes Outreach. It's a Christian ministry. During that period of time, we began to see that athletes were signing autographs on various sheets of paper and other things that kids would take and would then treasure. So we decided that we ought to get the athletes to come out with some kind of a little tract that would give their picture and their statement of faith. And when they signed it, the kids would take it and keep it.

It was so successful that some of us said, "Hey, if that will work for athletes, it will work for businesspeople." So some of us produced our own tract. We have a large number of believers spread through the company, and I even had people that would come in and take those pamphlets off the shelf in my office and pass them out. I didn't even know who had gotten them. These are very effective as a tool in allowing people to know where you stand—in a nonthreatening way.

You talked about how your faith impacted your dealings with other suppliers and companies. How about with your ever-expanding employee base?

I think it had a great impact. Over the years, my wife, Frances, and I have made a practice of being in the stores frequently. Frances has been an integral part of everything I've done. In fact I was in a store recently and Frances wasn't with me. The people immediately asked where she was. I told her later, "Frances, they don't miss me; they miss you." But the people recognize that we are Christians. I wear a little tie tack that is the fish symbol with a cross in it. I always said, "That's my brand." Back in Oklahoma, they branded the cattle, and I wanted people to know who I stood for—and so we would talk openly about our faith. Many times we would have people talk to us about the difficult things or the positive things in their lives. I always used that as a means of opening the door. People knew they could call me. They always knew that I would keep private things that needed to be private. We were very open. We also encouraged Bible studies in the stores and in the office.

In fact, as I made the rounds on my final retirement tour, I had a pharmacist in our Reno division tell me that he had been encouraged to be a witness to some of his patients who he knew were dying because he knew that I would encourage it. And he knew that he wouldn't be in any way threatening by sharing his faith with people. I never believed in hammering anyone. I wanted the door to be open and I would share where I could. I still do a great deal of speaking to Christian businessmen's groups, community leaders' prayer breakfasts, whatever and wherever.

130

How much influence have you had on whom Raley's hires?

Our human resources department does the hiring. All of my business life, I made a practice that when people came to me looking for jobs, especially people I knew, I would send them on to the people who did the hiring. I would be glad to give a recommendation, but I didn't hire. In fact a good many of the people that work for Raley's today are young people that came through my church and other churches where I would be speaking. When kids would get to be sixteen years old, they'd come running over to me and want to know how they could apply. I go in one store today that my newspaper delivery boy is running. Some of our vice presidents, people that hold extremely good jobs, are people that I was responsible for recommending years ago. I really think it is probably the most satisfying thing that you can do.

We had written principles at Raley's. As a company, we didn't talk about Christian principles, we talked about fairness, the employee's fairness to the customers, and fairness to the company. Those things are basics in any business.

Raley's has long been very active in various humanitarian causes, such as taking care of the hungry and helping with emergency disaster relief. Is that something that you brought with you?

Yes, absolutely. We have an operation we call Food for Families. I started it back in the '80s, and Tom Raley's daughter Joyce, who is the sole heir and one of the wealthiest women in America today, came in. Joyce and I had a great relationship. Joyce and her husband, James Teel, are cochairs of the company. Food for Families is responsible for furnishing a lot of the money that puts food in food closets. Raley's makes donations and coordinates donations from our suppliers and our employees. Then we have collection boxes in the stores where customers can make donations as well. All of that money goes into an account for food closets in the various areas. Raley's monitors the program, charges no fees, and the money is used to buy food for the food closets at our cost, which multiplies the effectiveness of it. So they can order direct out of our warehouse those items that they need. In addition, Joyce Teel donates hundreds and hundreds of thousands of dollars to various organizations that work with the needy in a lot of areas.

But that's not all you do.

We were sponsors for many, many years of the Senior Pro-Golf Tournament in Sacramento, and the monies raised in that tournament went to charity. We are sponsors for the Sacramento River Cats baseball team, which is a Triple A team. The profits of that operation go to various charities as well. Joyce recently donated a half-million dollars to the Boys and Girls Club in Sacramento. So the company is known for being community-oriented, community-minded, and for doing those things that I think are biblically based.

From a Christian businessman's standpoint, what advice would you have for a young person considering a career in business?

One wrong thing that we as Christians have done—and I'm talking about some of our Christian leaders here—is that we're trying to tell people, "If you don't go into full-time Christian service, you're not going to be effective in spreading the gospel." Christian businesspeople have opportunities far and above the average minister to reach out to what I call the "up-and-outers," as well as the down-and-outers. Some of the greatest ministry that I know of is done by people who run large companies. A lot of Christian businesspeople in this country are very effective witnesses for Christ.

So I tell people, "Take your God-given talents, go where God has called you, and then use those talents for the Lord." My faith is the important thing, but God gave me this talent as a businessman to use that faith and impact people positively.

One of the other things that I urge them to do is to give God a chance. Be aware of those God-intervening moments that come along in your life when all of a sudden he directs your path in a way that you may not even have dreamed of. I think every one of us can look back and see those times when a door opened that we just had no realization was there.

A good example is when I had the door open to come with Tom Raley. I was able to take a company that was struggling and help it grow. I took it into areas that we wouldn't have dreamed of before. For instance, we're now in food processing. We have a huge dairy processing facility where we process hundreds of thousands of gallons of milk a day. We also have a huge distribution center. I was able to get something done that was really unusual in our business. You see, we weren't big enough to compete with some of the national companies in some of these areas, so I brought together several different competitors in joint ventures. Here are people that you're trying to beat to death out on the street every day at retail, but we got them to come together and use our joint strength in our purchasing activities.

We had some of our competitors sit back and shake their heads, thinking, *How in the world are those people going to get along? They're competitors at retail, but now they're partners in the wholesale end of the business?* But it has been very, very successful.

Now that you've stepped back a little bit and you're an emeritus rather than being involved in the day-to-day operations, what are you using your new free time to do?

My wife and I are still doing some of the things we did before. We're involved strongly within our church. I believe everyone needs to have a home base, people who will support you. I still do speaking. I still serve on the board at Raley's. I am still involved in some of the planning process. I do a lot of fund-raising; my wife and I just completed our tenure as cochairs of the United States portion of a joint Canadian/U.S. effort to raise funds for the North American Baptist Association.

As God just opens the doors, we're still doing, though I'm not as active as I was. But then, I was seventy-six years old in 2001. I've told people that my prayer is, "Lord, don't let me die until I'm dead." I've watched people die after retirement. They just lie down and quit. And I don't want to do that.

Jeffrey W. Comment

Chairman and CEO
Helzberg Diamonds

The overriding mission that must motivate those who long to see our nation regain the integrity and moral stature that has characterized its history is this: to live and do business as if our future depends on it—because it does.

Jeffrey W. Comment, *Mission in the Marketplace*

Diamonds may be a girl's best friend, but Jeffrey W. Comment is a diamond's best friend. Comment is the dynamic leader of Helzberg Diamonds, one of the best-known and best-loved names in diamonds.

In 1988 Comment was handpicked by the family to follow three generations of the Helzberg family to lead the chain, founded by Morris Helzberg in 1915. The business was purchased by investment guru Warren Buffett in 1995. Today Helzberg Diamonds includes 235 stores across the United States and generates nearly a half-billion dollars in sales annually.

As for Comment, he has become a popular speaker both on faith-based and civic topics. The author of *Mission in the Marketplace,* Comment is the chairman of the board for the Greater Kansas City Chamber of Commerce, a director for the Heart of America United Way, and a former chairman of the National Board of Young Life.

Comment talks about his upbringing:

I came from a family where my mom and dad encouraged me to go to church. My dad kind of took us to church when we were young, but we were not what I would consider a strong faith-based family. But I give my folks a lot of credit because even though there wasn't a heavy spiritual foundation in my upbringing, they understood the importance of church. Just that instilled a discipline. That was my initial introduction to even hearing the gospel or the Scriptures. I will always be grateful and appreciative of my folks for that.

Can you pinpoint a time when faith became important to you?

Probably after I got all the way through college, sowed my wild oats, and did all that stuff that you're not supposed to do. It wasn't until a couple years after I got out of college and was working in Tampa, Florida, in the retail business that I began to really search and understand that something was missing. A Navy chaplain is really the one who introduced me to the gospel and the fact that Christ loved me and that there were a lot more things in life than just trying to make a sale today.

So your faith wasn't important to you in your earliest jobs or positions of leadership.

I graduated from college in 1966 and began my career thereafter. My initial job was with Maas Brothers in Tampa, Florida, in 1967. And, really, it was the Navy chaplain who introduced me to Christ.

How do your personal religious beliefs shape your business philosophy?

I'd like to think they have almost everything to do with the way I conduct myself in business and the way I conduct myself with family and friends. I've been a Christian since 1969 and along the way have learned to grow in my relationship with the Lord.

After thirty years, you learn a lot of lessons—leading people, mentoring people, training people, guiding people, and leading organizations. I basically try to use the lessons of the Scriptures all the way through, in all leadership opportunities. I like to conduct myself in such a way that ensures that the quality and character of the business reflects the way the Bible tells us it ought to be.

Having said that, I most frequently do that without talking about my faith. That's the old adage of "walk the talk." I've been here twelve years, and there aren't too many people in the company that don't know that I'm a Christian. I don't talk about it, they don't talk about it, but there's a tremendous appreciation for Christian values and scriptural values.

It's reflected in our character, the way we build our brand, the way we treat our customers, the way we build our stores, and the way we treat our business partners. This character trait permeates our culture, and I think it is one of the most significant reasons we are very productive.

Has there been a situation where your faith made a significant difference on how you responded to an issue?

I think the biggest way that people see my faith is in character. It's easy to lead when times are good. It's when times are tough, like now that we're in this economic downturn. But when you're selling diamonds, it makes a difference. It is during these kinds of times that your business partners, your customers, and your associates do look for leadership. People want to be around people with character. I find it time and time again. I think it's when we have to make difficult decisions that the honesty and integrity come through. That separates the talkers from the walkers. I call it a "subliminal Christian character of the business." We don't refer to it that way; we refer to it as the character of Helzberg Diamonds. But my inspiration is the Scriptures and my role model is Christ. It makes a huge difference.

I was on the phone this morning with a resource. We finished talking and he said, "You know, one thing that Tom and I appreciate is that you're always candid. You tell us exactly what you want, how you want to get there, and I know I can trust you.

And if I do what you ask me to do, you'll be faithful to your promise. With some other retailer calling in—probably not."

So it helps.

So your faith really shapes how you do business.

Absolutely. It's really my bedrock. Recently the senior pastor in our church said to me, "Would you do the sermon?" It would mean three services, and I said, "Sure."

Have you done that before?

I do a lot of public speaking. But in my case, my public speaking means that I go and I do a speech. I'm the kind of guy that gets a lot of adrenaline going, and I have a lot of fun with my audience. But I'd never done that three times in a row.

And never all in the same day.

Never all in the same morning! My wife almost had to take me out to the parking lot in a wheelchair when I was done.

But my pastor said, "I want you to talk. I don't care what you talk about other than to talk about something that the businesspeople in our congregation can relate to."

So I talked about leadership. I took the seven leadership traits that Christ displayed in leading the apostles. If you stop and think about it, that little group of eleven changed the world. There isn't a Fortune 500 company today that will make the difference that those eleven did.

After I finished each of the three services, people stopped and talked to me. The one thing that people said was—and it resonated in all the conversations after the sermons—"You really live your faith in the marketplace."

I said, "That's exactly what God wants. Once we've been blessed, not only does he tell us to share it with others, he expects us to live it in the marketplace." You can go right to the Bible and you can see that Jesus was the master at it. So it was fun—and very relevant.

Although you may not be wearing them on your sleeve, these are the strong beliefs that so many of our faith-based businesses are built around.

We're a wholly owned subsidiary. My boss is literally Warren Buffett. Nine years ago I wrote a little book called *Mission in the Marketplace*. I'm not sure where Warren's faith is, but I sent the book up to him and said, "I wanted to make sure you got this, that you don't find out about it from somewhere other than me." He didn't say much to me. But a couple of months later we were talking about something and he gave me an absolute quote out of the book. So he did read it.

Has your very strong value system ever presented any particular difficulty to you?

It happened at the end of my tenure as president at John Wanamaker in Philadelphia. The parent company was Carter, Hawley, and Hale. They were in trouble in a lot of different ways. They finally reached the point they were having such cash problems that they told their retail operations to delay payments with interest from thirty to sixty days. I took the position that our vendor resources were a valuable partnership with the company and that I wouldn't do that. Purchase orders were getting processed, and they needed the cash as much as we did. So I refused to do that. The chief financial officer said they were probably going to ask for my resignation.

I went home that night and my wife, Martha, said, "Well, what do our savings look like?" I replied, "They're good enough, but I'm not going to worry about it. At least I'm doing what I know is right."

Our accounting people knew what was going on and they had a great deal of respect for my position. Eventually my boss and the CEO of Carter, Hawley, and Hale had a meeting and they let us pass. All their other subsidiaries, to my knowledge, ended up doing what they wanted them to do.

As a result, I was told, "You're not a team player. When we phase out John Wanamaker, we're not going to move you someplace else in the company." So I was on a short leash and knew

I was going to be out of a job. I remember saying to Martha, "Sometimes life isn't fair. I did the right thing. As a result I'm going to lose my job." But we both knew it was the right thing and knew I did it the way God wanted me to do it. Sometimes it's not pretty, but you still do the right thing.

Six months later I was sitting at Helzberg Diamonds, running a one-hundred-million-dollar business with wonderful upside. Life doesn't always turn out that way, but I say to people, "It doesn't make any difference if it comes out that way or not, you've got to do the right thing all the time."

We have a code of ethics that we put in place about ten years ago and it's our bedrock. We really believe in it. Our people are really proud of it. We terminate people if they violate it. I've had to say good-bye to some really good people, but the company, long-term, is healthier because of it.

Do you have a corporate mission statement, and are there any faith statements in it?

No, there are not. We have an incredibly diverse group of people here. We are a subsidiary of a public company. I rarely talk about my faith, but like I said earlier, I would imagine—and I don't think I'm exaggerating—80 percent of the three thousand people in our company know that I'm a Christian. Often when I'm out visiting stores, people ask me. Sometimes you don't have to talk about it.

What advice could you give to young people entering the business world? What advice would you offer to other businesspeople, men and women, in the twenty-first century?

There are a couple of things I would like to say. First, life is about balance and certainly that calls for responsibility to shareholders. We have a responsibility to our parent company and our shareholders. I have a strong responsibility to be constantly looking for productivity in the business, to look for ways to make it more productive, to create a better return on investments. No matter where you are, whether you work in accounts payable, or you're the president of the company, no matter where you are in the organization, make sure there is a strong positive influence there. When you walk in the door in the morning, no one can question your performance. Do your best. God calls us to be the best performers we can be, not mediocre performers.

The balance is that God gives me responsibility and character. I share the gospel and am compassionate. When you can put those two side by side, you have an awesome look about you because you're not a hard, calloused, cold businessperson. You're the person who has a great desire to perform. At the same time, you're doing this in a way that, to put a descriptive phrase to it, it's got a sweet smell that people just like to follow. They want to be a part of it. Life is about balance. It's about both.

There are people who lean too hard to productivity. They become calloused, and people don't want to follow, while people who get too soft and warm and fuzzy around the edges usually don't get the productivity. So "find a balance" is what I would say to the young folks. And even if you're an old folk like me, it's not too late.

Kenneth Cooper

**Founder, President, and CEO
The Cooper Aerobics Center**

I believe there is a window of opportunity here to try and get our people in tune with the concept that it's not so much that we're sick, it's that we're killing ourselves. And if we can change our lifestyles, then there is the possibility of reducing death from all causes and prolonging life in dramatic fashion. We've proven that without question here over the last thirty years.

Kenneth Cooper

In Brazil they call running "coopering" or "doing the cooper." In Hungary the "cooperteszt" is the national fitness test. The *London Times* has said that, as a doctor, Kenneth Cooper is one of the "greatest of the last twenty years" and noted that "the drop in deaths from heart disease in America by 14 percent in the 1970s is commonly credited to Dr. Cooper, as is the jogging boom which put more than twenty-five million Americans on the road by the end of that decade." That figure ballooned to thirty-five million in 1984 and has grown exponentially ever since.

This grandson of a Baptist preacher is the author of eighteen books, including the groundbreaking *Aerobics: Running without Fear, Controlling Cholesterol, Kid Fitness, Dr. Kenneth Cooper's Antioxidant Revolution,* and *Faith-Based Fitness,* which have sold more than thirty million copies and have been translated into forty-one languages and braille.

Cooper puts his medical practice into action at the famed Cooper Aerobics Center in Dallas, where he oversees eight different divisions, each offering state-of-the-art research and facilities. The center is the medical home-away-from-home for a host of presidents, kings, and other world leaders.

But when it is all said and done, Cooper's message is breathtaking in its simplicity: "It is easier to maintain good health through proper exercise, diet, and emotional balance than it is to regain it once it is lost." And for someone who truly believes that the human body is a temple, there really is no option but to spread that word.

Dr. Cooper's Christian heritage prepared him for the life of service he has led.

My parents were raised in the Baptist church, primarily in Nashville, Tennessee. My father moved to Oklahoma from Tennessee to establish his dental practice many, many years ago. I was born in Oklahoma back in 1931 and immediately started going to church with my family. I was baptized at nine years of age at Trinity Baptist Church in Oklahoma City. So I do come from a very strong religious and Baptist family.

Has it been a steady walk for you?

At one time I thought I was being called to be a Baptist missionary. At age eighteen, at a Baptist assembly in southern Oklahoma, I dedicated my life to full-time Christian service. I thought that I was being called to be a missionary to China. But I was accepted into medical school and then I no longer felt that call to go into seminary.

I spent only three years of premed in Norman. But during my premed days, I was in charge of the noonday worship services or student activity services. We had the Baptist Student Union at the University of Oklahoma in Norman, Oklahoma, and I was quite involved in the church. During my junior year, I even helped start a little mission in Norman, Oklahoma. We went out on Wednesday nights and Sundays and would do our business in this little community. That little church developed into a full-blown, ongoing church that is still there. This was back in the 1949 to 1952 time period.

Even during my medical school days, I was still quite active. Once I got into medical school, we started a noonday program for medical students. We also began an evening vesper service that continued through my four years of medical school.

I was reminded back in 1991, on my first visit to China, that I really *was* a medical missionary, just like I thought I was going to be. Several of my books have been translated into Chinese. I'll be going back for the fourth time this October to speak in Beijing. The last time I was there, I was featured on the front page of the Beijing newspapers. My profession has given me a marvelous opportunity to bear witness.

But as to your question, yes, I have been fairly consistent, except during my internship. During that time I'd gone to Seattle and there was no church of the type I was familiar with in the past. I'd been very active in my church and the student activities in medical school, but once I got into internship, I got extremely busy—as happens with most interns. As a result, I kind of slipped from church. For about a three-year period, I had a hiatus in my Christian life. I didn't lose my faith, but I certainly wasn't as active as I had been in previous years.

You probably weren't sleeping much, either.

About four hours a night for about a year during the internship. So I had only about a one-year hiatus in which I really wasn't committed—not just in my church attendance, but my attitude too. I was just overwhelmed.

After that, I went into the military and was stationed at Fort Sill, Oklahoma. I did rejoin the First Baptist congregation at Lawton, Oklahoma, and became active in the church. I wasn't married at the time and was seeing a young girl from Seattle, whom I did not marry. I ended up marrying a wonderful lady. That was in 1959. I met her in Lawton. She wasn't an evangelical type of Christian, and she thought I was kind of a nut at first. She has become a very devout Christian, and we have a wonderful relationship now—and two outstanding children. Both are very active in their church, so it's come around again.

I left the military in 1970 to establish the Cooper Aerobics Center in Dallas. I had another lapse in my Christian walk during that time, again, because I got so busy. I've always said that if I keep God at the top, family second, and work third, I can have harmony in my life. Thirty-one years ago I was starting from scratch to establish this center. I had left the Air Force after thirteen years and had no retirement pay. I had no substantial income at all, except a few book royalties, and it was a very difficult time. I was having to work extremely hard again, just like my internship days. I was busy; I was traveling extensively; I was speaking all over the world. My wife and I started to drift apart, and it looked like it was going to be a real problem for us in our lives.

Then something changed. Up on the wall in my office is a picture taken October 7, 1974, at the Billy Graham Crusade in Rio de Janeiro, Brazil. Since then I've been to Brazil many, many times over the past thirty years.

Out of the blue, Cliff Barrows called about six months ahead and asked if I would give a testimony at the crusade on that Sunday, October 6, 1974. At that time, I didn't really have my life right with the Lord and I just didn't feel I could go. I told him, "I just can't do it." I was having a lot of emotional problems. My wife and I weren't getting along well, and I was under lots of stress. I just didn't know what was going to happen. I really wasn't walking with the Lord as I should have been at that time. So I said, "I surely can't accept that right now."

About six weeks before the crusade, Mr. Barrows called back and said, "I'm sending you a ticket."

I said, "What?"

He said, "I'm sending you a ticket. We want you to be down there and give your testimony."

Cliff made me angry because I thought he was pressuring me to accept the invitation. I just said, "I'm not going to do that. I've got all these problems; I cannot do this. It's impossible." I went on and on. Then I just hung up on him.

That was one of the most traumatic experiences in my life. In the weeks before the October 6, 1974, crusade, I really felt, for the first time in my life, that I'd turned my back on the Lord. I felt an emptiness; I felt a fear; I felt an anxiety.

I had a patient that was sitting in my office at the time. After that telephone call, I was emotional; I was deeply disturbed. He said, "What's wrong with you, Doc?"

I said, "I don't know what's wrong with me, but I've got to do something."

I stepped out of the room and called Cliff Barrows back. I said, "Cliff, I don't know why, but I'm going to be there."

It turned out to be one of the most marvelous experiences of my life, to be down in Brazil with Billy Graham. I was there for about a week, working with the Graham organization, giving my testimony before 240,000 people. The crusade was broadcast on national television and went all over Brazil. And that really turned me around again, and I've had no further lapses since then. I'll guarantee you.

Was there a difference in how you interacted with your staff and patients before your experience in Brazil and after that experience?

I would say I was more compassionate, understanding, and kinder, you might say, after I had that real change in my life. There has never been a major change; I've always tried to be very considerate of my patients and my staff.

The other day a gentleman was in, a very prominent person, for an examination. He was being taken by golf cart over to our north clinic for a scan. He shared with us later that he asked the driver, "What do you think about Dr. Cooper?" Actually, the driver was one of my higher ranking employees; he's been with us for several years. He just drove the golf cart that day.

The patient passed his driver's statement on to me. He said, "He's a wonderful boss; he treats everybody the same. There is no rank as far as he is concerned. I'm just as important as the physicians are. He makes you feel like you're worthwhile when you work here at the Cooper Aerobics Center."

I really appreciated that and I try to do that. I was taking Ross Perot on a tour. He's a patient and has been a friend for years. We walked over to the little cafeteria, to the pro-shop we have, and into the gymnasium. As I routinely do, I speak to all the people. I don't care whether they're cooks or busboys or whatever they may be, I introduce them to Ross Perot. Of course, they were just really excited about that. Afterward, he made this comment: "I've never seen an executive that has a relationship with his employees the way you do."

Likewise, when George W. Bush was here for his last examination in 2000, I took him over and introduced him to some of the staff that work behind the scenes at the cafeteria. They were just so excited about the chance to meet George Bush.

I do this just spontaneously. I do try to treat people the same. I think that's a result of my walk with the Lord.

The Cooper Aerobics Center has eight divisions and 450 employees. As your company gets bigger, I would guess that it would be harder and harder to maintain that personal witness.

I don't know everybody's name—that's impossible anymore—but I do try to speak to people even if I don't know their name. And I still do the same thing I've done in the past. When I have VIPs on campus, I introduce them to all the people I know. And even though I may not know the person's first name, I'll still mention their position, what their employment is here on campus, and introduce them to one of our guests. It's not possible, because of the size of the organization, to be as one-on-one as I was in the past.

Does the Cooper Aerobics Center have a philosophy?

We have a motto that we've used for years—"QE2"—quality, efficiency, and excellence. That has been our motto from day one.

But the other thing that I keep telling my physicians and staff here at the clinic is that the patients who come to this clinic come of their own accord. They don't come because they're sick; they come because they're healthy, because they want to maintain good health. Patients spend a lot of money to come to these clinics. We have a six-month waiting list. They come back in great numbers. And what I tell my employees and my physician staff is this, "Our patients don't have to be here, and they aren't coming back unless they feel their dollars are well spent." I'm convinced that our patients are as equally concerned about how much we care as they are about how much we know. That's what has made us successful. We spend an hour and a half with each patient. I see only four people a day. It means that we have four to five patients coming through the clinic a day for complete examinations. And so we try to limit our patients to three to four per day because of that time we spend with them, and the patients love it. They have a chance to ask the physician questions. They aren't rushed in or rushed out like at most doctors' offices. I've had many, many patients tell me that they feel a spiritual influence here on campus.

Mrs. Clairess Nichols, a very fine Christian lady, a southerner all the way, made a very interesting comment. She's now eighty-eight and she's been one of my very dear, dear friends. I was having lunch with her a couple of years ago over at our cafeteria.

I said, "Mrs. Nichols, isn't it wonderful how the Lord has blessed the Aerobics Center?"

She said, with this warm southern accent, "Hon, everybody knows that the Holy Spirit just hovers over the Aerobics Center."

I thought, *What a wonderful statement! I hope it's true.*

You have employees of all denominations and faiths here as well, right?

We're not restrictive at all. In fact the director of my clinic, who is a fine, fine physician, is a Mormon. Larry Gibbons is one of the finest people I've ever met. He's one of the top people in the Mormon church in this area. We have an outstanding Jewish gastroenterologist. He does a superb job with our patients. And there are many others.

The people who work here know that this is a Christian organization. But, as our Jewish employees know, we have no restrictions. We do not try to proselytize. We have prayer at our meetings—that's one of the things that I insist we do. We do have Bible study available here every Friday morning. But there in no way is any kind of coercion in trying to convert people to my beliefs. I believe in example; I don't believe in coercion. I don't believe in trying to convince people to my way of belief. I believe that people want to follow my example.

What advice would you have for a Christian young person who is going into business in general or into health care in particular?

The Prayer of Jabez has been number one on the best-seller list. I'm familiar with the prayer in that book in the past from Bruce Wilkinson. I think that prayer is such great advice for young physicians. It says, Lord bless me; expand my territory; place your hand upon me; keep me from evil so I will do no harm. I just paraphrased it, but that's the heart of it.

Dirk Dozier

**CEO and President
Austaco, Inc.**

> *We're all here to serve one another. So under-
> standing the true heart of what servanthood is, that's
> our motto. Our mission statement is, "We're here to
> take care of people on both sides of the counter, our
> employees and our customers."*

Dirk Dozier

More than thirty years ago, Dick Dozier opened one of the first Taco Bell restaurants in Texas. Thirty years later his son Dirk Dozier presides over an empire of restaurants that covers much of Texas—one hundred food concepts, employing more than twenty-five hundred people—under the banner of Austaco, Inc. Today Austaco is the largest chain franchise operator in the state, and its combined growth expectations are six to ten new locations per year for the next five years—not bad when you consider that the per store average of a Taco Bell is one million dollars per year.

What separates an Austaco Taco Bell or Pizza Hut from a run-of-the-mill fast-food restaurant is who is behind the counter. Dirk's father, Dick, coined the company motto "Here to serve." Dirk has been a leader in providing top-of-the-line benefits for employees. And Austaco was one of the first to retain the full-time chaplain service, Marketplace Ministries, for its employees.

Dirk Dozier's commitment to Christ has had a lot to do with the way he runs his business.

My family wasn't real strict, but I actually went to church as a kid. It wasn't until I was twenty-seven years old that I actually committed my life to Christ.

We had hired a lady to decorate my office, and she had something I wanted. It was the peace that she had. I asked her about it and she said it was Jesus Christ. I said, "I've tried everything else. I ought to try that." A few weeks later I accepted Christ. A few weeks later still I asked that lady—her name is Katie—to marry me. Three weeks later we were married. And here I am, eighteen and a half years later, still a happily married man and still on a solid walk with the Lord.

Is it true that you were running your own shop at age sixteen?

That's right. I started going to work with my dad when I was twelve years old. I worked there weekends and summers. I was the manager at a store when I was sixteen during the summer and trained an older person to take over when school started.

Pretty soon you were working there all the time.

Yes, I did. I had a little break in the action. I went to college and flunked out. I got back into business and made a career of it.

Was there a difference in how you interacted on a business level before age twenty-seven and after age twenty-seven?

Very much so. Before it was just work, work, work. I had my, as our President Bush says, "youthful indiscretions with drugs and alcohol," which I don't deny. I did cocaine for many years and really didn't have the understanding of what it took to care for people, to build a culture. It was just all work and numbers driven.

It wasn't until after I accepted Christ and started understanding the fundamental principles through spiritual teaching on how to run a business that my life took a dramatic change.

What did the Bible teach you about biblical and business principles?

Gosh, it's loaded with those principles. Probably one of the key things is that it is just the right stewardship of what the Lord has allowed me to be in charge of—the financial end and the social responsibility.

What specifically did that entail?

I first got started back when the business had about three hundred employees. Over the course of the last fifteen years, we have grown to something like twenty-five hundred employees. When we had three hundred, I was able to minister to them. If I saw that an employee was hurting or had problems, I was available to help them in whatever way I could. Maybe it was fixing the car or buying a washing machine or maybe it was helping with personal issues. As our company grew, levels of management got built in. You tend to lose some of the one-on-one directness with that many employees.

That was one of the reasons why we took on Marketplace Ministries. We have thirty chaplains on our payroll through Marketplace Ministries that visit our 115 restaurants. They're picking up that slack. When you're the president of a big company, employees sometimes get a little scared or intimidated to talk to the boss. Marketplace Ministries has filled that gap extremely well.

Austaco is one of the few companies in the service industry that has its own human resources division.

It's really paying close attention to your employees' needs. Our retention and turnover rates are very good, and we can't say it's just Marketplace Ministries—it's the whole program. Human resources has focused a lot of attention on our training and our people-development side, our benefits program, and all that comes with that.

As a result, some of your employees have been with Austaco for a long time.

We don't have any thirty-three-year employees, although my mother is still active in the business, so we have her. But we do have a good number of employees that have been with us fifteen to twenty years.

How has becoming a Christian impacted your dealing with other businesses?

I think just the overall attitude about interacting with other suppliers, brokers, and bankers is different. It's a different perspective—to stand firm in faith and stay with the biblical principles.

What is that perspective specifically?

Patience and understanding, being less demanding. Perhaps it is just the ability to work through issues, to investigate conflict resolution, to examine all of the steps of really analyzing the issue before we jump to any conclusions. Most of our contract vendors have been with us a very long time. We've built some long-lasting relationships. It's not merely based on who provides the cheapest service. It's the relationship that we have with our vendors that provide the service for us.

Has your faith made a difference in how you've projected your goals and future for the company?

We can start off with the motto of our company: "Here to serve." You can take that and go in many, many directions. But it's about servanthood. There's no job too big, no job too small, no person too lofty to do any function that's necessary. Whether it's cleaning the restrooms or cleaning tables, it makes no difference. We're all here to serve one another. So understanding the true heart of what servanthood is, that's our motto. Our mission statement is, "We're here to take care

153

of people on both sides of the counter, our employees and our customers."

Beyond our motto and our mission statement, we also have our four foundation pillars. The first one is our culture. Our culture is about character and integrity. It's about caring for people. It's about building the programs that substantiate that. There is many a company out there that says that they care for their people. But if you ask them, "What are your programs?" they're empty. The programs that we have are *not* empty. In addition to Marketplace Ministries, we have an employee loan program. We have what we call a Santa Fund, which is money that we just flat out give to our employees when they have a crisis, whatever it might be. It could be a funeral; it could be rebellious kids; it could be they need their electricity bill paid or the monthly rent paid. We've got single moms working for us for seven or eight bucks an hour with three or four kids and deadbeat dads that don't fulfill their responsibilities. We have a program where we just give money to our employees for those specific needs. You add to that the other benefits of insurance, flexible hours, and the other standard programs that you do in the workplace.

We're working on a low-income housing program now. We're putting up the money for the down payment, using some government housing monies that are available to help people that would never be able to have a thought of owning their own home. We're able to provide homes for them.

The second pillar is people development. Those are our training programs, our promotions, our advancement opportunities. It's just developing people, providing a working environment where they can fulfill their career dreams in our workplace. It's up to us to provide the development opportunities for them.

Our third pillar sounds strange. It's brand differentiation. We're in the Taco Bell and Pizza Hut brands and we have to be different than all the other fast-food joints out there, whether it's in our facilities, whether it's with our people, our product, our cleanliness, our service, or our hospitality. We *have* to be different than everybody else. We *have* to be a step up.

The fourth pillar is year over year improvement. That's not just in the numbers; that's in your own life. You strive to improve it each year over the past year.

Are these four pillars written down and distributed?

They are communicated to everybody that works for us. And nowhere in there did you hear anything about sales, and profits, and cost controls, P&L statements, and all of that. If we live our motto, if we live by our mission statement, if we fulfill the obligations stated in our four pillars, sales and our profits will take care of themselves.

What advice would you, as a Christian who is also a businessman and service provider, have for somebody who is thinking of going into this business as a career?

I'd have to go back to the mission statement. Business is about people; it's not about dollars. If you care for your people first, if you have the right character values, things will work out. As for your question, it is really summed up in our motto, our mission statement, our four pillars. That's the answer.

It's an ongoing, developing process. Like I said in that fourth pillar, to have that year after year improvement in our own business structure, we just can't say, "Okay, we've got it; now let's rest." You've *got* to continue to improve each year.

Archie Dunham

President and CEO
Conoco, Inc.

The mind of man plans his way, but the LORD
directs his steps.

Proverbs 16:9 NASB

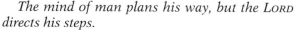

Conoco, Inc., didn't become one of the fifty biggest companies in America by being timid. Conoco's 17,600 employees scour the globe for oil. They also maintain the company's 6,000 miles of U.S. pipeline, work in its many refineries, or operate one of Conoco's more than 7,000 gasoline and service stations across America, Europe, and Thailand. And the man in charge of all of that production is Archie Dunham.

Dunham joined Conoco in 1966 as an associate engineer in Houston. He served in numerous capacities throughout the company before becoming executive vice president of petroleum products, and in 1985 he was elected to the board of Conoco. In 1987 Dunham became senior vice president of DuPont's chemicals and pigment sectors in Wilmington (Conoco was then a wholly owned subsidiary of Dupont) and assumed the same position for Polymer Products (another division of Dupont) in 1989. While in Wilmington, he was chairman of Dupont's Environmental Leadership Council. Dunham returned to Houston in 1992 as executive vice president of exploration and production, and he held that position until becoming president and CEO of Conoco in January of 1996. He retained this position when the company merged witih Phillips Petroleum in early 2002.

Dunham is active in a number of professional business and advisory organizations, including the United States Energy Association

I grew up in oil country. My dad worked for an oil company. While in high school, I wrote a paper on what I wanted to study in college. I had always been interested in paleontology and geology and so it was natural for me to pursue a degree in geological and petroleum engineering at the University of Oklahoma. I didn't even think about attending other universities because of the expense. No one in my family had ever attended college. Oklahoma was known globally as one of the world's great petroleum engineering schools, so it was an easy decision.

Did you come from a Christian family?

Yes. I grew up in a Christian family in the little town of Ada, Oklahoma.

Has it been a fairly steady walk for you, or have there been times that it seemed more real than others?

It's been a very steady walk. I became a Christian at age ten. Both my mom and dad were active in our local church, which was an active little Southern Baptist church of about a thousand people in a town of seventeen thousand. We had some great pastors over the years and an outstanding youth program. I met my wife there. So it's been a growing walk over a very long period of time.

But my deeper journey of faith began about twenty-five years ago when Conoco nominated me to become a White House fellow. The White House Fellows Program strives to identify future

157

leaders. You are invited to spend a year working in the White House or for one of the cabinet secretaries. It's an intensive interview and selection process. You spend months completing questionnaires and preparing for the interviews. About fifteen thousand nominations are submitted to the White House, and the selection committee's job is to narrow the list down to about 150 people for the final interview.

I really wanted to be a White House fellow. I thought it would be a wonderful learning opportunity and a great way to get involved in what was happening at the national level, so I devoted a considerable amount of energy and time in preparation.

The interviewers were a group of six or seven distinguished Americans. They asked difficult questions about policy issues and current events taking place around the world. I spent hours reading everything I could find about abortion, energy, foreign policy—trying to become an expert on these issues and a multitude of others. The Sunday before my interview, I was anxious, stressed, and very nervous. I was still reading, preparing, and scared to death.

Finally, my wife, Linda, came downstairs and gave me my Bible. She suggested that perhaps I was reading the wrong book. I opened my Bible and turned to Philippians 4:6 and 7. It reads, "Do not be anxious about anything, but in everything, by prayer and petition, with thanksgiving, present your requests to God. And the peace of God, which transcends all understanding, will guard your hearts and your minds in Christ Jesus." I reread that Scripture many times that day and then immediately before my interview. It's one of my favorite Scriptures because it meant so much to me at the time.

The next morning, God gave me peace, a calm heart, and complete confidence. I was convinced that I had "hit a home run" in the interview. I answered the questions with great clarity. I left the interview absolutely confident that I was going to receive a phone call the next couple of days from the White House announcing my selection as a White House fellow.

Of course, I *did* receive a phone call, but I had finished in second place. It was one of my greatest disappointments, but

God had a purpose in that experience because I learned very early in my career how to conquer doubt and how to rely on God during very stressful times. It's an important lesson that I've relied on many times since then.

What happened in your career after that disappointment?

The next two years in Houston were difficult years. I had a fantastic job, but I wanted more responsibility. I wanted greater challenges, and I was very frustrated. But God was working on me during this time period.

Linda and I were very active in a rapidly growing church in north Houston. It was one of those churches that grew from about two hundred members to two thousand in five years. And like many churches experiencing rapid growth, they were not prepared. We were landlocked on all sides with no room to park cars or grow. We discovered that six physicians owned the seventeen acres surrounding the church, which blocked our growth. The pastor asked me to chair a committee to purchase the land from the doctors.

I thought, *Piece of cake. No problem at all.* So I formed the committee, which included several prominent attorneys and a couple of CEOs and an elderly deacon, a real man of God.

We had numerous meetings with the doctors and their attorneys, negotiating hard but making no progress. I was getting frustrated. After every meeting, we would critique our performance to determine why we weren't successful.

Each time, this elderly deacon would say, "Archie, are you trying to do this with your own strength, with your own skills? Or are you asking God to help you?"

I would say, "Of course, I'm asking God to help us." But I wasn't. I was just trying to utilize the combined skills gathered around me to solve this problem.

Finally, after about six weeks, I realized that we really weren't seeking God's leadership. We were not seeking his wisdom in solving the problem. So the next time we met, we asked for his help. And, as you might guess, we were then able to quickly negotiate the transaction. The church purchased the seventeen acres, and today it's one of the largest churches in Houston, doing good for God's kingdom.

Did your involvement in leadership of your church ease your frustration with your job?

I was still frustrated in my career. But after the above experience, I decided to apply the lessons learned to my personal life and turned my career and my life over to God. I said, "God, you know I've learned a lot through this six-week assignment. If you want me to stay in my current job at Conoco for the next ten years, and if you want me to live in hot, humid Houston for the next twenty years, then I will be happy. I will be satisfied because I'm going to let you be in charge of my career and be in charge of my life."

That was the fundamental turning point in my career and in my life. I've learned that God really does have a perfect plan for each of us.

Within six months, I was transferred to California as executive vice president of a Conoco subsidiary—a super job. Linda and I moved to beautiful San Clemente and joined a wonderful little church in San Juan Capistrano.

Two years later the phone rang. It was the president of Conoco. He said, "I'd really like for you to fly to Houston this afternoon because I want to talk to you about a new assignment." Being a good Conocoan, I immediately responded. I'd never been in the president's office before. He told me that Conoco was going to move its corporate headquarters from its present location near downtown Houston to a new location way out on the Katy Freeway. The company had purchased a new site and was going to build a new college campus–style corporate headquarters. He wanted me to manage the construction of the new facility. He said, "Go back to California and talk to Linda about the opportunity and give me a call in about a week."

Linda and I talked about the opportunity and I tried to apply the lessons that I'd learned: Pray about the decision, seek God's leadership, and seek his guidance and wisdom in the decision.

After about a week, I became convinced in my quiet time and in reading God's Word I should *not* take the job, that I should turn down the promotion and stay in California. So I called the president and I told him that I'd decided to stay in California. He was very gracious and said, "Fine. You'll have other opportunities."

Fifteen seconds later the phone started ringing. My former vice presidential bosses were calling to inquire if I had lost my mind. "You really fell off the deep end. You can't do this. This is a great opportunity; it's a fabulous promotion. We've called the president's office and asked him to give you another week to reconsider your decision." So I said, "Okay, I'll think about it some more."

I kept praying about it, seeking God's decision, and ultimately I was even more convinced that I should stay in California. So I called the president again and said, "I'm really sorry, but I believe that I should stay in California." Of course, he was very nice about my decision and assured me that I would have other opportunities later.

Six months later I was elected president of that Conoco subsidiary, which was really the second-best job of my career—I'm currently in the best one.

I learned that, if you relinquish control of your life and seek God's will for your life, good things do occur. God had a purpose in us staying in California. Our church was experiencing problems. I was in a leadership role and able to make some contributions that helped the church remain strong. Also Linda and I were teaching Bible classes to young adults and, hopefully, we made a difference in many of their lives. By being faithful to God and doing what he wanted us to do, we were able to make the correct decision.

Talk about the challenges and rewards of being a public Christian in an equally public corporation.

You've seen the criticism that the Attorney General has received, even the President, for having a time of personal Bible study and prayer in their offices. They were severely criticized by the national media for doing this because it might impinge on others in their office that were non-Christians. If you're in a public company, you're certainly constrained. If you own your own company, you can do as you wish.

Conoco is a global company. We have employees of the Buddhist faith, Hindu faith, Jewish faith, Moslem faith, and Christian faith. The good thing is that everyone in our company, or most people in our company, know that I'm a Christian and that I believe strongly in my faith and that I practice it personally. I encourage *them* to practice their faith personally. Hopefully, my Christian walk and example have positively influenced other CEOs and others in the business world.

At the same time, you don't want to bully anybody, either.

That's correct, but the values of a company are important. One of the values of Conoco is that we value all people. Another is ethics and integrity. Your beliefs have an impact on how your values are practiced in the marketplace.

What advice would you have as a Christian who is a businessman for somebody considering business as a career?

It's a fabulous profession. Individuals should do what they believe God is calling them to do and use the gifts and skills that God has given them if possible. There is no conflict between faith and being a businessperson. It's not any different than being an athlete, an opera singer, or a minister. You can practice your faith freely and openly in all of these professions. That's a decision that each individual has to make.

Within limits, I believe that we can plan our lives, we can chart our careers, but God really does have a perfect plan for each of us. He's there to direct our decisions, help us discover that perfect plan for our life, but we have to ask for his help.

The verses that I started with in Philippians 4:6 and 7 mean that we really don't have to be anxious or stressed about anything. If we'll just seek God's help, he'll stand by our side; he will hold our hand; he will give us a calm heart. He will help us through the very difficult and stressful times in life, whether it's a health problem, career problem, or family problem. If we will just ask for his help, he will help. If you haven't turned your life over to God, to Christ; if you haven't turned your career over to him, then I would encourage you to do it. He has a perfect plan for each of us, and he wants to help us through the tough times.

George Farr

President and CEO
Children's Medical Center of Dallas

Children's Medical Center is dedicated to making life better for children.

Mission Statement

Children's Medical Center will strive to be the best by gaining widespread recognition as one of the nation's preeminent children's hospitals—an example for others to follow—and by identifying and realizing opportunities for change and improvement which go beyond, rather than duplicate, what is being done in other successful organizations.

Vision Statement

George Farr says he has the best job in the world. He oversees the hospital that *Child* magazine named one of the ten best in the nation. It's easy to see why. Children's Medical Center doesn't really look like a hospital. It is bright and airy, splashed with brilliant colors and kid-friendly playrooms and facilities. Since it serves children from birth through age eighteen exclusively, even the fixtures in the emergency rooms are to scale.

This private, not-for-profit organization has more than three hundred beds and fifty specialty outpatient clinics. It admits more than ten thousand patients a year, and sees nearly three hundred thousand on an outpatient basis. Children's Medical Center has grown from four borrowed tents in 1913 (the Dallas Baby Camp) to become one of the largest freestanding children's hospitals in America.

164

Farr says he looks forward to coming to work here every day. He has worked at Children's since 1977, holding several executive positions along the way. Farr came to Dallas from hospitals in Mississippi and Alabama. Today he promotes his profession and his community by serving on a host of boards, ranging from the Ronald McDonald House of Dallas to the National Association of Children's Hospitals and Related Institutions (NACHRI).

George Farr is quick to acknowledge his reliance on God throughout his career:

My mother and father raised my brother and me in the church. We didn't wait for the doors of the church to be opened. Most of the time we opened them. All of my life my Christian walk has been near the center of my life. Perhaps I matured more as a Christian as I matured as a man, but there has never been a time when being in God's plan wasn't important to me.

You have been involved in delivering medical service most of your adult life.

Yes, a significant part of it. I went to graduate school in '66, so that's thirty-five years—most of my adult life.

Was working in health care and helping people somehow related to your Christian calling?

I went into the hospital field as a result of trying to find something that, from a personal point of view, I could identify with. I guess it *was* part of my Christian heritage. I liked the fact that hospitals were doing things for other people and doing it at very critical times in their lives.

But the principal reason that I got interested in hospital administration was that I was searching. I wasn't happy with what I was doing and I wanted to do something else. Health care seemed to be an opportunity that was available to me, and I began to look to find out what I had to do to get involved. At the time, I was advised that the best way to get into hospital administration was to attend graduate school, so I began to pursue that path. That I was so interested in working in a field that involved helping other people probably does have a great deal to do with my Christian heritage.

What was your career goal when you were younger?

As a kid growing up, all I wanted to do was play shortstop for the New York Yankees. I was sure that would happen—eventually. It didn't happen. I was interested in sports and I went to college intending to be a football coach. Part of that was dealing with kids and being involved, but I principally wanted to do it because I loved sports. I went to Mississippi College, a Baptist school in Clinton, Mississippi, because that's the only college that wanted me to play football. I was not a very big guy and I wanted to coach. If I was going to coach, I needed to play.

But looking retrospectively at all of this—since I don't believe in fate—I believe it was God's guidance. I had an injury, and when it was clear that I was not going to be able to play football anymore, I changed schools and went to Mississippi State. I got a degree in business and intended to do whatever I could do to stay in my hometown. I certainly wanted to live in Mississippi. That was my goal. I don't know that I had much imagination in that regard! So I planned to get into the business field and stay in that area if I could.

I soon realized that business *as* business was not what I wanted to do. Instead, I got interested in the field of hospital administration. I went to graduate school, and the rest is history.

There is not a doubt in my mind that God, in spite of me, guided me to this field. As I matured and began to fully comprehend what health care was all about, it became a calling for me. I love the fact that Christ spent a significant part of his time ministering to the health care needs of people. I liked that. I felt like that was something I could build a life on. So health care to me was always different. It might have been a calling. So many times in my life, God was directing me and leading me to do things, and I didn't pay attention. But today

I know and believe with all my heart that I'm doing what God wants me to do.

Why do you believe that?

Because God gives us children. And to be involved in families, during perhaps the most critical time in their life, is rewarding to me beyond measure. I can't say it's not work, but I can't imagine doing anything else. It's just a great way to live out my faith and my total dependency on God. I see it every day.

I don't think it's by accident that we can transplant kids' hearts. I don't think it's by accident that we have ventilators that can breathe for kids. I don't think it's by accident that even a short time ago, 80 percent of the kids that had leukemia died—while today 80 percent of them are alive. I think those are the miracles that we don't always recognize as miracles in the biblical sense. But I think *whoever* "invented" chemotherapy or the MRI was given the ability to create or discover by God—thus given the ability to create or discover this treatment for cancer. Clearly God has his hand in it. I see as miracles every one of those things that I mentioned and many more. I believe that the things that occur today in medicine occur because God is alive and well and creates a willingness in men and women to search out the answers, to develop treatment plans, to perfect new technology, and more.

Some believe that all hospitals and healing places, regardless of religious affiliation, regardless of their original purpose, are houses of worship.

I can only speak for the hospitals I have been involved with, but I absolutely believe that. It's an awesome gift when a parent says to you at the most critical time in their life, "I'll let you take care of my child's heart" or "Treat my wife's breast cancer" or "my mother's emphysema" or whatever it may be. When somebody says that to you, *that's* a great gift.

167

I do think that hospitals *are* houses of worship. I can't say that we all worship the same way, or even that all of us worship the same God, because I've known people from the Middle East or European countries or the Far East, and they've all come with different backgrounds, hopes, and beliefs. When people come in need, and people minister to them by administering care, I think a form of worship has taken place.

Health care, to me, is a holy activity. I admire the doctors, the nurses, and the therapists. I know the people that clean our hospitals believe that what they do makes a difference. They're proud of what they do and they love Children's Medical Center. All of us, when you get right down to it, deserve to feel that way about the place where we work. Hospitals have an opportunity to generate that type of feeling, a much deeper feeling and a much more profound feeling about what you do than perhaps if you were cleaning an office building, a theater, or something else. Not that those activities are not important. They are. But a hospital is something different.

Yes. I think hospitals are places of worship. I don't think they are in the sense that we often think about them, or necessarily in the sense of organized religion, but I do think they're places of worship. I wouldn't want to say that a hospital is a substitute for the church or a synagogue or a mosque, but I do think that they are supplemental.

Although Children's Medical is not religiously affiliated, do you believe your Christian principles have an influence on how the facility operates?

I can't really answer that. Only the people who do the work of this hospital can answer that. I can only tell you that I will not, under any circumstances, *not* take the opportunity to express the fact that I'm totally dependent on God. I will not talk to a group or organization without in some way making sure that people know that the real difference in my life is the fact that I'm a Christian. This hospital offers me a forum. I feel so good about what we do, and I believe that God is so involved in it that I don't hesitate, and *wouldn't* hesitate, to express my beliefs.

168

I hope that at the same time I am sensitive to and concerned about other denominations and religions that are represented here. I hope that I would encourage them that if there *is* something different about me, to try to find out what that something is. I happen to be a Christian; I happen to believe that Christ is the only way. But I am not here to force my religious beliefs on anyone. I am here to live my life in such a way that other people would believe that there is something different about me or about my family or about the place I work or about our mission, and that it would cause them to think about their own faith-based walk, whatever that faith-based walk is. I would hope that everyone has a working, ongoing relationship with God, because I think we are all shallow and lost if we don't have something that is bigger than we are.

I don't apologize for my personal beliefs. I wouldn't dream of making a talk and not, for instance, saying at the end of that talk, "My prayer is that God will bless each one of you, that God will bless Children's Medical Center, and that God will bless the children of this community." I wouldn't hesitate to express that belief. As a matter of fact, if somebody tells me I *can't* say that, I won't go. It's my intention, every time I'm up in front of a group and have the opportunity to speak, to say something about my faith. If I don't do it, it's because I forgot. It's not because I didn't think it was the right thing to do. I would say that if I was speaking at a Jewish community center or a Catholic community center or a YMCA or a nondenominational facility, whatever it is. I wouldn't hesitate because that's the way I feel and that's in my mind. At the end of the day, that's all that matters. All this other stuff is going to pass away.

I find it easier to speak out now than it's ever been in my life. I don't know why. I truly think it's easier to talk about your faith-based walk than it's ever been. I believe I hear it more now on television and in the public, whether it is coming from athletes or the average citizen. I don't think that most TV shows reflect that awareness, but I do hear *people* taking a greater opportunity to say what they believe. If people are offended by what I say, then I'm sorry. But it's better that they be offended than I fall short of what I think I need to do.

As a Christian who works in the medical field, what advice do you have for a kid in the twenty-first century thinking about medicine as a future?

Some of the greatest people I've ever known—and the real reason I am in and stay in health care—have been physicians. I don't see those men and women changing from 1967 to 2001. I think it's a great way to make a living. Is it changing? Absolutely! But what writers do has changed. What lawyers do has changed. What schoolteachers do has changed. And what doctors do is changing. The thing that *hasn't* changed, in my mind, is the value that physicians, nurses, and therapists bring to the table. They provide a service in our community nobody else can provide. And they are there, literally, at the most critical time in people's lives.

If you want the joy of knowing that you're going to get paid, that's fine. But perhaps the ultimate compliment in our society today is that if you're going into health care, you're going to be trusted with people's lives. I think that is a great calling. It always has been and always will be. I think it's a great way to make a living. And if someone is smart enough, dedicated enough, and concerned enough to choose medicine as their profession, I would think it would be wonderful. It is very rewarding and it will continue to be a profession that we all look up to. In all honesty, whether we look up to health care professionals or not, sooner or later we're going to be dependent on them.

So I think it's a wonderful career. I think it is a marvelous way to build a life. I think it's like anything else. You have to be careful that you don't let the fact that you are building a life take a backseat to your career. I love doctors, I love what they stand for, I love what they do, and they make a difference in people's lives. If that's what young people want to do, that's fine—plus you can make a living at it! You can always find a job if you're in health care. What a great decision to make from a career point of view!

Have you given that advice to your own children?

My son is thirty years old and he's a hospital administrator. When he came to me years ago, I told him that exact thing. He's a bright kid. He could have done anything he wanted to do; he could have gone anywhere he wanted to go. He asked me about hospital administration and I told him, "It's a great way to make a living if you want to work in a profession where your life makes a difference. I just can't see any vocation, other than the church, that has a higher calling than being in health care."

I'm proud to say that he's a hospital administrator in a religiously affiliated institution. He was originally going to be a minister and he asked me what he should do when he began to question his call to the ministry.

I said, "Son, I don't know. I was not called into the ministry. I've heard all my life that if you believe there is *any way* that you could be happy outside of the ministry, then that is probably not your calling. But the one thing that I do know is this: I believe with all my heart that if you stay close to God, if you listen, and if you pray, you'll know what you're supposed to do."

And my son, in a car driving back from Mississippi, told me, "That's easy for you to say. You're *doing* what God wants you to do." If *anybody*, if *any* group of people, was going to endorse what I do and believe that I am doing what God wants me to do, I would want it to be my wife and my children.

It's obvious that hospital administration is your calling.

Hospital administration and being in the health care field is an extension of my faith. It's special. It's different. I love what I do. I love this place where I work. It has a mission to make life better for children. That thrills me. I love to tell people where I work. I believe that what we do, and what I do, is an extension of my faith. I believe that for me. I have met a lot of hospital administrators, and I think that most of them would believe that as well. It may not be a religious thing with them, but I do believe that they are there because they want to help other people. They chose this field because it is an industry that is based on giving and supporting others.

I would guess that the percentage of people in hospital administration who just completely change and get out of the health care industry is smaller than in most industries. It's a terrific way to build a life, and I can only tell you that I've enjoyed it. I couldn't see myself doing anything else. Unless it was playing shortstop for the Yankees or, better yet, the Texas Rangers!

Thomas S. Haggai

Chairman and CEO
International Grocers Alliance

If you are destined to be a leader, one of the things you have to do is to be sure you associate yourself with magnificent patrons. It will be surprising how good you'll look, despite any weaknesses you might possess.

Thomas Haggai

What do you do when you're the world's largest voluntary alliance of supermarkets, with more than four thousand stores and ninety-two thousand employees in forty countries worldwide? You hire a preacher to run your operation!

Lecturer, author, minister, and CEO Dr. Thomas S. Haggai has been chairman of International Grocers Alliance (IGA) since 1976 and CEO since 1986. It was under Haggai's leadership that International Grocers Alliance (formerly Independent Grocers Alliance) expanded abroad and became the first U.S. grocer in China. And just as IGA is in all fifty states, so has Haggai spoken in all fifty states, along with thirty countries, to audiences ranging from corporations and educational institutions to civic and benevolent organizations.

Haggai's rags-to-riches achievements and powerful motivational outlook have been chronicled in his four books, including *How the Best Is Won* and *Today*. His daily radio program, *One Minute, Please,* has been on the air for thirty years. He's received the Horatio Alger award, the National Secretaries of State Meritorious Medal, the Chauncey Rose Award for Free Enterprise, and the Boy Scouts of America's highest award, the Silver Buffalo.

173

And when he's not at IGA's corporate headquarters in Chicago, he can be found in scenic High Point, N.C., home of Tom Haggai and Associates, a nonprofit organization dedicated to education.

Here is Thomas Haggai's story:

When I was a lad of twelve, I was at a conference in Rumney, New Hampshire, and Cliff Lewis was speaking on the last night out by a campfire. He said, "There is a pile of sticks, and those of you who feel that God wants to use your life, and you're willing to give your life to be used of God, pick up a stick and put it in the fire. Then say 'God use me for your glory and may I be consumed by you.'" And so I did that at age twelve.

I came back home that summer and had a very strange illness. As I look back at my father's diary, it was not life threatening, but it was very serious. It seemed pretty serious to my family and me at the time, anyway. We went to the doctor who, after x-raying me, said, "It's going to take some delicate surgery. I want to review the x-rays again in two days and then set a date for the operation, if we have to do it."

My father said, "How important is it that I be there for the second visit?" The doctor said, "Well, not absolutely important."

"I've committed myself to speak to the New England Laymen's League, so I'll let my oldest son, John, bring his kid brother."

So John brought me. I hadn't eaten for several days. Back then, you had a long period of time between the x-ray and the time it was developed. While we were waiting, I said, "Gee, I'm hungry. Can I have something to eat?"

Dr. Moore winked at the nurse and said, "Despite not eating for several days, I guess this boy who smiles all the time does keep a sense of humor."

I said, "No. I really am hungry."

So he said, "Let's get him some cookies and milk." That was the first thing I had eaten and held it down.

That evening when we were having supper, a knock came at the door. I was just having broth because I couldn't tolerate anything that substantial. A man at the door said to Dad, "I'm on my way home, but I was in your audience at noon today, and

174

when we came to prayer time, you requested, 'If you don't mind, my youngest son is having some challenges right now. Could we remember him in prayer?'"

Checking it out, that was at the exact same time I had turned to Doctor Moore in Brockton, Massachusetts, twenty miles away, and said "I'm hungry" for the first time in several days.

When it was all over, John said, "You know, Tommy, God used Moses at eighty, but he used Samuel as a boy. You never know when God may be saying that you should serve him now."

Were John's words prophetic? What happened?

Subsequently, and this sounds like coincidence as well, I got a request to speak, of all things. Then that followed with another request to speak. So I talked to Dad, and he was totally against the idea of a "boy preacher." He didn't wish for me to be caught up in the novelty and publicity of it. Finally, he said, "I can't argue, though, against God if he is in it. But we have to lay down some principles. One is, I am your father, and therefore I am not to abdicate my responsibility. You can speak once a month, because you won't be able to prepare more than one message a month, if even that. And it can only be those months that, number one, you're obedient to your parents. Because if you're not obedient to your parents whom you do see, why would anybody trust you to be obedient to your heavenly Father whom you don't see?" Which was pretty good logic.

The second thing he said, "You have to make straight As in school." Which wasn't hard to do. This was just a small community and you had eight grades in four rooms. The teachers wanted to give you As. You really had to mess up not to get them.

"Third," he said, "on your paper route, you have to make a profit, because the purpose of business is to make a profit. Then, of course, if you do that, you not only give a tithe but then, being under grace, you have to give more than a tithe to the church."

Then he said, "Number four, because your grandfather is a well-known baseball player, when it's baseball time, you have to do well in that sport."

175

That set a tone for my whole life because Dad was saying, "God doesn't sort of save the soul, like it's a piece of you. Instead, the soul is the total person in whom God is interested." So that's the way it was later in my ministry. I guess my sermons always dealt with the total person. And so businesspeople would come and say, "That's a good sermon. I need it for my corporate sales meeting." First it was IBM, then the Borden Company, followed by the Belk Stores, which are America's most successful department stores by far. Then it just started happening.

You were a pastor at this time, weren't you? How did you get into a full-time speaking ministry?

After a while, in 1963, I looked at my diary, and besides preparing a couple of sermons a week in the pastorate, which I'd try to do meticulously, I'd spoken two hundred more times outside the pulpit during the year—when the average speaker does around seventy-five speeches a year. So I figured, *This is God's next step,* and I retired from the pastorate.

In time, as I was speaking, I was asked to join some corporate boards. Then I did a little radio program, as corny as could be, called *A Thought and Tune in the Afternoon,* which came on at 4 p.m. each day. I spun my own records and just chatted informally.

About the same time, J. Frank Grimes, the founder of IGA, had retired in La Jolla, California. He was succeeded by his son, Don. He heard of me from a friend. He called his son and said, "Don, whenever you're going to have a meeting in the South, check this fellow out. I'm just curious." About two hours later Pete Covington from Lake City, South Carolina, called Don and said, "Don, you know I'm the program chair for our meeting. It's going to be held at the Grove Park Inn. Hold on to your seat, but I want to have a Baptist preacher keynote that meeting." He gave him my name. Don's first comment was, "Who is this guy? First my father called from La Jolla at sunrise his time, and now you're calling from Lake City."

So that's how the IGA relationship began. I started speaking for them several times each year.

When did you join the board?

Later they were embroiled in challenges and asked me to attend a board meeting. When called on to make some comments, I said, "Look, you've run out of money but you're not broke. There is a big difference. When I don't know which way to turn, I call on the One who cares more about us than we care for ourselves. So, gentlemen, may I suggest that we ask the Lord for guidance? Let's spend some moments in prayer." That's highly unusual for a boardroom, but the little plan we developed worked.

Shortly thereafter in 1972, they said, "We've never had a non-food person on the board. Would you come on the board?" In 1974 I was elected vice chairman and in 1976 nonexecutive chairman. By 1986 I guess I'd made such a mess that the IGA board thought I should be forced to straighten it out, so I was elected CEO! So that's the long story, or explanation, of how I became part of the food business.

By that time I was pretty well versed in all types of business, either as a corporate board director or as a speaker. From 1963 until 1986 I thoroughly enjoyed being a world lecturer. Now I knew I was the world's second-best speaker because my colleagues printed colorful brochures claiming to be the best. My wife thinks I was insane because when Vietnam was on, I was speaking up to 350 times a year, and one year I made over 400 addresses. These appearances were for the United States Air Force bases around the world. We'd start with a breakfast with the noncom leaders then fill and empty the theater as many as eight times during the day, followed by a dining-in or dining-out banquet for the officers at night. Also I was fortunate enough to be under contract to lecture for the Belk Stores, General Motors, and Mayflower Worldwide Movers.

Then in '75 the Boy Scouts faced problems, and *Time* magazine gave scouting a cover for all the wrong reasons. The BSA National Board asked if I would come in as national director of personnel with carte blanche authority to do anything and everything necessary to turn the movement around. I committed for twenty-four months but it took twenty-seven. By the grace of God and people like my right-arm assistant, Frank Parachini, this, the largest nongovernmental agency in the free world, reclaimed its radiance. With the professionals, family, and volunteers that make up Scouting, you might be able to abuse such an institution, but you can't destroy it.

You recently received an award from IGA.

The year 2001 was our seventy-fifth anniversary, and the highest award we give is named for our founder, J. Frank Grimes. To my shock and total surprise, IGA initiated a new award in my name to be given to someone, within the arena of our four thousand stores in forty countries, who has done the greatest work in their community in keeping with our theme "Hometown Proud."

In addition the IGA board had secretly arranged to have our family flown in for the occasion. When my wife, Buren, and I regained our composure, I think I responded this way: "I'm grateful to those many colleagues whose leadership has impacted IGA, such as our J. Frank Grimes award recipients this year, Lorraine Smucker (J. M. Smucker Company) and Bill Johnston (Morton Salt). When the board asked me to join this marvelous organization, I had only one prayer and it was somewhat like Solomon's prayer. I said, 'God, whenever you are finished with me at IGA and one reflects upon the growth throughout the world, the only explanation will be that *God did it*. If that happens, then I shall be happy.'"

What is the intersection between business and Christianity? IGA is obviously not a Christian company, but you are the Christian in charge.

It's never been a problem. We start off our meetings with prayer. At our last Global Executive Conference, we had my respected friend Horst Schulze, the president of Ritz-Carlton Hotels, as our keynote speaker. He's a very wonderful believer. His wife, who is Lebanese/Syrian, as I am, was already a very devoted Christian. He then was sort of nominally a Christian.

After some health challenges, he really became a very committed person and is very active in the Church of the Apostles in Atlanta, pastored by Dr. Michael Youssef. Dr. Youssef is the former president of Haggai Institute, the international leadership organization founded by my brother John.

Horst asked me, "How do you get by with what I just witnessed?" I really didn't catch on to what he was asking. He said, "The opening prayer and the atmosphere charged with religious overtures. You had people there from all around the world. Some had to be from other faith traditions. How do you do it?"

I replied, "Horst, I've never been challenged. I guess it's 'the baggage' that comes with me. Even those who are of a religion that I'm not part of would rather have somebody believe something. Maybe they believe that the secret of this unusual energy at my age does come from a Source outside of myself. Regardless, we just do it." I don't think you have to compromise. At the same time, I don't think you can use a bully pulpit.

At the Horatio Alger meeting this year, which I've been part of since 1980, the organizers mistakenly, just by setting dates way in advance, had the meeting at the beginning of Passover. And we had quite a number of Jewish recipients who weren't pleased with the timing anymore than we would have been had it been scheduled on Good Friday.

When I was asked to deliver the invocation at the Friday evening awards banquet, I asked God for the right words and simply prayed: "What a wonderful moment this is! The eve of Passover and we are reminded with our Jewish friends that there is never a Red Sea so deep nor so strong of current that you cannot part the waters. But also remind us that when we wander forty years in the wilderness, it is not your will but our unwillingness to follow the cloud by day and the fire at night that you have given us. Wandering is not your will but our stubbornness. At the same time, remind us that, despite our failing, there is that promise of redemption and a Promised Land."

179

Christians don't have the best track record of being inclusive, whether it is because of religion or race.

I feel pretty keenly about that too. For instance, when I came to High Point, North Carolina, every pastor was given membership in the country club. I just automatically said, "I'm sure you have a good number of Jewish families. How many families would you say you have?" And there was this deafening pause from the membership director.

Finally, he said, "Well, we probably will have one someday."

I said, "First, that's not right. Second, when I was a little boy in Massachusetts in Depression years, Mr. Miller, a Brockton shoe store owner, used to call my mom and say, 'Mrs. Haggai, I have some shoes. I've got them on special. You can afford them, so please come by. I'll save a pair in Tommy's size.' Mr. Miller didn't have shoes on that much of a sale. He knew my mother couldn't afford them, but he also knew she had pride and he couldn't give them to her. I think all the shoes I wore for nine years, from grades one through nine, came from Mr. Miller.

"If I accept your gracious invitation to enjoy country club membership, every time I look down at my feet, I would be erasing my gratitude to Mr. Miller. Also I would be denying my faith by rejecting the religion of those who cradled my faith and, through Abraham, received a special promise. So I thank you, but no."

Today . . . oh how I wish I'd been better than that! I wish I'd said something about blacks, but I wasn't that far along in 1956. I felt that way about them, but I didn't say anything then. Years later, I had another chance.

One of my closest friends is Bob Brown, who once served in the Nixon administration. He says, "I happen to be an American who is black. I'm not an African American." He had been a close pal of mine and serves on corporate boards such as Duke Energy, Sonoco, and Republic Service. He came back to High Point in the early 1960s to handle public relations and diversity challenges for companies like Sara Lee and Nabisco. At that time I had a secretary who was too good to fire and not good enough to keep.

One day Bob said, "I need more space."

I said, "Bob, there are some offices open right next to my office at the bank."

He said, "Well, I can't do that."

I said, "Bob, the office is really attractive and the rent is reasonable."

He said, "No, I can't."

I said, "I don't understand." I didn't know up to that moment that we had never allowed a black person to have a business office in downtown High Point. I was just ignorant or I'd have done something about it. When he told me, I said, "Bob, you can have those offices. Let me think about it and what I'll do about it."

The next day I went to see the head of the bank and told him that I wanted Bob and his company, B & C Associates, next to our office. He looked at me and said, "Are you serious?"

I said, "I'm dead serious."

He said, "You know that's going to break custom."

I said, "Good. Because otherwise, you'll have more offices to rent than you thought." So that's how it came about.

What happened? How did others deal with the change?

On the day Bob started moving in, my secretary came in white as a sheet. She said, "Oh, oh, oh."

I said, "What's the problem?"

Then she said, using the very worst, most offensive words, "*They* are coming."

I said, "Why is that a problem?"

She said, "How can I go to the water fountain and use the restroom facilities?"

I said, "I guess you have to understand. They're coming at my invitation. So I guess you'll just need to find another position."

The nice thing is, had that not happened, I don't know whether I would have ever had the guts to let her go. But Mary Helen replaced her and she's been with me thirty-three years.

I haven't written a check for thirty-three years. She does everything for me, everything. I couldn't accomplish near what I get done without her. In every sense, Buren and our four children and grandchildren consider her not an associate but family. To me, she is a gift from God.

It really is the principle of the thing. I try to say to young people, "Do the right thing, every time that you can. We're all going to fail, but even if you fail doing the right thing, it's surprising what doors it opens."

I couple that with another idea. Whatever you do, do it the best you can, because God is always preparing you for the next opportunity, far beyond what you can imagine.

Some people set more specific goals than I choose to set. I've never had specific goals. Maybe it shows; maybe I'm trying to cover my bets; maybe it's because I'm cowardly, but I've always figured that, so far, my life has been so much more than I could have dreamed. I've just had one desire and that is to be better today than I was yesterday and, if the Lord lets me, better still tomorrow. I try to be prepared, not knowing what I'm preparing for. Don't set your goals too hard and fast as it may compromise what God really has for you. What's the old line? The only time God really does snicker is when we make plans without him.

Ultimately, you've been able to combine your faith with your profession.

I've found no problem. In fact what has often happened is that I've had my counterparts of large corporations call me and just want to bend my ear. They know that I am a very private individual, that I hold confidences because they are sacred. And they'll call and conclude the conversation saying, "Could you just have a word of prayer over the phone with me?"

So I'm glad for every aspect of my life. If our family had an adopted verse, it would be these words. I heard them from my father when we had food and when we didn't, when Mom was deathly ill and when she recovered, when brother Ted was in submarine warfare and when he came home, when John almost lost a leg but unbelievably won a gold gymnastic cup landing on his one good leg:

> He was better to me than all my hopes,
> He was better than all my fears,
> He made a bridge of my broken works
> And a rainbow of my tears.

Billy Ray Hearn

Chairman
EMI Christian Music Group

*Create a challenging and rewarding environment
for each other and those we serve.
Impact popular culture and resource the church
with music and related content consistent with a
biblical worldview.
Lead with excellence and be profitable.*

EMI Christian Music Group Vision

Billy Ray Hearn is one of the legends of contemporary Christian music.
He founded what are arguably the two most influential contemporary
Christian music record labels of all time, Myrrh and Sparrow. It was
during Hearn's watch that artists like Steven Curtis Chapman, BeBe
and CeCe Winans, the late Keith Green, Steve Taylor, Kirk Franklin,
Steve Green, John Michael Talbot, Margaret Becker, Charlie Peacock,
and others joined the label.

In 1991 Hearn moved Sparrow to Nashville and, a year later, sold
the label to EMI Music—a worldwide music conglomerate forming
EMI Christian Music Group (EMICMG). Today, as chairman of the
board of EMICMG, he oversees more than fifty artists and is a strong
presence in film, video production, publishing, and distribution.

In 1997 Hearn was inducted into the Gospel Music Hall of Fame.
Two years later both he and Sparrow were given Lifetime Achievement awards by the Gospel Music Association. He's also won both
Dove and Grammy awards along the way for his production wizardry
in the studio.

In the past year Hearn has stepped back from day-to-day operations of Sparrow and EMICMG, but he remains an enormously influ-

ential figure in Christian music: "I am chairman, which is more of an honorary title, but I do special projects for the company each year. My son, Bill, is now the CEO and president and is carrying on the spirit of the company as it was in the beginning."

Music and the church were important parts of Hearn's childhood:

I was raised in a Southern Baptist family. Mother played piano and organ for church services in Calvary Baptist Church, Beaumont, Texas. One uncle was a minister of music and education and two other uncles were Baptist pastors.

Even though I lived in a Christian home and my lifestyle was what you would say was Christian, my faith was not important to me until I was in the Navy, age seventeen to nineteen, stationed in Pensacola, Florida. Dr. Wallace Rogers, pastor of the First Baptist Church, influenced me greatly, and under his mentoring I dedicated my life to music ministry.

After being discharged from the Navy in 1948, I entered Baylor University to earn a bachelor of music degree in church music. My faith was very important to me while a student at Baylor. I was very active in the Christian community of the campus. I was a member of the original *Baylor Radio Hour* choir, I was the first student to lead the hymn singing in the Baylor chapel services, and I was active in the Baptist Student Union.

What jobs did you hold after graduation?

My first jobs were directing music in churches and leading music for youth revivals sponsored by the Texas Baptist Convention Youth Department in the summers of 1949 and 1950. The U.S. Navy called me back to service for the Korean conflict in January 1952 and stationed me in San Diego, California. While there for sixteen months, I served as minister of music at the Highland Avenue Baptist Church, National City, California. As a minister of music, I expressed my faith and beliefs regularly, hoping to influence other people to give their life to Jesus Christ.

While I was a minister of music in several large churches for fifteen years from 1954 to 1968 (including Trinity Baptist, San Antonio, and North Fort Worth Baptist), I continued my graduate studies at the Southwestern Baptist Seminary in Fort Worth. I also served at the Baptist Tabernacle in Atlanta, Georgia, and the First Baptist Church in Thomasville, Georgia.

How did you get into the recording business?

In 1968 I was hired by Word Records in Waco to be director of music promotion. For the first four years at Word, I helped establish contemporary music in the church by helping Ralph Carmichael and Kurt Kaiser promote their youth musicals *Tell It Like It Is* and *Natural High* and the Jimmy Owens musical *Come Together* to the evangelical churches.

It was about this time that I began producing children and youth musicals for Word, which eventually developed into my founding the Myrrh Records label for Word in 1972. The motivation and mission of these endeavors was evangelistic, especially to young people.

These works were very successful both commercially and spiritually. The Myrrh label introduced an entirely different style of Christian music to the world. The artists were mainly part of the Jesus Movement that was taking place in the whole country, but especially on the West Coast. This movement too was evangelistic in nature. It was born out of the peace, flower child, and hippie movements. Jesus was the answer to their search for the meaning of life, so they wrote music to express their newfound faith. It spread nationwide during 1970 to 1972, causing the establishment of huge Jesus Music festivals, which were similar to Woodstock in the secular world. Many of these festivals are still annual events, attracting as many as thirty-five thousand young people.

As a leader in the commercialization of this music, I was able to work with many artists and youth leaders of the churches trying to make this music and movement effective in winning young people to Christ. We were taking the gospel message to the current culture in their style of music. Throughout history, music has been a viable and effective tool to win people to Christ and teach the gospel truths. The first hymns were radical in the church, but Martin Luther used them very effectively to teach his doctrine to the masses.

My own faith and commitment to minister was the motivation in all these developments. I felt God had called me to do this. However, many times I felt like Elijah crying in the wilderness. The "establishment," or the traditional church, was slow to accept us. I would have quit and gone back to being a minister of music in a local church had I not thought that God wanted this to happen. Being a choir director was a lot easier but not nearly as rewarding.

How did your position at Myrrh help you grow in your faith and as a businessman?

During the four years as head of the Myrrh label at Word, I made a lot of mistakes and learned a lot of things *not* to do if I was to stay true to my spiritual mission. I was in a leadership position with no models. The label and I both slipped into a more commercial attitude and I sometimes began producing product for the wrong reasons. This caused me to want to start over and do it on my own—and do it right.

In January 1976 I left Word and founded Sparrow Records in Canoga Park, California, with the financial backing of a publishing company called the CHC Corporation. The motto or mission for the new record company was "Quality contemporary Christian music by artists who lived the life they were singing about." My goal was to have a label of artists who were very ministry minded. That is borne out by the list of our first few artists: Second Chapter of Acts, John Michael Talbot, Terry Talbot, Barry McGuire, Janny Grein, Keith Green, and the Agape Force, who produced the history-making children's album *The Music Machine*.

My religious belief or God's will for my life had come to fruition. I was confident I was put in that place to do exactly what I was doing. The days as a minister of music and at Word had prepared me for this day.

You felt confident, then, in your ability to lead a record company?

As to the business side of Sparrow Records, I was totally unprepared. I was a musician. I had no knowledge of balance sheets, P&Ls, debt ratios, cash flow, *anything*. Fortunately, my investors, the CHC Corporation, had a very good staff of backroom people. They began teaching me the business side. God gave me a good brain for logic and math. I learned very quickly but was still an amateur. There was never a question in establishing company policies in regard to paying royalties and other bills. We would be totally honest and Christian in all our dealings and contracts. We were determined to build integrity and we did.

When I became 100 percent in control of the company, I hired a wonderful Christian businessman, Gene Holloway of Newport Beach, as my consultant and teacher in the ways of running a business. We met regularly. I used a dedicated Christian man, Bentley Mooney, as my corporate lawyer. The accounting firm was also a group of fine Christian men, especially Marlin Summers. My business affairs lawyer, the one who wrote my contracts, Richard Green, was a newly converted Christian with years of great experience in the secular record business. He became one of my most trusted spiritual advisors and still is to this day. We established a fairness in our artist contracts that set a new standard. In other words, I surrounded myself with like-minded businesspeople. We were always striving to do what is right, no matter whether it was good for the business or not.

How did that work out in practice?

One instance was when our largest-selling artist, Keith Green, came to me and asked out of his contract, which had two years' commitment remaining. He said to me that God had called him to move to Texas and establish the Last Days Ministry and that he wanted to give his albums away for a donation instead of selling them at a price. He did not believe we should "sell" the gospel. Of course, I could not give albums away and keep a business running, but I believed that if God was truly calling him to establish such a ministry, I could not stand in the way. I released Keith, believing that if God *was* in this, he would take care of me. And he did. He sent me Steve Green and others to make up the lost sales very soon after.

My concept of Sparrow Records was, and is, that it is *not* a ministry to the people. Our place is to minister to the artists and they in turn minister to the people. We provide a good record company as the platform from which the artists can launch their ministries. We are not a church. We are a good business run by Christians based on Christian principles and ethics.

Still, some of our artists and employees have thought that we should be like a church. On some occasions, employees and artists thought I should excuse poor performance because we were a Christian company and that I should be more compassionate and forgiving. Dropping an artist after they were no longer contributing to the success of the company, even though they were still effective as a ministry, was difficult for me to explain. But I was not a pastor. I could not jeopardize the solid base of the company for one artist, because we were committed to supporting *all* the other artists. Most of the time, the artist in question had come to a place in their career or ministry where they could do as well or better in some other place or they needed to reevaluate their situation. Sometimes what they needed to do was produce their own records and become independent of a record company. Sometimes I advised them to start their own record company or label. Looking back, almost every one of the artists I gave this advice to became more successful and happier that way. It was always a painful and disappointing time for them and me, but in the end they saw that it was best.

As to ineffective employees, the old saying comes to mind: "Too heavenly minded to be earthly good." This may sound harsh or unchristian, but poor work cannot be excused because someone is a dedicated Christian or works in a company run by Christians. We are competing against the world. We cannot be anything but the highest of quality in our work or product.

What would you say to someone thinking of a career in business?

My first advice to young people entering the business world is that they need to follow the passion that God put in them. What you are passionate about is probably what you do best, and that is where you will probably succeed. And the term *success* should not be judged in monetary terms. Happiness and the sense of doing what God put you here for is most important. God does not give you talent and not expect you to use it. But God *does* expect you to get the best education possible and develop your talent.

I tell young people, "Always try to recognize your shortcomings or weaknesses and align yourself with people who can cover you. Do not be afraid of admitting your weaknesses. People are always willing to help when they know you are open to help."

One of my legacies is that I hired the best people possible to surround me in my company. I hired very qualified people and then let them do their job. I am not a micromanager. Today the executive staff of twelve people at EMICMG has a combined experience of 159 years, not counting me. They are still young thinkers and great professionals. They have built the best company in the industry. It was never about *my* ability or *me*.

For the young person at the entry or junior executive level, I say, "Do not get impatient or anxious to move ahead of yourself. You always need time to develop your skill and create your network. You must be good at what you do at your present level before you can move to the next. Time is on your side." I was forty-six years old when I founded Sparrow Records. The track record and the relationships I built were my greatest assets. I constantly hear and see young executives who want to do what I did and do it now, and they are still in their twenties. Patience is a great virtue.

Love God, life, family; work hard, do good work, and be enthusiastic. It is contagious. And he honors it.

Jack Kinder Jr.

Cochairman of the Board
Kinder Brothers International Group, Inc.

May the God who programmed you to win,
May the God who computerized you to succeed,
May the God who showed you how to conquer
Death itself—and live an eternal life—
May that God be with you this day
And forever.

Jack Kinder

Any enterprise is built by wise planning, becomes
strong through common sense, and profits wonder-
fully by keeping abreast of the times.

Proverbs 24:3–4 (Jack Kinder translation)

Jack Kinder speaks to two hundred audiences a year, usually as a sales management consultant to the several hundred corporations that employ his services. But when you talk to Jack Kinder, you're not going to hear that he's past president of the insurance industry's exclusive Million Dollar Round Table or that he was the managing director for Purdue University's Management Institute for more than twenty years. What you'll hear from Kinder is enthusiasm—and Scripture.

Kinder loves Scripture. It bubbles from him in casual conversation. He writes "Galatians 6:9" ("Let us not become weary in doing good, for at the proper time we will reap a harvest if we do not give up.") after his signature. He freely hands out cards titled "Spiritual Vitamins for Daily Consumption," each with a carefully chosen list of Bible verses.

Kinder (with brother Garry) has developed a host of CD-ROMs and audio- and videocassettes on attitude building, sales strategy, and personal effectiveness. They've authored a number of books, including *Upward, Winning Strategies in Selling* (with Roger Staubach), *Positive Power of Successful Salespeople* (with W. Clement Stone), *The Selling Heart, The Making of a Salesperson, 21st Century Positioning* and the upcoming *Building the Master Way.*

Jack Kinder's love of Scripture, reflected in his work and philosophy of life, can be traced to his growing-up years:

We grew up in a home environment that had us at church every Sunday and always with a few coins to put in the offertory plate. Back then the name of the church was St. Paul's Evangelical and Reform Church in Pekin, Illinois. They had Saturday morning catechism classes. These catechism classes were taught right below the gymnasium. You came in the morning and you had to commit everything to memory. If you did that successfully, then in the afternoon you were able to go up and play in the gymnasium. If you weren't successful, then you stayed downstairs—and you heard the roar of the crowd upstairs, right above you, playing basketball. At the end of that two-year, maybe three-year, program, they did something that was just remarkable. In front of the congregation, they had you tested on how well you retained this Scripture. In other words, about twenty of us would stand up there, and they would ask us to respond with Scripture when they called out the chapter and verse. That was very effective. If you passed all of that, then you were awarded a diploma that said you had graduated.

You've had two careers: your very successful career in insurance and then as a motivational speaker.

There are actually three careers because when I was eleven I recognized that I had a competitive edge. While everybody else wondered what he or she was going to do with their lives, I knew what I was going to do. I was going to be like Big Jim. Big Jim was the high school football coach. I had a role model to follow and I never intended to do anything else. Had I been selected for a college coaching job, I never would have done anything else. I would have stayed right in there.

But when that didn't happen after three years, I left coaching and went into the insurance business with Equitable Life. I've almost always been with Equitable. I had two years when I went over to Southland Insurance, and I ran that operation with my brother for a couple of years. And twenty-five years ago we embarked on a consulting practice. It's now the largest of its kind in the world of financial services.

We speak, we write, we record, we film, and we consult. I start out a few of my speeches, or I have in the past, by saying that when I was in New York as a senior officer with Equitable, they thought that I needed some speech training. So they engaged Dorothy Sarnoff—she played the lead part in *The King and I* on Broadway and later built a speech consulting practice that became quite well known—mostly in the East. One day she asked me if I had any questions. I said, "I have one. How many points should a good speech have?" Without hesitation, she said, "Jack, at least one." So I tell the audience, "Since then, I've always carried one point around with me. That is, up until today. Today I've got two." Then they start to chuckle.

The first of the two points I give them is something a wise man once said to me: "Never get so discouraged over those things that you can't control that you lose the blessing and the joy that would come your way if only you would focus on the things you *can* control."

The second one is, "We teach; we preach; we try to live by three basic principles in business. The first one is, If you're expected to be there, be there. In other words, show up on time and show up dressed ready to play, attitudinally and physically. Second, Make good on all commitments. A commitment made is a debt unpaid. Number three, Always strive to do the Christian thing; always try to do what's right regardless of the politics of the situation.

Those are the kinds of things that we do and write about. We've just had a very successful career staying brilliant in the basics.

193

How has being a Christian had an impact on the decisions and choices you've made?

I started my insurance career, not in Chicago where I was coaching, but in a little central Illinois town called Pekin, the home of Sen. Everett McKinley Dirksen. I started out selling insurance, and I soon decided that I wanted to stay in Pekin my entire career. After eleven years, my manager convinced me that I could leverage my skills and my Christian influence a whole lot more if I moved up the ladder and became what most people would call a territorial manager but was then called an agency manager. They convinced me to go to Louisville, Kentucky. It wasn't very long before I became convinced that I wanted to live *there* the rest of my life. I wanted to live and die right there in that great state of Kentucky.

Then they came to me again and put together an opportunity in Detroit that most people would jump at, but I still wanted to live in Kentucky. They wanted me to go to Detroit and head up the company's number one agency. Again, I turned my back on that until they reminded me what a wise mentor of mine had said: "Your Christian influence, your aura of influence as a Christian, can be leveraged and can be enhanced greatly by taking advantage of some of these opportunities that are placed in front of you." So I went to Detroit. From there I went to Chicago as the company's youngest vice president. Then on to New York. And in all of those moves, I made the decision to go because I felt led to do it, believing I would be able to have a stronger influence in the marketplace.

Today in our consulting practice, we cut across all company lines. We consult with more than three hundred companies. You see what influence you can have, and your impact can be great.

Can you talk about some of the specifics of how you were able to make that happen at each step?

I have always been influenced by the people that I know, the mentors that have taught me, and the things that I've read. We say to our audiences, "Move the clock ahead five years and look back. And in that short sixty-month period, you will discover that

194

you don't change much except for the people you meet and the books that you read." Of course, today we would add to that, the videos that you watch and the cassettes or CDs you listen to.

For an example, I came across Dr. Edward Rosenaw, who became famous as a heart surgeon at the Mayo Clinic. He liked to tell the story about the incident that sealed his commitment to go into the field of medicine. He says it happened while he was growing up as a young man in Minnesota, in the north woods country.

They shook him awake in the middle of the night, out of a deep sleep, and told him to go next door quickly and have the neighbor go into town to get a doctor because his brother had taken very sick. He went and roused the neighbors, then came back and sat in the corner as they waited for the doctor to arrive.

He said, "I couldn't help but notice those anxious expressions I saw on my parents' faces. Before long the doctor arrived and very quickly examined my brother. He looked in his ears, his eyes, and his throat, felt his pulse, and took his temperature, listened to his heartbeat. In just a few minutes, he looked up. And with a smile on his face, he said to my parents, 'You folks can relax now. Your boy is going to be all right.'"

Young Edward Rosenaw, sitting over there in the corner, just eleven years old, was so impressed with what that announcement did to change the expressions on his parents' faces that he decided that very night: *One day I'm going to be a doctor so that I can spend my life putting that light in other people's faces.*

There are very few jobs that carry with them that opportunity. But it's the opportunity that the Christian can carry with him every day in whatever he does. You can enlighten people, if by no other way than as a role model.

Another hero of ours, of course, was Everett McKinley Dirksen. We peddled him newspapers and shoveled his walks when it snowed. He was quite a guy. I used to follow him around. One day, as a young lad, I followed him right into an interview. I don't even know how to this day I got there. But I'm glad I did.

The reporter asked, "You have known the greats and near greats all over this world. In your opinion, who is the greatest individual that walks this earth today?"

Dirksen, in his somewhat theatrical manner, said, "Oh, I just wouldn't know. But I can assure you of this, it's somebody you and I have never heard of before."

I've often thought about that, the people that I meet who are great. My dad was one of those people. He was great, but there probably weren't fifty people that knew him. If you can be led to expand that Christian role, you can influence thousands upon thousands of people. But most people that are great, they're great doing what they do and, as Dirksen said, most people have never heard of them.

I would think that in insurance you have the opportunity to come face-to-face with a lot of people in the course of a day.

The thing we do today is knock down the walls and talk to the world through video, audio, and CD-ROMs. You can touch people that you're never going to see, meet, or hear from. Of course we hear from a lot of them, but we never see them or never meet them. We don't know who they are or where they are. But the good news circulates.

Are you still able to maintain the strong Christian message that you've had through most of your life, or have you had to adapt it for your consulting career?

Some people think I'm versatile, but I don't adapt easily. I guess the older you get, the more independent you become. I just kind of call them as I see them. But the Bible is just loaded with things that are as relevant today as the morning newspaper. You can roam around in Proverbs and never go to another book. I've got to watch the way I say this so it's not misinterpreted, but sometimes I'll hold up a Bible and say, "You know, if you'll take this book and clip out every reference to salvation and eternal life, what you have left would still be the finest 'how-to manual' that you could ever put in your hands."

For instance, take Proverbs 24:3–4 where it says that any enterprise that is built by wise planning becomes strong through common sense *and* profits wonderfully by keeping abreast of the times. It doesn't get much better than that.

I've got a closing illustration that I use for most every speech I make. This year the prestigious Million Dollar Round Table asked us to speak to their audience. On a Power Point, I show a cross and say, "Now, this was first introduced to me by Dr. George W. Crane, a professor at Northwestern University. Dr. Crane said, 'You want to carry this symbol here with you because it will remind you of the word *balance*. The reason balance is more important today than it has ever been is that we're finding that more and more people are failing in life for reasons that have nothing to do with the way they perform in their jobs.'"

So at the top of the Power Point I flip on *professional*, and it's displayed atop the cross. Then, "Down here at the bottom," I say, "we've got the *physical*. How much time do we spend here and what shape are we in physically? Then we come over here to the right to the *financial*." At that point I talk about that and how important it is to manage that part of our lives effectively.

And then we come over to the fourth part, to the left, and here we have the *personal*. Those are the relationships that evolve and are built around, for the most part, the kitchen table.

Now the key, of course, is keeping all of these in balance. And Dr. Crane offers a marvelous way to do that. It's to make sure that you have a fifth dimension in there, right in the center and that's the *spiritual*. If you begin to put that in the center and if you can keep it there, you've got a much better chance of living your life in balance.

Carlisle said, "One life, just a little gleam of time, between two vast eternities. There is no second chance for us for evermore." So I say, "Now, that's reason enough to take this one life and live it to the fullest, live it in balance and to the glory of God."

Sometimes when I come back, they'll say, "Jack, you may want to tone that one down just a little bit." I shake my head like I acknowledge what they said. But instead of toning it down, I tone it up! And then there are other cases, fewer in number, where they will tell me to be *sure* I get to that balance part.

What advice would you, as a Christian who has been a successful businessman, have for a young person thinking about going into business?

I'd say a couple of things. First, *pay attention*. We often quote from Ezekiel 44:5: "Look carefully, listen closely and give attention to everything." Just pay attention. Some people look, but they don't see anything. Some people listen, but they don't get it; they don't hear anything. So that's the starting point—pay attention.

Then I would tell them to be a student of their business. Move quickly into the top 10 percent of your field; find a way to quickly do that. And you do that by being a student.

Then I'm strong on commitment and staying power. I would ask them to remember to make good on all commitments. *A commitment made is a debt unpaid.* I would also point them to Proverbs where it says, "Have two goals: wisdom that's knowing, and doing right and common sense." And don't let them slip away from you because they will fill you with living energy.

And, of course, stick to the task until it sticks to you. There's an old poem that goes something like this: "Beginners are many and enders are few. Success, power, and praise come to the one who sticks and stays." There is always a good reward for sticking with things.

Finally, like I said before, stay focused on those things that you *can* control. Don't get caught up wasting energy on those things you *can't* control.

And then never, ever, ever get tired of doing what is right. That's Galatians 6:9 [KJV]: "Let us not be weary in well doing: for in due season we shall reap, if we faint not." What that means is you keep doing the right thing, in the right way, at the right time, in all situations, and you're going to reap a great reward.

Douglas M. Lawson

Founder and Chairman
Douglas M. Lawson and Associates, Inc.

More Give to Live holds forth a bold promise: If you want more out of your life and are willing to take some simple steps, you can have a richer, fuller, happier existence. I invite you to try the program of action set forth in these pages. I invite you to believe me when I say that you have everything to gain and absolutely nothing to lose from a life of giving.

From the introduction to *More Give to Live*

When it comes to philanthropy, few people in American history have done more to promote and understand the benefits of giving than has Dr. Douglas M. Lawson. He's perhaps best known for his book *Give to Live: How Giving Can Change Your Life* (1989). This best-seller is in its sixth printing and has been published abroad in Spanish, Italian, and German. Lawson cites the evidence of top doctors, psychotherapists, and scientists to prove that we can help heal ourselves when we reach out to help others. Later books—*More Give to Live* and *Volunteering: 101 Ways You Can Improve the World and Your Life*—have done nearly as well.

But Lawson also walks his talk. He is the founding chairman of Douglas M. Lawson and Associates, Inc., a fund-raising and management consulting firm that has to date raised more than one billion dollars for more than a thousand clients around the world. Those clients include the American Red Cross, Habitat for Humanity International, Special Olympics International, C.A.R.E., the United States Committee for UNICEF, Girl Scouts of America, and Robert Schuller Ministries.

199

Lawson is also in great demand as a motivational speaker and author, having written dozens and dozens of articles for a variety of magazines, in addition to his monthly newsletter, *Philanthropic Trends Digest*.

When *More Give to Live* was released, M. Scott Peck, the author of *The Road Less Traveled*, had this to say: "This is a brilliant book, waging spiritual war against our assumptions, in order to save our society and the world."

Lawson talks about his early years, which prepared him for the influential life for God he now lives:

I was born into a religious family in Newport News, Virginia. My parents were Methodists. I was baptized in the Methodist church when I was a baby and brought up in the Sunday schools in the church and what they called in the Methodist church the MYF—Methodist Youth Fellowship.

I went on to study for the ministry. While I was a college student at Randolph Macon College in Ashland, Virginia, I was appointed by the bishop as an accepted supply minister in the Methodist church, and I built a church in Hampton, Virginia, from 1954 to 1957. I left that church with 450 members and a parsonage. I was replaced by a full-time Methodist minister.

I went on to Drew University, in Madison, New Jersey, where I became an associate minister of the Madison Methodist Church on campus and earned a bachelor of divinity degree. From there I went to Duke University where I studied religion and history and received a Ph.D. I came back to Randolph Macon College in '62 as their first full-time chaplain. From there I became dean and vice president for development. Later I went into my career as a professional fund-raiser, which I've been doing as a company for thirty-two years and professionally for thirty-five years.

It's no longer that big a step from being the head of a school to a fund-raiser, since that seems to be what a lot of college presidents have to do these days.

All of them do. It was natural for me to get into fund-raising, although I certainly didn't train to do it. I never thought I was going to be a fund-raiser, but it has been wonderful. My company has had over a thousand clients all over the world, and many of them have been churches. Many of our clients have also been religious organizations like Habitat for Humanity International, Youth for Christ, Young Life, Youth With a Mission, the Haggai Institute, and so forth. But I've also had many secular clients, such as museums, hospitals, and universities.

All of my professional life has led to the love of my life, which is giving. Everybody wanted me to write a book on how to raise money. I said, "I've already lectured on that, and people have already written that book, but nobody has written anything about giving." So if you read *Give to Live* and scratch under the surface, you'll see the religious roots there, which are very firm with me. They are the foundation on which my whole philosophy of life is built—giving.

Is there a difference in fund-raising in the secular world compared to fund-raising for religious organizations?

There really isn't any difference, although most people think there is. Religious people believe there is the religious-type fund-raiser, and secular people say there is a secular-type fund-raiser. I never go into that with my clients. I use the same principles with both. Giving is universal. It has nothing to do with secular or religious. It's the foundation on which we are as human beings.

The Christian faith is built firmly on John 3:16 [KJV], "For God so loved the world, that he gave his only begotten Son." The only response to that is that we give back. That's the Christian slant, but the point is that in gardening or farming, you cannot get corn if you don't put seed in the ground. You cannot get cotton if you don't cultivate the field. Nature, like the Word of God, is totally built on giving, and there's nothing—whether it's a marriage or friendship or growing corn—that will exist or even happen without giving. It has been simple for me to combine the two, secular and religious, because the glue that holds either together is giving.

I am who I am, and it's very obvious if you read *Give to Live*. The Rev. Robert Schuller wrote the introduction, and religion

201

is all over it. But it's not a book that turns a secular person off. And this is still true in the updated version of the book, which is titled *More Give to Live.*

Do you find that secular businesses are receptive to this idea of give to live?

Yes, very much so. One of the biggest problems in America today is throwaway children. These are the underprivileged kids who don't get the education they need. They don't live in homes that are decent, and many of them have only one parent. They are the crisis children of our time. Corporations are very open to giving to these children. In fact many corporations adopt a school because they realize the education going on there is no good. They'll adopt a school, put money in it, send their employees out to tutor—all because they're hoping that they can do something about this crisis that we have with children who are being brought up in neighborhoods and schools that are worse than subpar. Corporations have responded and they are giving as never before.

I'd say that forty years ago corporations did not give anything to secondary or elementary education. They gave only to universities. They still give to universities, but increasingly they're giving to elementary and secondary schools.

Corporations are becoming more responsive to this, not just in giving money but in giving volunteer time. A corporation today that allows its employees to volunteer—and also gives money—is better thought of in the community. Corporations are increasingly finding, from a selfish point of view, that a corporation that gives of its time and of its money has a better image, a better public persona, and it sells more products.

The classic example of this in America is a company called Phillip Morris. Phillip Morris sells cigarettes and beer. In recent years they have bought Kraft and other food companies because they are trying to get into other things so they don't just sell cigarettes and beer. But when they were just selling cigarettes and beer, they started a campaign to give to the arts. They are today the biggest giver to the arts in the United States. From time to time you will see a full-page or a two-page ad in magazines with a ballerina flying across the page. And down at the bottom it will say Phillip Morris. But it will not say cigarettes and it will not say beer. It will say art—and that Phillip Morris is a patron of the arts.

Is it easier to convince corporations or individuals that if you give, you'll get something back and become richer for it?

Corporations give primarily out of self-interest. A corporation is in the business of making money. Unless they can see something that they can get back, they will not give. Unless it is a company that's owned by an entrepreneur who controls the purse strings and is really committed to causes. But if it's a public company, they have to rationalize, "What's in it for us and the stockholders?" And if they can't do that, they politely decline.

Whereas an individual is much more prone to see or to feel the individual benefits, which are everything from better health, longer life, personal self-esteem, to a better life in general. Corporations don't really respond that much to the personal benefits of giving. Although they *are* seeing that their employees are happier if they volunteer and that their customers like them better if they give. Corporations tend to give more, however, out of self-interest than the spiritual roots of giving.

Let's create an imaginary, publicly held company. It produces a product that is not damaging to the environment or people in any way. It's a neutral product, so they don't have any corporate guilt. What strategy do you use to convince them that it's in their best interest to give?

First of all, it depends on the charity, but let's just pick one. Let's say UNICEF. That is a charity involved with underprivileged children in foreign countries. What in the world would convince a corporation to support UNICEF? First, I would ask if they are selling any product overseas in the countries where UNICEF is located. Well, UNICEF is everywhere. Generally speaking, UNICEF will be in those countries. I would make my case to this company that in the country where they are selling Coca Cola or selling IBM computers or whatever, the children there will be better customers if they are cared for better. That would be a very important part of the pitch to the company. Their giving would be a mixture of helping children to live a better life, which is what UNICEF does, and the selfish side, which is to sell more products. I'd combine those two.

Is there ever a point as a Christian in business where the principles of your faith are challenged? Or does that even have to be a problem?

If it makes for good business, it makes for good life. When you rub it in, if you start bordering on proselytizing or something, then you'll run into a wall. New York City, where my company is located, is a very Jewish-oriented city. But just the other day a group of Jewish people, Yemenite Jews, invited me to come to a fund-raiser. Yemenites speak Aramaic, which was the language of Jesus. They are the only religious sect that speaks Aramaic today. It's all that's left of Jesus' language. They need support and I made a pitch that Christians need our Jewish friends to support this Jewish sect. That was interesting. But I guarantee you this. If I had even hinted to those people that they ought to convert to Christianity, you can forget it. It wouldn't work. But if you practice the principles of Christianity in your solicitation, in your gratitude for the gift, it's well received, because Christian principles are universal.

Your latest book is called *Volunteering: 101 Ways You Can Improve the World and Your Life*. That seems to be a logical outgrowth of what you're doing.

Yes. Volunteering is a vital way to give. It's a giving of your time and your talent as well as your treasure.

Everything you do seems to have its underpinnings in your Christian background.

That's why I'm still an evangelist, but the best evangelists are not in churches. The best evangelists are people that don't mention Jesus Christ. They just practice the principles, and people follow them. And yes, I'm able to persuade more people to move over to that side by not advertising the Christian side of things.

There are a couple of mistakes that dedicated Christians make. They believe that they've got to quote Scripture; they believe that they've got to rub the Bible in people's noses. And it doesn't work. They're nice people and I don't even argue with them, but they're not talking evangelism; they're just preaching to the choir. But most people are outside the choir. They aren't going to listen. I feel that I practice a sermon every time I ask somebody to give, every time that I help my clients raise money in order to make the world a little better. I practice Christian principles, but I do not state it in a Christian context.

I'm always reminded that Jesus was a Jew, not a Christian. He was not talking about us feeding just Christians. He was talking about us feeding *everybody*.

What advice would you have, as a Christian who is a businessperson, for somebody thinking about going into business as a career?

The first thing is, the best business school is in the Bible. Jesus talked more about money than about love. There are more Scripture passages in the four Gospels about money than anything else. And if you do not believe that, just go read one parable, the parable of the talents. Read that several times and see what you think about what he said about the person who buried his talent in the ground as opposed to the person who took his five talents and multiplied them to ten. You can't multiply five talents to ten unless you're in business. Business to Jesus was as normal as the sun coming up. When we have made business the evil bad thing, we don't understand the New Testament.

My advice would be to look to the Scriptures, but particularly the four Gospels, and read and reread what Jesus said about money. If you look at that, you begin to learn that earning money is okay.

Now, once you've earned it, the Bible is very quick to say that you should share it with others. The point is, in a capitalistic system, the idea is to earn a profit and not just make a living. When you earn the profit, what do you do with it? You share it with others. Giving comes from people who have money. How did they get the money? They earned it.

So the interesting thing is, if you really want to change the world, you must first become a Bill Gates. Become a billionaire and do what Bill Gates has done; he's given his money back. Think about that. Wouldn't it be nice if we had four or five Bill Gates who are practicing what Bill Gates is doing? He has given more than 21.6 billion dollars already, and he is only in his forties. Think about that. Nobody on earth in the history of humankind has ever given away that much money while they were alive, *ever.*

Mr. Gates, who has never talked publicly about any kind of personal faith, and Ted Turner, who has publicly spoken against organized religion, are two of the biggest charitable donors in history.

Bill Gates, as you may know, is married to a Christian. Melinda Gates is from Dallas, Texas, a Roman Catholic, and a very fine Christian. So that family is Christian-oriented, very much so. Their works speak louder than a lot of words of a lot of Christians who are tight as ticks. They practice what they preach.

Cary M. Maguire

President
Maguire Oil

You don't know what student out there may become a future leader. In business today, you will have crises and how you deal with a crisis, when you deal with it, and who deals with it counts. If you can have a moment of ethical thought, it can make a significant difference. Leaders should find ethical approaches to solving problems. Some of these ethical lapses have cost companies more money than any technological shortcomings.

Cary M. Maguire

Cary Maguire knows oil—crude petroleum, natural gas. And, of course, in an energy-hungry world, people know Cary Maguire. Two presidents and British Prime Minister Margaret Thatcher have been guests in his home. He has held leadership positions in some of the most powerful oil and gas industry trade and professional organizations, including National Petroleum Council, MidContinent Oil and Gas Association, and Independent Petroleum Association (past director).

But Maguire believes he will make his greatest mark not as a wild-catter but as a supporter of education. At Southern Methodist University (SMU) in Dallas, Maguire established both the Maguire Energy Institute and the Cary M. Maguire Center for Ethics and Public Responsibility. He is a generous donor to education and currently sits on the executive committee of SMU's board of trustees.

Cary Maguire is a quiet, modest man who doesn't wear his religion on his sleeve. And yet his passion for ethics, not just in business but in all walks of life, in all professions, bespeaks a strong and vibrant faith.

We grew up Episcopalian, but I like to think of myself as ecumenical. I do have a Baptist story, though. My father was a friend of Billy Graham. When he was in town for one of his crusades, my father and I walked out with Billy Graham—the three of us together—on the Cotton Bowl field in front of seventy-five thousand people. At that time, the crowd was larger than for any football game ever played there. It was the first time—and only time—I'd been on the Cotton Bowl field. That was quite an experience. While we were Episcopalians, my father supported Reverend Graham because he thought he did a lot of good work.

By the way, one of my ancestors on my mother's side was married to someone who inaugurated more presidents than anybody else. Billy Graham and Supreme Court Justice John Marshall have sworn in more presidents than anybody else. And that's my Baptist story.

When you went into the oil business, was it difficult to maintain your belief system?

No. But I think all business has a certain amount of challenge. When I first got into the oil business, I did find that there were some people who would attempt to bribe somebody or to give them what appeared to be an attractive oil deal from a major company. We decided that no matter how attractive the deal might appear, we're not going to do that. Somebody might ask, "I wonder why that guy got this deal rather than somebody else?" So there was some of that being done. Although I will say that today in the United States currently, I think very little of that is being done. It's still being done a lot internationally. There are always some stories with a lot of the companies about where some oil minister or another somewhere gets bribed, or there is an attempt to bribe, to get some oil concession. But I don't see that much in the United States.

Once you got in a position of leadership, were you able to operate under the same principles you operated under all along on a company-wide basis?

Yes. I think that anybody in a leadership position normally sets the tone for the operations of the company. So whoever is in a leadership position will generally establish by their behavior what is acceptable and what is *not* acceptable. I think the problem many people have is trying to do something that's legal only—*without* actually staying within the spirit of the law. I think anyone with even some religious beliefs realizes the importance of complying with the spirit of a transaction. This is one reason I funded the Maguire Center for Ethics at Southern Methodist University.

How did that come about?

It's important to know that it's not just in the school of business. I was on the long-range planning committee of the university when the subject of ethics came up. There were two reasons not to do it initially. Someone said, "Look, we're already doing it. Do we want people to now think we're doing something unethical? Why do we have to do anything additional?"

My position was that by hiring a professional in ethics, it can help guide this dialogue. There were some who felt that it was not necessary, that it had never been done before in the fifty years of the university, and this was a totally new concept.

When we finally established the Maguire Chair for Ethics, it became the first all-university chair. Ethics is something that can be woven throughout the entire university. The rationale was that ethics was something not just for the business school, not just for the law school, but it was something that should be addressed university-wide. I didn't want it in the Perkins School of Theology because we wanted this reflection on ethics not just for somebody who is going to be ordained as a minister but for everybody, for those who had a lot of religion in them and those who had very little religion in them.

The other objection to it at the time was, "We don't have space in the curriculum for this." That's when I said, "Can we address

209

our priorities? I'm not saying let's substitute the study of ethics for, say, geography." Of course, academics tend to get a little bit defensive when you come on a new concept. There is a priority problem, which is difficult for academics. If you keep adding classes to the curriculum, such as computer science classes, at some point you're going to need to make some relative choices. You can't do everything, no matter how good.

My view, and we finally agreed, was that ethics should be a high priority and we should make time for it. And that is what happened.

About ten years later, we said, "Let's put more emphasis on it and make a center out of it, a center for ethics and public responsibility." The words "and public responsibility" were added at that time. Dr. William F. May, who had the Kennedy Chair of Ethics at Georgetown University, became the first director of the Maguire Center for Ethics. He thought "and public responsibility" was good to add because he felt, and I agreed, that not only did we want the concept to be part of the university, but we also wanted outreach to the community itself. We didn't want the discussion of ethics just to be isolated to the campus, we also wanted to reach *into* the community.

And in that connection, I am funding the Maguire Chair for Ethics and American History in the Library of Congress in Washington, D.C. Dr. James Billington, who's the Librarian of Congress and a historian, is quite interested in this concept. The idea is to try to raise the ethical awareness in Washington by addressing the historical instances where ethics was important for the country.

What are some of the things the center does?

We have conferences on various subjects. For example, we had a conference on the ethics of philanthropy where we addressed the ethics of giving and receiving. That's a very interesting area because a lot of people, when they give, won't spend the time to refine what they really want to do with the money. There was a case study on the Carnegie Foundation. Andrew Carnegie, close to death, signs something, creates something, but there was not enough detail as to the direction of the foundation. Then you end up with a staff charging off in some other direction after you're gone.

And the people you wanted to help don't get helped.

Right. So the ethics of giving addresses the issue of not just giving of your money but also giving of your thought and time to *how* it is going to be done. It's not just saying, "Here's a million dollars."

The ethics of receiving, of course, gets into spending the money for the purpose in which it was desired. I was on a school board once when a donation was made for new books. Somebody else on the board said, "Look, we don't need any books. Why don't we just use this to relieve operating expenses?" I said, "No. They gave the money to buy the books." The ethics of receiving deals with doing what the donor of the money actually wanted. A lot of people may say, "What difference does it make? This is an equally worthwhile thing." But again, it's keeping the deal.

Then we have ethics in contracts, which deals directly with the subject of keeping a deal. I was asked to be on a panel as one speaking to the merits of keeping the deal. There was another professor who was supposed to speak on the ethics of breaking a deal in some instances. That's not my sense of ethics, but we've always presented two sides of a coin so that someone can weigh the relative merits.

We also hosted an ethics in sports conference. Then we had one, which was very interesting, on ethics in media. That usually gets a laugh. But what I found was that a lot of the executives in the media were quite interested in this because they didn't want the government to come in and dictate something. They'd rather find out how to clean up their own houses.

Then we had ethics in health care. One of the issues, for example, was about a patient who had gangrene and needed six days to recover completely. He called his insurance representative, who said, "We'll give you four days." But the man died because he didn't have the needed six days to recover. So much of this now is attorney—and insurance—driven, but the doctor's original oath is to take care of his patient. That should be the primary consideration, as opposed to budgetary considerations. There are a lot of problems in mental health care on that same issue.

We've had a number of joint conferences as well. There was one with doctors, lawyers, *and* clergy. There we dealt with the ethics of doctors not honoring the living will agreements of patients.

I'll bet that one stirred up some interesting discussions.

Yes, it did. I signed a living will and my wife—who feels very strongly about it—wants somebody to honor what she did. But the lawyers and hospitals many times will advise the doctor not to honor that request because somebody might contest it in court.

What we've found through all of this is that the number one cultural force in America today is not the same cultural force it was when I was a young boy. When I was a young boy, religion and the military were two of the most prominent cultural forces. Today the media has supplanted religion as being the number one cultural force. That's a sad commentary. But that deals with another ethical issue in religion and that is this: How many religious leaders do you see with the courage to come out and speak about the media on national television? Relatively few.

Our ethics professor just gave a great talk on that subject because he called the media "the unordained ministers of culture." In other words, the media today speak as if they were the ordained ministers of culture.

What advice would you have for a young person thinking about going into business as a lifetime profession?

I think it is this: Do what's right. The spirit of doing what's right is far more important than a whole bunch of rules, regulations, and legalistic concepts. View each thing you do by asking, *What would it look like if this were in the newspaper tomorrow?* That is a measure of guiding the behavior.

I also feel strongly that if you give, you receive. I've got a bronze at my house. It features two Indians climbing up a cliff. And the Indian at the top is reaching down to lift up his friend. The inscription says, "They rise highest who lift as they go." When I show that bronze to most people, it makes an impact. That's a very important concept—they rise highest who lift as they go. So part of my advice is to try and help others and you'll find that helps you, as well.

Another thing I would say is, if you recognize that there is a God, there should be some sense of fairness in what you do.

One more thing that helps very much in business is that if you will take the time to be specifically clear, you're not only helping your own company, you're helping create goodwill with others, as opposed to being vague in your dealings with people on the theory that if you're not clear, well, you'll just have the lawyers try and straighten it out later. That's not really an ethical religious concept. And so part of that is the willingness to make some effort to be clear as you go.

One thing we do in our company is that we have a matching contribution so that when people give to their churches, we match it. And that encourages people to give.

Finally, I think it is good to try and teach people to thank God for their blessings on a continual basis. And even though you may have some things you're not too thankful about, express thanks for those blessings you *do* have. In the end, I think that goes along with the original concept of giving and receiving.

213

Gary Martin

President
Whitmore Manufacturing Company

It was very apparent to me at the beginning of my career that one's own intellectual furnishings were a minor part of the overall requirements to successfully lead others. Having, sharing, and encouraging faith in the broadest sense is natural to goal achievement.

Gary Martin

The world moves on Whitmore, or, more precisely, Whitmore's lubricants, greases, and oils. Since producing the original lubricants for the center pivot and roller bearings necessary to build the Panama Canal, the Whitmore Manufacturing Company has been a world leader in making sure that shovels, draglines, dozers, haul trucks, and crushing, grinding, and milling equipment run smoothly.

With state-of-the-art plants in Texas and Ohio, Whitmore produces among other things the well-known brands Air Sentry, KATS Coatings, and Horizon Lubricants.

And the man who makes Whitmore move is Gary Martin. Martin is a worthy heir to S. W. Whitmore, the Cleveland pharmacist who invented the first really effective manila belt dressing—a key component in the American Industrial Revolution. Under Martin's guidance, Whitmore was one of the first companies in the Southwest to adopt the Total Quality Management plan. Additionally, all employees are required to complete a course in quality systems, problem solving, decision making, process improvement, and analytical controls.

214

Not surprisingly, Martin has been equally concerned about his employees' spiritual well-being, quickly contracting with the then-new Marketplace Ministries to make chaplains available to all employees.

In 1972 Martin joined Capital Southwest Corporation (CSC), the largest publicly held venture capital organization in the United States. Today he serves as both a director and an officer in the organization. Whitmore is a subsidiary of CSC. Martin also serves on the board of directors of a number of corporations, both public and private, is chairman of the American Management Association's General Management Council for Growing Organizations, and is past chairman of the Chemical Specialties Management Council. He's also held several publicly elected and appointed positions on councils, boards, and commissions in the Dallas area.

Martin talks about his Catholic family and his faith:

My mother's strong Catholic background was the dominant force in our home. Growing up in a conservative Southwestern environment in the 1950s and early '60s meant a very formal mass, well-endowed with Latin. My brother and I often wondered why our non-Catholic friends had such a good time at Sunday school. Faith became a key part of my life when my family and business career started accelerating during my thirties.

Did your faith play a role in your early jobs and leadership positions?

Initially faith was not something I shared or felt I needed to share with others at the workplace. Again, from a conservative 1950s' homelife, it was natural to maintain a quiet perspective on faith in general and specific religious beliefs in particular.

As I became more involved in general management, the importance of individuals' striving in concert with others toward a unified goal revealed the need for more open discussions about one's faith in self, the family, and worthwhile group efforts. Such discussions seem more effective within an overall business setting without reference to specific religious beliefs.

215

Did your strong value system ever present any difficulties in business dealings?

No. As maturity develops, I believe we gain an important perspective to identify the early signs of improper actions. Wise business managers, equipped with strong value systems, can usually derail, or at least sidetrack, potential difficulties before they blossom into real problems.

Does Whitmore Manufacturing corporately have a creed or message or statement?

The senior management of this organization determined many years ago that our collective outward expression of faith, values, and beliefs should exemplify a very wholesome inner core. To help accomplish that objective, we have well utilized, on a company-wide basis, the chaplaincy program of Marketplace Ministries. I hope our actions speak in place of creeds, messages, or posted statements.

What advice do you have for young people entering the business world?

Organize your minds and businesses toward acts of fairness.

Drayton McLane Jr.

Chairman and CEO, Houston Astros Baseball Club
Chairman, McLane Group

We have people of all different faiths working with us, but I quickly try to talk about integrity, honesty, and morality. To be successful as a leader, you've got to feel good about yourself. The only way you can feel good about yourself is to have the proper values. And if you approach life correctly, you'll feel good about your achievements.

Drayton McLane Jr.

One man, two mega-corporations. At a time when most of us are struggling to keep one enterprise afloat, much less make it internationally known, Drayton McLane Jr. has done it twice. And don't bet that he won't up and do it again.

McLane's first success was to make the family business, the McLane Company, Inc., one of the country's largest and most powerful grocery wholesalers and distributors. In late 1990 Wal-Mart purchased the McLane Company, although McLane stayed on as CEO until 1993 and served on Wal-Mart's board of directors until 1995.

Today he heads up the McLane Group, a multifaceted entity that manages his many business ventures and investments, including McLane International (wholesale consumer product distribution centers in Poland, Spain, the U.K., and elsewhere overseas), Classic

Foods (manufacturers of "genuine" Texas foods), Leading Edge Brands (specialty soft drinks and spring waters, including Frostie, Grapette, Dads, and others), Lone Star Plastics (plastic film products, including trash can liners), M-C International (export management), M-C Pacific (distribution in the South Pacific), CSP Information Group (global multimedia communication company), and M-Group Systems (business management software design and development).

McLane's other success story has been the Houston Astros and their world-class ballpark. Since McLane purchased the club in 1992, only the Atlanta Braves have had a better cumulative record in the National League. Just as important to McLane, Astros players have become the most involved players in their community through the Astros in Action Foundation, continuously supporting area charitable and educational causes.

But then, that's McLane's way. Even with his twin responsibilities, he is still actively involved in the Boy Scouts of America, the Children's Miracle Network, the United Way, Scott and White Hospital, Baylor University, and a host of civic and religious activities in his hometown of Temple, Texas. He's even past chairman of the deacons at his church and continues to teach a Sunday school class. All of these involvements attest to his commitment to God.

I grew up in Cameron, Texas, a little town of five thousand. My father was a Presbyterian and a very religious person. He was extremely active in the Presbyterian church. My mother grew up in the Baptist church and was a devout Baptist. So, when they married, rather than one joining the other's church, she went to the Baptist church and he went to the Presbyterian church. That was back in the late '40s and the '50s. But my two older sisters and I went to the Baptist Sunday school and church every Sunday morning. Then we went to the Presbyterian church, back when they had church services on Sunday evenings. I went to both the Baptist *and* Presbyterian vacation Bible schools each summer *and* went to both summer camps. So I had all the doctrine of both the Presbyterians and the Baptists. Our parents were just really fine Christians, and they really set the proper example for my sisters and me.

Did you go straight into the McLane Company after graduating from college?

I went to Baylor University, graduated in 1958, and then I got an MBA from Michigan State University in East Lansing, Michigan. That was a two-year program and I graduated in 1959. I was single at the time, and I had a job opportunity in San Francisco. I was really looking forward to that. After I graduated from Michigan State, I stopped in Cameron. I was going to spend a couple of weeks with my parents and some friends.

At the time, my father headed up a small family business, doing about two million dollars annually, with sixty-six employees. I told my dad that someday I'd like to go into business with him. He told me, "Son, the business has changed dramatically, and we really haven't changed the business to fit the current needs. But if you want to go into business with me, you'd better do it quickly, because if you wait a few years, there might not be a business here to do."

That disappointed me because I was anxious to move on and live in California for a few years. But that night, I thought, *I've always wanted to own my own business and to be in a family oriented business.* So the next day I told him that I changed my mind and I was ready to go. I'd had six years of college and I had all this knowledge and information.

He said, "The only available job is working at night on the second shift, loading trucks." There were seventeen people on this loading shift and I thought, *At least I'll be in charge.* But I wasn't. I was just one of the seventeen. For almost a year, I worked physical, manual labor at night.

He later told me, "Son, with your education, if you couldn't have won the support and the admiration of those seventeen people you were working with at night, then you weren't going to be a very good leader. I wanted to see if you had the skills and the ability. You don't anoint people to success; they earn it." That was the first step.

In addition to working on the second shift at night, I eventually worked in all the transportation areas too, driving trucks, supervising drivers, and all that. I also worked as a

219

salesman and as a buyer. Eventually I did almost every job in the company.

Later I had to go to my father and apologize and say, "Dad, that's the nicest thing you ever did for me, because I learned the business from the ground up." I earned the respect and admiration of the working people. I learned how they do things, how you gain their respect, and how you communicate and motivate them. He taught me business skills I didn't learn in college.

Was your faith important to you even at that stage?

My faith has always been very important. In my early life, my mother was a powerful force. I had two older sisters and she talked to us constantly. When I make talks today, I say that my mother shaped a great deal of my life. Thousands of times, she told my two sisters and me, "The most important thing in life is your Christian faith and your belief in God and Jesus Christ. The second most important is the love and respect that you have for your whole family."

Then she said, "The third one totally shapes your life. That's whom you select to be your friends. Select them wisely and they'll lift you up. Select them badly and they will certainly pull you down."

Mom had spies all over town. I had to sit with her in her bedroom, in her rocking chair, as a little boy, and she would lecture me awfully hard about some of the people I was hanging out with. When I went to Baylor, I thought, *Boy, I'm done with that.* I remember the first time I came home after about six weeks at Baylor and she brought me into her bedroom and she told me, "Now I want you to sit here and I want you to tell me about all your new friends at Baylor." So until she passed away at eighty-nine, even when I was fifty years old, I constantly had to talk to my mother about who my friends were. She was such a positive Christian person. So that certainly structured my life early on.

When I became a teenager, and particularly when I went into business with him, my dad had such an outstanding moral

220

value system. I saw the way he did business; I saw his moral, Christian ethic; I saw the way he made decisions based on integrity and values. So he too became a very powerful force in my life. I was very fortunate in having both parents who were truly outstanding Christians.

Talk about being a Christian in the business world.

I learned from my dad that you run a business by having great personal integrity. Every executive that I've ever recruited has to have that. We had an executive in here from Phoenix on Saturday. I'd talked with him previously and we're going to send him to Lisbon, Portugal, to run a business we have there. I've told him every time that integrity and honesty are the greatest values of a leader. You can have all the education and skills, but you've got to have integrity. Otherwise, people see through you over a period of time.

We have people of all different faiths working with us, but I quickly try to talk about integrity, honesty, and morality. To be successful as a leader, you've got to feel good about yourself. The only way you can feel good about yourself is to have the proper values. And if you approach life correctly, you'll feel good about your achievements. You've got to set standards.

Does your company have a mission statement?

Back in the '70s it became the vogue in strategic planning to have a mission statement. We had a very complicated mission statement. I was the only one that really understood it because I wrote it. At that time in the McLane Company we had about eight to nine thousand employees—and I probably was the only one that really understood it at all.

One day I really felt, *We've missed the message.* A great communicator gets his ideas across where people buy into it. I just threw that old mission statement in the garbage can. We then established a new mission statement that said, "The mission of McLane Company is honesty, integrity, high Christian principles."

221

The McLane Company now has eleven thousand employees. Each division president has several thousand employees, and he has to meet with every employee at least once every thirty days in groups no bigger than thirty-five. I learned a long time ago that if you're really going to communicate with people and get things accomplished, you've got to get their interaction. If you put them in big groups, the loudmouths do all the talking and the real, genuine people do not. So the division president spends about 50 percent of his time in doing nothing but talking to employees, communicating the values of the company, understanding the operational things that we need to be doing. We have meetings with no more than thirty-five. The division president mixes different people each time—truck drivers, forklift drivers, accountants, and computer programmers—and he talks to them. When he starts the meeting, he's always supposed to say, "The mission of the McLane Company is honesty, integrity, high Christian principles—and hold us accountable for that."

We've had divisions all over the United States, and now internationally, and we've got a lot of people who aren't Christians. I've had people say in the meetings, "I'm Jewish or Hindu or whatever, and I don't like this Christian stuff." I say, "Great. I'll make a deal with you. I'm trying to convey values to everyone about doing the right thing. I use the word *Christian*. You don't have to be a Christian, but I use it as a descriptive word of what we're trying to achieve." There was a Jewish fellow one time in California who really got after me. I said, "You find me a better word and I'll use it." He came back a few days later and said, "I've thought and thought and thought and talked to my rabbi. Why don't you just keep using the 'Christian' word? That probably conveys it better than anything else."

So, we're not trying to convert them to Christianity. We're trying to set integrity and honesty as the principles of business.

Is there any difference in how you run a baseball team and how you run a multinational corporation?

Absolutely none. I've been in the grocery industry since I got out of graduate school when I was twenty-two years old and have dealt in the grocery business with a large number of people. I don't wear my Christianity as a sign on my shirt. But I *have* wanted people to see the way I've thought, the way I've conducted myself, the way I've behaved.

I noticed very young that, particularly with my mother and her family, when her sisters and brothers were around her, they acted in a much more gentlemanly manner. I noticed that they had such high respect for her because she had such great ethics. My dad was as straight an arrow as you'll ever see. He never used any bad language, he didn't tell crazy stories, and he was just very straightforward. People respected him for what he stood for. I've always tried to conduct myself in business that way and be the same kind of person—whether I'm going to Sunday school on Sunday or in a business meeting in Chicago on Monday—with the same values and the same integrity.

As I hopped over from the grocery business that I was involved in for thirty years into the baseball business, I've conducted myself in the same way. If you go into the locker room, baseball players will be all over the place sometimes. But they act a little different when they see me coming. I think they appreciate that I'm not just another guy that wants to hang out with baseball players, that I try to lift them up and have high standards.

I said in a news conference when we bought the Houston Astros in 1993 that we had two objectives. One was to become a champion team—to go to the World Series and to win the World Series—and the other was to make a positive difference while doing it.

Nothing communicates in America like sports. It gets everybody, whether you have a Ph.D. or didn't go to college or you have no money or you're a multimillionaire. You have the same interest in it. I'd like to use the athletes and the admiration the public has for the team to do good things, to get deeply involved in the society, and do public service. We were the first Major League baseball team, and still the only one, that has a full-time chaplain who works with the players. But his main role is to get the players involved in the community. We have a very extensive community service program where we're involved from daycare centers to senior citizen groups. I think that is one of the obligations, one of the responsibilities we have in dealing with a professional sports team, to use it to set a good example for all people.

Some owners won't take a chance on a truly gifted athlete who is a troubled individual.

That's true in business too. I've noticed that there are a lot of talented people in business who have great skills and accomplishments, but personally they are on the razor's edge. Even though they're brilliant, they don't really motivate the people that work for them because their employees see through them. Because of the way they conduct themselves, or because they're so upside-down personally, it affects them when they're involved in business. People can see this in a hurry.

I like people that have stability, people that have a focus in their life, people with Christian values. They're more successful; they're the better leaders. I've always said, "If you're getting on a 747 flying from Los Angeles to Sydney, you want a pilot that has stability. When troubles occur, he doesn't get frustrated. He knows exactly what to do." That's discipline. Integrity, Christian values, and discipline—those are what we've worked hard to do. In my business, when we would get people that had a lot of accomplishments and ability to achieve objectives but just didn't represent the same values that we did, I would slowly move them through the organization—and then move them out. The same is true with our team. I want to be a champion team, but with players that have great personal values and integrity. We've moved a bunch out, but you sure don't read negative things about Houston Astros players.

As a Christian who is a businessman, what advice do you give to young people thinking about business as a career?

Business is just like sports or writing a novel or anything else. Being a farmer, I've been out in the country. When you see a guy farming, you can tell how good a farmer he is by how straight the rows are that he plants. Or you can tell how good he is by the appearance around his home and his barns and all that. If he takes great personal pride, if he has great appearance, it shows.

People have asked me, "You must be really having fun being in baseball." I say, "I've been in the grocery business for over forty years and *that* is exciting. I enjoyed every day I went to work. I find business interesting and challenging. I loved the competitiveness of it. Business is as competitive or more so than sports. I love the teamwork with other executives."

I've said for many, many years in management meetings that you can read all these management books you want, but if you'll just go back to Genesis, to when God selected Moses, you'll see that Moses said he wasn't qualified. God said, "I'll show you how to do it." In Genesis you'll see how God told Moses to divide up the different camps and to put people in charge of the camps. That was the first management plan.

And that's the fun part of business—taking something really complicated, breaking it down, putting people in charge, giving them the responsibilities, teaching them how to be successful, and *then* letting them use their ingenuity. And don't say that you've got only one way to do this.

I remember years ago at McLane Company, as we were growing (I had gone to graduate school where they showed us how to write policy manuals and procedures and all that). I looked up one time and discovered that we had about two thousand employees, and we weren't really responding to unusual conditions as they came up. People were looking in the policy manuals for answers.

So one day I had a big meeting. I took all the policy manuals and threw them in the garbage can. I said, "We don't have them anymore. I know only three things you've got to do in business. You can't ever violate any laws, because you'll go to jail. You can never, ever violate the other person's moral values. And you've got to make a profit, because if you don't make a profit, either you get fired or you go into bankruptcy.

"Outside of that, just use your God-given creativity. These are the ways I started doing it. You can show me a different way to do it, but you've got to stay within these boundaries. You've got to believe in customer service. Then you've got to show respect and motivation and leadership for all the employees. If you'll do these things, business turns out to be easy."

I think business *is* fun. It's exciting. And I have tried to use those business principles as I've been involved with the Houston Astros.

Charles Miller
President (Retired)
Reese Products

We believe business principles should conform to the teachings of Christ.

Plaque on the wall of Charles Miller's office

Reese Products is the world's premier producer of towing equipment and trailer accessories. Charles Miller was an early employee, a very early employee. In fact in the third grade he painted the die-cast nameplates for each trailer, at a fee of one cent each.

Miller has been working hard ever since. After stints with the Air Force during the Korean War, the Dexter Axle Company (a manufacturer and assembler of axles, hubs, brakes, and drums for the RV and mobile home industry), boat trailer manufacturer Republic Industries, Inc. (founder and president), and Stoutco, Inc. (vice president and member of the board of directors for thirty-five years), Miller has been at Reese ever since, serving as president from 1977 until his retirement in 1990.

Along the way, the son of noted inventor Milo E. Miller has served on a host of national safety and industry-wide boards and committees, as well as in several service organizations: the Elkhart Community Leaders Prayer Breakfast (cochairman), the Rotary Club of Elkhart (board of directors), the Recreational Vehicles International Annual Leadership Prayer Breakfast (founder and chairman), the Christian Businessmen's Committee of USA (board of directors and four-term board member), the Christian Businessmen's Committee, International, (board chairman and board of directors), and twenty-four years with the Gideons International.

My mother and dad were great parents. They tried to teach us to be good citizens. Going to church was one of those lessons and was a regular thing at our house. My memories of this do not carry any feelings of resistance. In fact I looked forward to this routine because it meant fun with my buddies.

I was comfortable with Mother and Dad's reputation of being churchgoers and the fact that I had been born into a Christian home. I took on that reputation for myself as well. I was comfortable being part of this Christian family, which I believed surely made me a Christian as well.

We moved to Elwood, Indiana, where Dad started the National Trailer Company in 1938. They were producing 22 trailers a day at a 140,000-square-foot plant employing 478 men. It became a model of how to set up a production line for recreational vehicles. My father was given the title "School Teacher of the Industry" for this production technique.

Dad soon took in a partner who had a son, Richard, my age. Richard and I spent a lot of time together. We rode our bikes around town together, went to the same church, and were good friends. I was about nine at this time.

One Sunday before church, Richard and I were together in front of the church. It was about time for church to begin, so we were going up the front steps headed for the front door. Richard then asked me a question that startled me. He said, "Charles, have you become a Christian yet?" I was so startled that I didn't answer him. We just went on inside and sat with our parents, which was the custom.

As I was sitting there, I remember thinking to myself: *What did he mean by that question, "Have you become a Christian yet?" Why would he even ask me that question? He knows the kind of kid I am; we play together. He knows the kind of family we are because he has been at our house a lot of times. He knows we have a Christian home.*

I was kind of getting upset with Richard for asking that question. However, I couldn't get it out of my mind that morning. I then began to remember the vacation Bible schools we had attended together. And I began to reflect on some verses from the Bible that we had to memorize at every Bible school we attended, such as, "For all have sinned and fall short of the glory of God" (Rom. 3:23); "The wages of sin is death [separation from God], but the gift of God is eternal life in Christ Jesus our Lord" (Rom. 6:23); "For by grace you have been saved through faith, and that not of yourselves; it is the gift of God, not of works, lest anyone should boast" (Eph. 2:8–9 [NKJV]); and "For God so loved the world that He gave His only begotten Son, that whoever believes in Him should not perish but have everlasting life" (John 3:16 [NKJV]).

I thought about those verses and others and Richard's question all during church time. It was at this time that I recognized that I didn't become a Christian by being born into a good family. I wouldn't get to heaven by my dad and mom's reputation or experience. I needed to make that decision on my own. It had to be my own personal experience, not one acquired by osmosis.

It was that morning in the quietness of my heart that I asked the Lord to forgive me of my sins and to accept me as one of his children. I still remember the importance of that decision that morning and have never regretted it. In fact it was the most important decision I have ever made in my life. It changed my eternal destiny!

Ever since that time, it has been a wonderful experience to know that God responded to my prayer and forgave me of my sins, and that I can live with the confidence of his promise to be with me always. That is exactly what he says he will do in the book he wrote for us and left for us to read.

Is Reese a privately or publicly held company?

Reese started as a privately held company when it was formed by T. J. "Terrell" Reese and his son Robert in 1952. It was in the business of manufacturing trailer hitches and tow bars for the recreational vehicle, marine, and automotive industries. In 1973 they merged with Masco Corporation in Taylor, Michigan. So Reese Products became a wholly owned subsidiary of Masco, which is a large conglomerate. I joined Reese in '66.

What, if any, are the differences between being in a private company and a public company?

When it was private, we naturally had a lot of freedom to administer the company the way we wanted. One of the choices we made was that with every shipment that went out, we included a little pamphlet titled "The Best Things in Life." That practice continued for years, and we received many positive responses to that booklet over the years. Then, as the product and packaging changed somewhat, that practice was discontinued.

When I became president in 1977, Terrell Reese had passed away. There was a plaque that I found in his office. The plaque said, "We believe business principles should conform to the teachings of Christ." So I put that plaque on the wall in *my* office, and that kind of describes, I think, the basis for all good business. That's the way employees want to be treated; that's the way customers want to be treated; that's the way suppliers want to be treated. After I retired from Reese, my son Doug duplicated that plaque and gave it to me one year for Christmas. I now have it in my home office.

I think a private company has more freedom to display management's personal beliefs, feeling it is a benefit to everyone with whom they have contact.

Could you talk about some of the ways that this specifically played out both in your personal life and your business life? What does that mean in practical terms?

It blends together in a policy and a method of managing. You treat the employees the way that you think Christ would have wanted employees, customers, and suppliers treated.

The Bible has a lot to say about that topic. If there is a problem with confrontation with anyone, there is a method for resolving that. The Bible talks about goals, it talks about money, it talks about planning, it talks about procrastination, and it talks about stress. All of those together give the format for success in business and in life in general.

I don't think that is necessarily always exclusive for a Christian businessperson. There are a lot of businessmen who adhere to the format, but they probably don't know where all those principles came from. But the Bible is the source.

At the same time, when folks hear that you're a Christian businessman, does that put extra or different expectations on you?

I think if you have the label that you're a Christian businessman, yes, it carries a different responsibility. That carries over into a warranty policy, for instance. We generally had a very liberal warranty policy. Our basic way of treating a customer who had a complaint was that whatever the customer felt would be a fair resolution to a problem, that's what we tried to do. Usually people are fair in what they feel is a fair resolution. So, yes, that does carry some additional responsibility. And although not everybody in our organization necessarily was a Christian, everyone felt very comfortable with that method of doing business.

It seems that excellence would be one of the biblical mandates for Christian businesspeople.

It certainly does. Yes. And not only in your warranty, but it also extends a responsibility in the paying of bills, for instance. You don't encroach on the terms unless you have a very clear understanding with your supplier as to why you're doing it and you have an agreement. That applies to the way you handle your customers as well.

There is no difference, then, between someone's Christian life and his or her business life? One just flows naturally out of the other?

Yes, because when you have that relationship, it becomes a lifestyle, and those rules or principles are not exclusively for a Christian businessperson. They're just really good business principles. And all of those come from Scripture. They're all just good principles that lots and lots of businesses follow, even though they may not be Christian businesses.

A Christian business is going to suffer setbacks and market share declines like any other business. Does a Christian businessperson respond differently to adversity?

I would say the big struggle comes when it involves the necessity of laying off employees. That is a hard, hard struggle. We did have cases where that needed to happen. Usually we would do our best to explain in pretty good detail to the workforce what was happening and try to give some kind of a warning, if we could, as to what we saw coming and the struggles that we were going through. It was an attempt to have open communication as to what was happening. That did not alleviate the pain for those involved in being let go, but I think that they understood. At least that's always your hope that they understood what you were going through and that it was a necessity for keeping the business whole for everybody. From an emotional point of view, that usually was the hardest struggle.

What advice do you have for young people who are thinking of going into some kind of business as a career?

They need to prepare, skill-wise. And, assuming that they *are* prepared skill-wise for managing a business, then they need to be prepared ethics- and morality-wise as well. It's not 100 percent true, but I would say the key to success is the longevity of consistency of an honest business. There are lots of honest businesses that go under for other reasons; some of those could be management reasons or market-related reasons. But if you're going to be competing in a market, you need to build the reputation. And you build the reputation by consistency and not by hyping the ads or spins.

Truly liking people is very important. We need to value, respect, and enjoy working with others. Those working for us will quickly sense the genuineness of our interest in people. We will enhance their job satisfaction and sense of worth by our healthy people skills.

The most important point is that we're always struggling with the managing of our time. That will always be a constant pressure. Where do we spend our time? We need to decide to protect our priorities from the beginning.

Priority number one ought to be to develop your spiritual growth with Jesus Christ. That's the most important thing for this life—and not only for this life but for eternal life as well.

Number two is to nurture your family, not just providing food and housing but making a home. Set aside enough time for nurturing and developing a healthy relationship with your wife and your children.

Number three is to make sure your job and your career fit in this order as number three because priorities one and two can be done only by you and no one else. Things about your job can usually be delegated, but you can't delegate number one and number two.

Number four is the good things you do outside of work for the community or charitable organizations. We sometimes do these good things, substituting them and confusing them with our number one priority—the personal development of our growth with Christ. These are two distinct priorities.

That, in a nutshell, is the order of priorities. If we get them out of balance, it is like a wheel going around that has its weights in the wrong place. It will wear out prematurely. So keep your priorities and your time allocation in balance.

Norm Miller
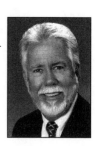

Chairman of the Board
Interstate Battery System of America

Fulfillment in life is based on having a loving relationship with God. That's twenty-four hours a day. That's seven days a week. If Christianity is the truth, then embracing God in life and through business will yield similar results.

Norm Miller

To glorify God as we supply our customers worldwide with top quality, value-priced batteries, related power-source products, and distribution services. Further, our mission is to provide our partners and Interstate Battery System of America with opportunities which are profitable, rewarding and growth-oriented.

Mission Statement

Nobody sells more batteries than Interstate Battery System of America, the top replacement battery company in North America, to the tune of more than 12 million units sold annually. Those batteries are available through 300 distributors and more than 200,000 dealers. The home office's 450 employees also enjoy a full-time chaplain, voluntary prayer meetings, and Bible study groups. What they may not know is that Miller has quietly committed more than 1 million dollars to see that the popular *Jesus* video is distributed worldwide—and for free.

Not surprisingly, Interstate's entry into the fiercely competitive world of NASCAR is just as successful. The green Interstate Batteries/Joe Gibbs Pontiac Racing team with driver Bobby Labonte won the Winston Cup in 2000.

Miller is a popular speaker and author *(Beyond the Norm)*. Interstate Battery's entertaining corporate web site features his full testimony—and extensive NASCAR links. He was deep into the business world before his faith became an integral part of everything he did.

My boss, John Searcy, who founded the company, was twenty-two years my senior. So by the time I got with him, he had pretty much figured out a niche, if you will, in the market. He'd discovered a way to go. In some places, his people were doing well, but it was primarily those people who had their own initiative. Even though we had the system put down, it really wasn't honed. We were able to impart a system of operation to people who had only a marginal understanding of what to do in the battery business, which sheltered their risk factor.

And at the same time, you were going through changes in your own life.

I got involved with John Searcy in '62 as a distributor with my dad. In '65 when I went to work for John on a full-time basis, I moved back to Dallas and started traveling the United States, working with distributors, setting them up, troubleshooting them, and marketing. It wasn't until 1974 that I became a Christian.

Did things change in your business life about the same time?

I'd say they changed pretty radically in the spring of '74 because I quit drinking. I'd become an alcoholic and spent a lot of time partying on the road. So a lot of that quit then. I'm sure, in general, I became more stable.

I began to study the Bible right after I became a believer. As the Word of God was built into me and as I embraced it, I began to try and employ his truth in my life. Then there were two major changes within a couple weeks after I received Christ. First, fear went away from me. I had set a bunch of goals as a young guy getting out of college. I had actually accomplished them ahead of time. But the only problem was that my motivation was fear of failure. So I was driven and, as time progressed toward reaching these goals, I became even more anxious. I'm sure this helped accelerate the drinking.

After receiving Christ, I began to just accept my circumstances as what he had intended for me at the time. In essence, that's what it says in the Scriptures, "That which you have, you have because that's what I have intended for you right now." So, I still tried hard, made plans, set goals, and sought excellence. But I leave the results to him, accept them, and thank him for them. In the midst of all that, I received a deep peace. Peace grew into my life, which my wife will certainly testify to.

The second thing that happened was that love came into me when I first read in Galatians that the fruit of the Spirit is peace, love, and joy. I know it says more, but I looked just at those three. The love part just didn't really sit with me right. It's almost like when you eat something and it just doesn't settle on your stomach for a short time, but you have this remembrance. I had that.

I remember I was in a supermarket, walking down the aisle, pushing a cart two weeks after I had received Christ. And on that day, as people started coming toward me in the aisle, I realized that *I loved them*. I looked them in the eyes and I realized that *I loved them*. Shortly thereafter, contemplating all that, I realized that I had never really loved *anybody*. Prior to Christ, I had affection for people, but that was all based on how they served me. It was all conditional. If they made me laugh or if they were fun to run around with or fish with or if they helped in business, *then* they became my friends. I didn't go deep down. It was all surface as far as love was concerned.

So in the days that followed my transformation, those two things—the fear leaving and then the love coming in—affected my business behavior.

When did your mission statement for Interstate Battery emerge?

I read where the Scripture tells you to be alert for opportunities. I came to Christ through people that had a heart for evangelism and discipleship. Then I hooked up with Campus Crusade for Christ, whose driving force is evangelism. And so my heart was in evangelism. I began to be alert for every opportunity how we might be able to further lift up Christ, but in a sensitive manner. Our prayer was that we would be perfectly bold, yet perfectly sensitive.

Did you come up with that phrase?

It just came up at our meetings. We asked God that we not offend anybody because we wanted to win them to the Lord. From a business standpoint, that was an overriding goal. We came up later with our mission statement. Before then, my brother Tommy and I ran the company by the seat of our pants.

But there came a time when I started losing interest and passion for business. It became mechanical. When I saw that happening, I decided that I needed to let Tommy run it because I knew he had a passion for it. At the same time, we needed to not operate out of our back pocket. That's when we identified the top ten other people in our company besides ourselves and we decided to start over with a mission statement. We met for hours weekly for several months, redefined what we were going to do, and came up with the mission statement.

Do things change when a mission statement goes from unsaid to said?

Somebody once said, "Habits are caught and not taught." My brother became a Christian about the same time I did, but totally separately, which was interesting. We began to try to honor God with our life in business. I think the company was small enough in '74 that the behavior of the company came from the top. The statement put some tire on the wheels. Still,

I think that people had a pretty good understanding of who we were, where we were going, and why.

Do you think new employees coming in have a sense of what Interstate is all about? And do you believe that certain kinds of people are drawn to a company that is faith-based?

I think so. Because I think we make it pretty clear who we are and what we're about. When our distributors bring their employees to Dallas for training, one of the things I tell them is that our belief is to treat people the way that we would want to be treated if we swapped spots. I tell them I believe that because I think it is a mandate from God.

I say, "If you believe it for that reason, great. If you don't, it's all right. I believe it is also the wisest philosophy to follow in running a business. Therefore, I want you to put yourself in the customer's place. Who would you rather have dealing with you? Someone that has their own interest at heart or someone who has your interest at heart trying to treat you the way you'd want to be treated? The answer is you'd rather have the second. Consequently, we want you to understand that we desire and expect you to operate under this philosophy so that we can build the business."

Has your being a Christian company caused other companies to behave differently in interactions with you? Have you had any incidents relating to your beliefs as a company at a corporate level?

I can't recall that it's caused any problems at all. We have a newspaper that we send to our two hundred thousand dealers. In it we have some, but not many, references to the Bible and God and Christ. Sometimes on the masthead page, we will quote a Scripture or say something like, "If you have any interest in understanding how you can receive Jesus Christ as your Savior, contact Chaplain Henry Rogers."

At different times I've sent out both my book *Beyond the Norm* and the book *More than a Carpenter* to every Interstate dealer. We use Christmas as an opportunity to send something that is Christian to our dealers. We're figuring, "Hey, it's Christmas! We're all thinking holiday."

But I had a distributor in Skokie, Illinois, whose dealer started giving him a bunch of flack about the Christian references to our stuff and they didn't want to receive it anymore. So we did stop sending them Christian-oriented materials. That's fair too.

To my knowledge we haven't lost any business. We lost a couple of accounts that were pretty good, but we sent a man in there for a week to sell and to build the account level back up for the distributor and that eliminated the problem. We went on down the road. We obey the law; we don't hire only Christians. We try to look for the best. We pray for God to bring us the people he wants and then we try to pick the best person. And if things are equal, we try to pick the most needy.

Let's say, for example, that we had a wealthy guy's wife wanting to work and then we have a single gal with three kids—and both want work. If they are outright equal, then we'd probably hire the gal with three kids.

You have stepped back a little bit from the day-to-day operations, and you've left something of a legacy with your brother and the other people who have been with you from the beginning. From a Christian standpoint is it scary to have this thing you built gradually no longer quite in your hands? Or is it empowering?

The three who actually run everything are my brother, Tommy, Len Ruby, and Carlos Sepulveda. Len was involved when we restructured the company and created our mission statement, end goals, and intentions. It's sort of our manifesto. It was all done with my total agreement. Today I am chairman of the board, and we meet quarterly to set policy. I trust Tommy and Len and Carlos. Through all of that, I've never been uncomfortable with the way things are going either spiritually or in business.

Goals have always been important to you. Do you have any goals left?

Yes. We just want to try to, in an excellent fashion, follow God's lead in what he would have us to do from a business standpoint. We recently expanded our line of batteries and are going into retail. We're establishing retail stores and our tag line is, "Every battery for every need." We're setting up these little 1,500–1,600-square-foot retail stores with five or six parking places in front where you can zip in, get something, and zip out. Our intention is to try to provide the market with any kind of battery they need in one spot. Today the average family of four with no teenagers has twenty-eight different batteries.

"Every battery for every need" means we need to provide everything from defibrillator batteries to batteries for cranes, boats, motorcycles, flashlights, wristwatches, fire alarms, telephones, and computers. We intend to be a specialized, expert battery store.

What's the name of the store?

Interstate All Battery Center. What's interesting is we also have a technical department in each little store. It's almost like watch repair. Replacement batteries are not made for many of the devices out there. A customer can bring in an old tool that he or she can't find a battery for, and we can put one together right there in ten minutes and send the tool out working. We buy these little cells, solder them together, seal them, stick them in your equipment, and off you go.

What a great idea! Any advice for someone thinking about going into business?

The first thing I would do is I would try to research the proposition. Determine that it is sensible, that you can find some kind of proven success in a similar venture. Then I would try to find the mature, Christian people that have been in the business who could inform you as to what it all really is about and what it is going to require. All of that would be covered in prayer—and I mean very specific prayer: "God, lead me to the right people."

After appraising all of that, I would try to establish the gift God has given me—what I have to work with. I'd try to establish, Could I with God's help reasonably do this?

Let's say that you want to open a dentist's office, but you've got a wife and three kids and it's going to take you seven years to go back to school. Apart from divine intervention, that would be a pretty hard task for a lot of people. So I would have to feel real strongly that God was leading me in that, and then I would have to have 100 percent approval from my wife. After I felt that it all looked good and reasonable and that I had the wherewithal to do it *and* I felt that God was leading me into it, then I'd just pray and go.

When I don't know what to do, I always ask God to stop me. I always back up and couch it with, "Lord, you know I want to do what you want me to do. I don't want to do what you don't want me to do. This appears to make sense to me and it seems like it's okay with you and so I'm going to go. But I ask you to please stop me. Please judge my heart that I'm being honest here. If this is inconsistent with what you want from me, then please stop me." And after extended prayer, I go and accept the results as his intention for my life.

Jay S. Pifer

President
Allegheny Power

Remember, Christ said, "He who is greatest among you shall be your servant." And so I, more and more, have tried to mold my leadership style on that servant-leader model. That's where my faith comes in—trying to set the model for being the servant leader.

Jay S. Pifer

Jay Pifer is a very powerful man. As the president of Allegheny Power, he oversees a corporation that supplies power to more than 1.7 million customers in five Middle Atlantic states, and presides over a workforce of 3,300 people.

But Jay Pifer is a man who understands that the real power in his life and the world around him rests with God. Through his leadership in the business world, his many community activities and more than thirty-five years' part-time activity in ministry, he evidences his faith to all who encounter him. He embraces the model of the servant leader and brings the energy and enthusiasm of his faith to every project he tackles.

Active in the United Way, the Boy Scouts, several college boards, and numerous other community organizations, Jay Pifer brings the power of heaven to all those he touches.

I came from a religious family. My mother and father were very active in the church, and so, when I was a young child, they took me to Sunday school and church. I really was kind of raised in the church. I had excellent parents, whom I came to appreciate even more when I became a parent.

My father worked for the company that I work for. He was a surveyor, and on Saturdays I would help him do property surveys. My parents saw to it that I went through college, and they sacrificed everything they could for my sake.

Do you have siblings?

I have a half-brother, who is eleven years older. Because of the age difference, for most of my youth he was out of the nest; so in many ways I was an only child.

When would you say that you began your personal relationship with the Lord?

As I said, I was raised in the church and so was my wife. My wife was the daughter of a dairy farmer. We were married in 1958 when I was still in college.

We began attending a church in the town where I was going to school, and the minister there led me to a personal relationship with Jesus Christ. That's when I moved from "religion" to a real relationship. And that really changed my life. It gave me a whole new perspective on my faith. It was much different than the way I had been raised as a church member.

After graduation from college I started working for West Penn Power Company, but my life was changed. I decided I'd like to enter the ministry. I felt a call to the ministry.

Would you reflect back on that personal relationship and the impact it had on your life as your career began to develop?

What happened once I developed a relationship, once I accepted Christ, I turned everything over to God from then on. I pretty much yielded to God and did whatever he wanted me to do. I saw him beginning to direct my life, whether it was opening doors or closing doors. And I developed a sense of God leading me and pulling me and tugging me all through my life. I was sold out to Christ. In other words, I was totally sold out to what he wanted me to do, and I am, even to this day, guided by what he wants me to do. I believe the success I've had in my career has been totally the result of God leading me and directing me and wanting me to be in this position.

So I left my job and went back to college and received another degree and actually started seminary in Ohio. That didn't seem to work so I returned and got my job back at West Penn Power Company. I completed my seminary work through correspondence over a ten-year period and was ordained. And everywhere I moved with the company, the bishop would appoint me to a small church in the area. I recently retired after serving various churches for thirty-five years.

Looking back, I see that apparently God didn't want me in the full-time ministry. God wanted me to work in a business and be a "tent-making" part-time minister. He has decided to take somebody with limited abilities and use me for his glory. And he has blessed me with a fabulous career, a wonderful family, and wonderful opportunities.

In your business career, do you find that your faith plays a significant role? And by that I mean, are you aware, as you're involved in the day-to-day business decision-making process, that your faith might help you make a difficult decision or handle a challenging situation?

Let me first make a statement about our company and its corporate culture. I'm very fortunate to be in a company where the chairman and the board of directors have always done what is right. Our company will go to any lengths to make sure that what we do is based on integrity and honor. So it makes my faith very compatible with a company that values doing what is right. For as long as I've been here, there never has been a time when there has been any question about doing what is right. I'm not faced with any decisions where my faith says I should do one thing, but there is pressure from the company or from the business side to do something contrary.

Now where my faith comes in, I think, has to do more with dealing with people and trying to be more compassionate, more understanding, or trying to be what I view my role to be, the servant leader. Remember, Christ said, "He who is greatest among you shall be your servant." And so I, more and more, have tried to mold my leadership style on that servant-leader model. That's where my faith comes in—trying to set the model for being the servant leader.

That aspect has changed somewhat over the years. Back in my early career, when I was a young supervisor, we were more in a command-and-control environment. Fortunately that has evolved so that there is more teamwork, there is a more participative management style, and so it lends itself much more to my goal of being the servant leader. So it's in that role that my faith has, I think, helped me to set the example for others as a servant leader.

The corporate world today projects an image in many cases, to people on the outside, that there is a lot of corporate greed. My sense, though, is in many cases that really isn't the case. I have met so many very good people within companies who are, as I think you've so well said, servant leaders—walking the walk, which I think is a responsibility that we have as Christians. Can you comment on the general business climate that you see?

Let me do it in two ways. First of all, there has been this perception, because corporate executives today are paid very well, but it's based on what the market is. In other words, a company is trying to recruit people that have leadership talent and to retain the talent, so it's a market-based compensation approach. So, unfortunately, we have a lot of people who see the salaries of senior executives, and they view it as greed because the pay scale is so high. But it's what the market is, it's what you have to pay to attract and retain talent in business today.

Second, in business you have to look at how leaders interact with the people who work for them and with them. I view myself a little bit like a Barnabas, who was the encourager. My effort on the job is to try to encourage people, to try to affirm their skills and their abilities, to try to coach them, to try to help them succeed. I spend a lot of time meeting with employees. We have seventy service centers around the five states, and I try to get to most of them every year, some every other year. One of the skills that I believe I have is trying to encourage employees, to help them be successful within their own potential.

In your company, as the corporate leader, do employees seek you out, knowing that you are a man of Christ, a man who seems to be a strong moral leader? Are you ever sought out by employees, asked questions about faith or morality, or put on the spot about your faith?

Yes. Because many people know of my background and ministerial activities, quite often people will come to me to inquire or to get confirmation or for guidance. Now I try not to flaunt my faith. I don't go around trying to impose it on anybody, but it's pretty well-known throughout the corporation where I stand and where I come from and who I am.

Like so many senior executives in America, you're in a position that you can have great impact on a lot of people both within and outside your organization. Can you think of a good example where your role as a senior executive has put you in a position to have an effect on someone?

I'm not sure that I could just put my hands on a specific example. However, I'm very involved in my community, first of all, because it's part of being a corporate citizen, and second, because it's also something I enjoy doing. I'm involved in the Boy Scouts and the United Way and all kinds of community activities in the five states where we do business.

I've been on the board of trustees of a private Christian college for fourteen years. I'm also on the Educational Alliance. So I'm in lots of community activities throughout the whole five states, and fortunately I think my faith has been evidenced in my activities through those organizations. God has taken me and transformed me into one of his vessels, fit for the master's use.

What are some specific ways God has used you?

You know, I used to be so afraid to get up even to say my name before a group, and yet God has used me. I now do a lot of public speaking; for example, I've been commencement speaker at a number of college graduations. So God has taken me and transformed me into something that he has used. That's really a miracle. Maybe it's in that sense that people are seeing what God can do with somebody that has very little ability and turned him into someone who can accomplish a great deal in his name.

To return for a minute to the idea of a servant leader, I'd just like to mention, I also try to break down the barrier between corporate president and employees. For example, in recognition of Earth Day, we asked our employees to come out on a Saturday morning, on their own time, to go collect tires from dump sites around the area and turn them in to a recycling operation. My wife and I joined a group of our employees, and we went out to a couple of dump sites and collected tires.

It was amazing. Overall, we ended up with over eight hundred of our employees on that Saturday who collected thirty-seven thousand tires to be turned in to the recycling stations.

As a servant leader, I saw my role on that day as going out and getting my hands dirty in the dump site with employees to help collect tires. I keep coming back to the example that Christ has given us when he took the basin in the upper room, when he cooked the breakfast by the sea of Tiberius after the resurrection. He keeps speaking to me that I have to constantly be trying to be that servant leader.

Was there a particular time when you were having a career or life struggle and your faith really became a foundation that you fell back on?

I really can't go back to a crisis or a struggle. It's almost as if my life has been so miraculously blessed. And I've grown tremendously, as I have become more keenly aware of how God leads and directs me. It's amazing. I can just sense his leading, and I feel his tug on my life all the time. So I've grown immeasurably as I'm more aware of how God leads. But I cannot look back to a single struggle or a crisis, and it's because I'm really like the clay. I'm very malleable; what God wants me to do, I do.

Is there a business tip that you might be able to give us in terms of how you've been able to weave your faith and your business skills together?

I think the biggest tip would be to let people see in your life that you walk the walk as well as talk the talk. They need to see and hear your faith, in your speech, in your actions, and in your interactions with people. Your faith will come out if you believe it and live it. The philosopher/theologian Nietzsche once said, "If you want me to believe in your redeemer, then look more redeemed." So I guess the tip I would have is to be more intentional, more proactive about being the model, about being the example for others. And I think people need an example today. You may encounter a person that's a Christian who is looking for a model to follow in their leadership style. You could be that model if you live out your faith.

Lonnie "Bo" Pilgrim

Chairman
Pilgrim's Pride Corporation

INVITATION!

Will you now receive CHRIST *as your personal* SAV-*IOR? You know you are a sinner . . . you know* CHRIST *died for you, for* YOUR SINS.

Will you, by faith, pray this prayer: "Lord Jesus, be merciful to me a sinner. Save me now . . . I give you my life now and forever. Amen!"

Please let us know of your decision for Christ. Mail us your name and address. We have some helpful material to send you that will help you in your Chris-tian growth.

Excerpt from "Good News for Modern Man"
by Bo Pilgrim

From a single feed store in the small east Texas town of Pittsburg, Pilgrim's Pride has grown to become the second-largest chicken processor in the United States. Each week, Pilgrim's Pride's 24,500 employees process and ship 10 million birds throughout North America, Eastern Europe, and Asia.

While prepared poultry products comprise 43 percent of sales (now more than 1.5 billion dollars annually), at the heart of Pilgrim's Pride is the ramrod-straight patriarch, Bo Pilgrim, and a 20 dollar bill. Pilgrim joined his late brother, Aubrey, in founding Pilgrim's Pride in 1946. Pilgrim still knows many of his employees by name (some are second- and third-generation workers), still teaches Sunday school in his local church, and still remembers his small-town roots. Bo and his wife, Patty, donated the beautiful Witness Park and Prayer Tower in downtown Pittsburg, featuring a 75-foot chiming bell tower and 24-hour chapel.

As for the twenty-dollar bill, perhaps that is a story better told by Pilgrim himself:

My father died when I was ten. I accepted the Lord two months later. I left home when I was very young, and I promised the Lord that if I ever amounted to anything, I'd always honor him. I've been into a progressive business all my life, and I have to give him credit for it all the way.

How has your faith impacted what you've done as a businessperson?

It has been the strongest impact of anything on my success, because I have a high school education, but I have never had any fear of the President of the United States, or anyone else. I think that comes from the fact that I know the Lord is always there with me. And as long as I apply the principles of the Bible, the outcome, whether I'm having a good year or a bad year, is pretty level with me as far as my emotions go.

Pilgrim's Pride has a reputation for operating under Christian business principles.

I think there are a lot of principles in the Bible that talk about how you do business as far as integrity and honesty and as far as having faith. So we've always applied them. And I've tried to exemplify them in my leadership. And I know that the people who work for me in responsible places read them and know that I expect them to do the same thing.

Can you talk about the specific ways that Pilgrim's Pride has operated according to your beliefs?

For one thing—honoring contracts. We've had contracts that have been favorable to us and unfavorable to us. But in all instances, we do as we contract in supplying chickens at different prices over a period of a year or more—deliver the kind of products that we're proud of, at a reasonable price—and that service and integrity maintain customer satisfaction. In our business, it's very, very competitive. You can spend two or three years getting a customer and you can lose a customer in one day if you foul up. But we don't have a history of losing customers because of our service and integrity.

Pilgrim's Pride has a reputation for excellence. Is that rooted in your Christian background?

Yes. One of the standards that the Lord expects us to live under is excellence. Although you can't achieve that, you have to seek to achieve it. And once you fall short, that's the glory of the grace of Jesus Christ. He forgives you of that. Excellence is one of our goals. We have different programs that teach excellence throughout the company at all levels. We employ 24,500 people, and they all know what we stand for and what's expected of them.

Do you feel like God's hand was on your life to get you where you are?

I don't have any question about it, because in our family we have a medical problem, hardening of the arteries. My father died at the age of forty-two. I had a brother that was a partner with me in 1946 when we started out, and he died at the age of forty-one. I had a brother who died at forty-seven and another one at fifty-nine. I had open-heart surgery in 1975, a heart attack in '82, and I've had three TIAs or mini-strokes—where you lose your memory for thirty minutes or so. And I had still another medical problem in 1973. But I'm still here. So I know the Lord has had his hand on me as a Christian businessman, setting an example for customers, suppliers, and employees, that there is a standard that God expects us to live up to.

What advice would you have for someone thinking of business as a career?

First of all, I think you have to seek an industry where there is a need for the product, where it's economical, where it's con-

251

venient, and you have to try to apply a high level of excellence to your products and your services. Next, you have to have a product that's more economical than the competition. But you have to apply leadership that involves integrity and respect, not only for you as a leader, but to instill this in your employees. All of us are in God's sight every day, so we don't need to think that he skips days or that there are times when we're not accountable to his expectations.

What's the secret of Pilgrim's Pride's success?

I think number one, the Lord's been with me all the way through. Number two, we have a product that has been in strong demand for the last twenty years that is economical, versatile, and is good from a standpoint of nutrition. So there has been an industry-compounded growth of about 5 percent per year over the last twenty years. But our growth has far exceeded that. We've exceeded twice the growth of the industry.

Do you have a favorite Bible verse or passage?

I can't say that I do. I have been teaching a Bible class since back in the '50s and, from time to time, it appears that different Scriptures exceed the others.

There is one verse in Luke where it says that if we are ashamed of him and his works, he may be ashamed of us when we appear before him in heaven. I take that literally to heart and I carry a little pamphlet, a plan of salvation that I put together in 1982 when I had a heart attack. Since then, I've handed out hundreds of thousands of these and I practice it every day. I carry these pamphlets with me everywhere. It gives a plan of salvation that you can say in thirty seconds. And then it has a sheet of ordinances on how to live.

I started a number of years ago putting a twenty-dollar bill, folded, in the back of it. I go through this pamphlet and I say, "This is a plan of salvation, which will save you. This is how you should live in the meantime. And I put this twenty dollars in there so you won't throw this away." It always makes the recipient chuckle. And they are very appreciative because they realize that you are sincere about what you're giving them and the value of it. It causes them to read it more than I think it would otherwise.

I made a pledge a number of years ago that I would never speak to a crowd too large that I wouldn't put the twenty dollars in the pamphlet, and I've spoken to crowds of three hundred, five hundred, and up to eight hundred. But I always put twenty dollars in there and hand them out to the entire group.

I still put them in my pocket every day and replenish my pocket every morning. I say I have a goal of at least forty a week, but I exceed that most of the time. When I go to New York or travel anywhere, I carry a supply. I literally give them to anyone that I have thirty seconds with, when I can make the presentation.

Boone Powell Jr.

Chairman
Baylor Health Care System

Baylor Health Care System will, before the end of this decade, become the most trusted source of comprehensive health care services.

Baylor Health Care Vision

Boone Powell Jr. happily presides over one of the nation's largest not-for-profit medical networks, the sprawling Baylor Health Care System, which serves seven metropolitan counties in north Texas and includes the famed Baylor University Medical Center.

In 1990 *Business Week* named Powell one of the "Five Best Health Care Executives" in the United States for his steady handling of Baylor's one-billion-dollar operating budget. Powell has received several honorary doctorates and was appointed by then-Governor George W. Bush to the Blue Ribbon Task Force on the Uninsured in 1999. In addition to Baylor, he's active in Young Life (national board of trustees), the Healthcare Leadership Council (past chairman), the American College of Healthcare Executives (fellow), and the Greater Dallas Chamber of Commerce (board of directors).

Baylor has been part of Powell's life since childhood:

I grew up in Dallas and my father used to be CEO of the Baylor Health Care System. Mom and Dad attended the First Baptist Church here in Dallas, so I grew up there. The two points of influence in my life as a kid were the good youth group and Young Life. I'm still active in Young Life. It has been fifty years since I first attended the camp in Colorado. So I've been

254

associated with it both as a high school kid and through college as a volunteer leader. My wife and I got the program started in Abilene, Texas. I've been on the Dallas board and the national board of Young Life for many years now, so I'm still very involved with it.

How old were you when you made a decision for Christ?

I actually joined the church before I had that real significant experience. I thought I'd done it right. But somewhere in junior high I remember having a very distinct sense of apprehension that things were not right if I were to die. It was very significant for me, and it was about that time that I accepted the Lord in an old-time church revival. I got confirmation of the decision—this must have been around '50 or '51, whenever Billy Graham was in Dallas at the Cotton Bowl—when I went up at the last service. I never will forget the sight of all the people holding candles. The Rev. Graham talked about heaven, and I had a sense of peace. And that took care of that issue. I think that apprehension accentuated my going ahead and finally dealing with the question. I've really been reasonably steady ever since.

My wife and I were tested, however, when we left the Baylor University environment. I put all my possessions in a U-Haul trailer and went out to the University of California at Berkeley. It's quite a contrast between Baylor and Berkeley. The only thing I could find in common was that the mascots at both universities were bears! Other than that, it was night and day. I began to sense how those in a minority must have felt. I felt fairly isolated at Berkeley.

We went to a little church that had two hundred members. Fortunately it had a pastor from Texas and that gave us some sense of stability. But that was also a growing time for us and I wouldn't take anything for it. I love California, but that was a testing time for us both. Ever since then we've been right in the middle of Texas with Texas churches and Young Life and all the rest.

255

As head of Baylor, are you doing what you always wanted to do?

No. In fact, since my father was so active in health-care management and had built a pretty strong national reputation in the field, when I went to Baylor as a student, I had pretty well vowed I *wasn't* going to do that. I had some sense I wanted to do something ministry related, but not necessarily a vocational ministry. I thought about banking; I thought about law; I thought about a number of things. Finally, I entered the business school and about halfway through my college career, it clicked that my interest in business and my interest in ministry fit nicely in Christian hospitals. It was my sense of calling, and I immediately started making plans to go to graduate school. And I've never looked back.

But with those two elements—business and ministry—you have to figure out *how* you blend them together. And, of course, the environment I work in now allows me to do it.

Is it easier or harder being in business where it's publicly stated, "This is a Christian corporation"?

I've been on corporate boards. In fact I was just talking to the CEO of the Fortune 500 company that I've been a director with for many years. If I were in his seat, I would probably have a different view of how to do it than what I have at Baylor. Since we have been Christian-based for ninety-eight years, the way I've approached it is that I take the creation of the institution and its original founding statement very seriously. I feel that I need to nurture it, protect it, and enhance it.

Now, having said that, you realize that in a complex organization like a big medical center you've got people of all faiths and those of none. Just look at the founding statement of George Truett about Baylor Medical. I can't imagine that anyone other than the Lord gave this to him or that he could make a statement like this in 1903: "Is it not now time to begin the construction of a great humanitarian hospital, one to which men of all creeds or those of none may come with equal confidence?" I've never seen anything stand the test of time, and all the currents that run against it, like that statement has.

That statement has been particularly significant to our Jewish friends, both those who support Baylor financially and the great number of Jewish physicians that practice and feel very comfortable here. To me that's a very fine case study of how your Christian statement can survive and how it can relate to others who might not share exactly what you want to do, but it's value-based and it does draw people to it.

When you claim to be a Christian corporation, does that mean you are held to a higher standard?

Yes. And I think that is, again, the sense of stewardship you feel when you have a mission statement, when you have a set of purposes that have been created to carry out Christ's ministry of healing. All my life, my concern—and I've only worked in two medical centers, but they've both been Baptist-related—is not to mess it up, not to create a *faux pas* that would hurt what all the years of investment allowed to come into play. It has been so fortunate how this place has evolved and developed over the years, as well as the level of respect that it has. As I would drive up to this campus and see how mammoth it is, I would often ask myself the question, *What are you doing here, trying to operate this thing?* It was my way of keeping things in perspective, but it was overwhelming in many respects. But here we are, preparing for our one hundredth anniversary.

I'll tell you another thing I haven't forgotten. I heard Billy Graham say one time that organizations that have been created with Christian purposes very seldom survive fifty years.

Why did he say that?

Over time, those who join it can dilute its purposes and mitigate some of its early vision. Or it can come from some of the cultural views new arrivals have. You've seen how the country now modifies certain past principles and values that we held to be important. For example, many of our most famous uni-

257

versities began as Christian institutions. You can't even say the word *Christian* there now. So what happened? They were founded correctly, they had mission statements that were correct, but over time people stripped it down.

This is just personal philosophy, but one of the things that bothers me that is now coming out of the academic community is that they would say that the greatest virtue that any American ought to have is tolerance. But they have put a new definition on the word *tolerance*. The old definition, I could accept. And that is this: You could have a point of view and I could have a point of view. They could be different, but we would respect one another's point of view. Today's definition goes much farther than that. It says your point of view is *equal* to my point of view and neither one is necessarily truth.

If you start taking that equation and applying it on a spiritual basis, then they're basically diluting what God has to say. I think it's just a total aberration of the whole Christian faith. If I were a Moslem, I would think the same thing. So I'm really disturbed about this whole tolerance issue. I do fundamentally get disturbed about the movement toward tolerance. Politically, you see it all the time. I won't accept that definition. I will accept the first one. And I'll explain to people, "I respect the fact that you can have a viewpoint. I hope you respect mine." But I won't let it go any further than that.

What have you done, what have your predecessors done, to keep that vision of a Christian hospital that's open to everybody stay focused for nearly a century?

It's not taking your eye off the ball. And, in our case, the ball would be our mission statement. It's our purpose for existence. I have trained myself through the years to make the major decisions, both adjusted to the industry trends and checked against the mission statement, to be sure we haven't violated it. I've always come back to that statement, that's been my gravity point. I measure what we do against that mission. I don't know how else to be a steward. If the board changes the mission, that's one thing. But if they don't, then my obligation is to nurture that mission statement. As a result, I've focused a lot on that.

I expect our people to do that as well. I don't have any faith requirements of them, but one of the expectations if you work here is that you need to be comfortable with who we are and what we represent. If a person can't be comfortable with that, they have one of two options. First is to have a better understanding of what it means to work in our organization and see if they *can* get comfortable with it. Second, if they can't, then they're certainly free to go where they are comfortable. We don't allow those fundamental purposes to be seriously challenged.

Is this mission statement part of everybody's initial interview packet?

Through the employee orientation, yes. Our purposes and the mission and the founding statement are all shared with employees.

As a Christian organization, how do you deal with vendors and suppliers? Do these people see a difference in how you deal with them?

I never will forget Judge Abner McCall (former president of Baylor University) saying that there is no such thing as Christian chemistry. So there is not a Christian gall bladder operation. What I think it means to be a Christian organization is that you operate in such a way that the tenets of Christianity are upheld, not imposed on someone, but upheld. And that means a vendor would not have a reason to discredit our operation for sloppiness, late pay, chiseling, or other things of that nature because those things don't meet the definition you'd want for a Christian organization. You work your way through all the elements of your business and how each of us relates to the community. We try to do it in an honorable way, with integrity and with conflict of interest statements that allow us to take the general guiding principles of operating this hospital in a Christian manner and applying them in such a way that's respectful to other people.

Is there a central mandate for any Christian organization?

I have believed deeply for a long time that mediocrity and Christianity are exclusive to one another. There is a slang term for it—"sloppy agape." That's when we go do something in the name of the Lord and we do it in such an ill-prepared manner that it's sloppy and mediocre. Christ was *never* mediocre. He's the great standard bearer. He's the greatest leader that we've ever seen on this planet. Excellence fits into that notion, so I don't think we ought to do things in a second-rate fashion. And I think those that do so basically discredit the whole image of what Christianity is about.

How do you continue to promote that awareness or that attitude with the people that work for Baylor Health Care System?

We have to segment what we do. If you come over to the medical staff side, where the clinical decisions are made on behalf of the patients, we have very high standards for the physicians on the medical staff. My dad was once called by the editor of a religious magazine about whether or not there were any Catholic doctors on the medical staff. Dad said, "Sure."

The editor said, "You shouldn't have any. You're a Baptist hospital. Do they wear those long black robes?"

Dad said, "No. They're in scrubs and suits like anyone else."

The editor said, "Well, you shouldn't have them."

And Dad, as he tells the story, said, "Let me ask *you* a question. If I had two surgeons that could perform something that you needed to have done and one was a Catholic and one was a Baptist, but the Catholic was a superior surgeon, which one would you choose?"

The editor said, "That's not a fair question."

We go after very high-quality physicians. The doctors decided that many years ago. Clinically speaking, they wanted to be associated with the very best. In a hospital, you have the whole medical staff organization, credentialing committees, quality review committees, tissue committees, things of that nature, that all make sure you stay at a high standard. We've got some of the best clinical programs in the world right here, and it's because of that philosophy of quality.

On the employee side, you've got to set up your personnel policies so that they are right too. My guiding principle there came from the man that I trained under in Abilene, Mr. E. M. Collier. He was a great gentleman. He was at that hospital in Abilene for forty years. The thing I noticed about how he worked with his employees was he was always fair. That was a value that he personally had, but it also carried over into the life of the organization. You want to treat your employees appropriately, so not only do you give them the opportunities for educational enhancement but you encourage them to grow and develop and take more responsibility, if they're so inclined. At Baylor we have leadership development programs called Leadership Baylor. The participants spend a full year going through all the dimensions of our system. They have a chance to be better prepared and take on greater responsibility.

There is a wonderful culture in the Baylor employee ranks that was here before I came. I was determined, once again, not to mess that up. A couple of times we've had a crisis for the organization, and I can't tell you how much I personally appreciated the sense of culture that people have here. Many of them consider this more than just a job. They consider it a calling. They consider it working with a purpose.

If feeding people is one of the two best jobs in the world, then healing people must be the other.

I think it is. If you go to the miracles in the Gospels, you'll find that over 75 to 80 percent of the miracles were related directly and indirectly to the healing process. It was a big part of how Christ demonstrated who he was when he was here. I think that's why you've got a whole series of hospitals spon-

261

sored by church groups all over the U.S.—Catholic, Presbyterian, Methodist, Baptist, and so on.

Through the years, I've had businessmen serve on our board of trustees, and they've begun to get a sense of what taking care of people really means. They've come to understand the stories, to understand people getting organ transplants and getting a second chance at living. Often it's that intangible feedback that they get that makes serving on the hospital board their favorite volunteer effort.

I went to my forty-fourth high school reunion about a year and a half ago at the Lakewood Theater in Dallas. About 250 people were there and a lady came up to me from South Carolina. She said, "You're not going to know this, but my doctor in South Carolina referred me to your hospital where I had a liver transplant. It has saved my life. It gave me new life and allowed me to come back to this reunion."

You tell me how much that's worth. I've had that all of my career. Those are the intangibles of ministry and service.

I gave a talk Friday on leadership development to a group made up of a lot of companies, including some of our vendors. I didn't give them the whole ball of wax, but I did talk to them about the philosophy of leading by serving, about the servant leadership model that's been very good. We've been sharing certain leadership principles for a number of years with our managers, and we often do it from a Christian point of view.

How do you leave a legacy? How do you leave the place where you work better than you found it?

Some years ago, I came across a story about William Wilberforce. He was a young Englishman who lectured to the Parliament and was aghast at the fact that slavery was so institutionalized in England. He'd just become a believer and felt that slavery was very inappropriate. So he struck out to see what he could do about getting it eliminated. He ran into all kinds of resistance. Even the royal family had an investment in slavery, so it would be like overturning every chamber of commerce in Texas to take on that subject. But he did. And he started building alliances. He was vilified, very hated for his crusade. But through the years, he continued to build his network and continued to work toward his goal.

At the same time Wilberforce started his crusade, there was a young sailor who sailed the ships that were transporting the slaves. On the boats from Africa to England, the slaves were stacked like cordwood, with only inches between them.

But this reprobate sailor had an experience with the Lord in his young life as well, and he eventually went into theology, into the ministry, and eventually became a composer.

The thing that caught my attention about that story is that these two people ended up with marvelous legacies. Wilberforce stayed on this task for forty-seven years. He was in Parliament the day that they voted to abolish slavery. Three days later, he died. At his funeral, he was called "The Washington of humanity." He who had been called a "villain" was called "The Washington of humanity." Did he make an impact and leave a legacy? He did!

The reprobate sailor moved nicely into the Christian world, and he ended up writing a song that's the most loved song in all the world, "Amazing Grace." His name was John Newton.

Do you enjoy getting up in the morning and coming to work?

I do. You've read *The Prayer of Jabez?*

It seems like it's really talking to doctors.

It's talking to all kinds of people. I've given the book away so many times. I know Bruce Wilkinson. We went to Israel with him in the early '80s. My wife and I heard a tape in our car one day on this prayer. It made so much sense that I came to our management staff and said, "You know, this is the kind of prayer we ought to pray for Baylor." And I started praying for Baylor that way. I have that prayer on the wall that faces me. It was given to me by my management staff. The date is 1985, years before the book ever came out.

That's another way we have of saying, "This is what we're about. This is how we can hold up the institution with a Christian purpose."

What do you tell someone thinking of a career in business?

You really have to have a passion for what you do. Mundaneness works against you. If you can feel that what you're doing makes some kind of contribution, you can get energized to do it. You can see the efforts of your work are going to be meaningful.

For me, the mission of this place, the Christian ministry of healing, was always bigger than who I am. So I have felt that motivation comes from throwing myself into something more important than who I am. It becomes a real privilege, then, to do the work.

You've got to find it yourself. Somehow you've got to determine what the value of the work is.

Some people may not be able to find that. But then they can follow Bob Buford's example. Some years ago, I gave his book *Halftime* to all our managers. It's subtitled *Changing Your Game Plan from Success to Significance*. The director of public relations here at Baylor read it. She came to see me and said, "I'm going to change directions." I said, "What are you going to do?" She said, "I'm going to go to Fort Worth and enroll in the seminary at Texas Christian University. I want to be a chaplain." She did, and she's now back here working with our senior centers as a chaplain and is happier than she's ever been. So it *can* work.

Charles E. Ragus

Founder
AdvoCare International

Our goal every day is to live our faith and to rep-
resent the Lord. That's what we feel we're here for.
I'm on assignment; I'm an ambassador for Christ.
People see Jesus, hopefully, through a relationship
with this company or through a relationship with
me.

Charles E. Ragus

Editor's note: Shortly after this interview was completed, Charles
Edward Ragus died unexpectedly at his home. He was fifty-nine. Ragus
is survived by his wife, Peggy, and their three daughters. Officials at
AdvoCare indicated that they would like to see the interview published, saying that the beliefs he espoused in it will live on in the
company he created.

AdvoCare International is the culmination of one man's dream.
Charles Ragus wanted to create a nutritional supplement company
with leading-edge products that would help people be proactive about
their health. The key, he believed, was a company founded by and
for distributors. He named it AdvoCare. Charles Ragus was an advo-
cate who cared.

Since the company's inception in 1993, it has grown geometri-
cally, from two products and one distributorship to roughly seventy-
five products and one hundred thousand distributors from Hawaii to
Maine. Ragus was twice named a finalist for the Ernst and Young
Entrepreneur of the Year Award—in 2000 and 2001.

Developed by a medical and scientific advisory board chaired by Robert Hackman, Ph.D., AdvoCare products are made with the highest-quality materials and based on the latest research. (Board member Richard Schekenbach, executive director of the Institute for Biomolecular Nutrition in Oregon, says that Ragus was the only person who ever walked into his lab demanding top quality and stuck with it, even after learning the cost.)

The company also earns credibility with its unpaid endorsers—pro and world-class amateur athletes who praise the products because they work. That list includes seven pro football coaches; Steve Watterson, strength coach for Tennessee's professional football team and a licensed Drug Enforcement Agency researcher; Petty Enterprises' Race Team strength and conditioning coach Mark Mauldin; Hall of Famer Joe Seay; coach of USA Wrestling (AdvoCare is the official nutritional products supplier); Dallas hockey star Mike Modano; Tennessee quarterback Steve McNair; and Chicago's Brian Urlacher, the 2000 defensive rookie of the year.

But it was always Ragus's desire to reach the rank and file of America. "I didn't get into this business to be a vitamin salesman," he said. "I got into this business to change lives."

The quintessential entrepreneur, Ragus truly believed that, with a forty-dollar AdvoCare distributor kit, people really can start their own business and take the first step toward living life on their terms.

These are business values as new as the twenty-first century and as old as the teachings of the Christ, whom Ragus called his Savior and his light.

My parents were both devout Christians. I grew up in a Christian home and grew up in the church. I was a very active participant in all aspects of a Southern Baptist denomination from the very beginning. I received Christ as a young child—about the second grade is when I realized that my life was without God, and so I accepted Christ. Later in my life, I realized what it meant to have a relationship with Christ on a different level, a relationship where he actually became the Lord of my life. That occurred back in 1977.

Was AdvoCare your first venture into business?

No. I went to school at Northwestern State University in Louisiana on an athletic scholarship. I grew up in Shreveport, Louisiana, and eventually married my first date to the sweetheart banquet at Queensboro Baptist Church. She and I dated and then got married my junior year in college and have been married ever since.

I have a business degree from Northwestern State. I started selling life insurance in college. After I graduated, I spent a short period of time with the Kansas City Chiefs. From there I joined Fidelity Union Life Insurance Company, which is a good old Southern Baptist type of company. I sold for them for a long period of time and became very involved in the insurance business. After that, I went into real estate development. We then moved back to Louisiana, where I worked with my parents. It was there that I was introduced to the direct-selling industry in 1983.

During these earlier jobs, was your faith part of how you did business?

My faith's always been a major part of my life. I can't say I have lived a life totally sold out to Christ. But my faith has always been kind of a dividing point for decisions in life. God has always directed my path and has caused me to make decisions that have kept me out of major difficulties. However, I was not spared from challenges and difficulties through which my faith has been perfected over the years. But it's always been a major part of me.

Back in my senior year, I was a participant in the founding of the Fellowship of Christian Athletes chapter at Northwestern. So I've always been very active in the church and the affairs of Christianity.

How did you become involved in direct selling?

My family and I owned several retail stores in Shreveport, and a man came into my store and told me about the direct-selling business. That was with Herbal Life. I became one of their top distributors in the early '80s and was reasonably successful.

In 1989 I founded a company by the name of Omnitrition, and then sold my interest after a couple of years to two minority partners. I was basically going to retire. But God just didn't have that in his plans. I always felt that my direction in life was mandated by the Lord, and that was the reason I started Omnitrition. When I sold out, it was because I was having partner problems. Two of the people I was in business with were just not Christian people, and even though they were minority partners, it was a difficult situation. So I sold out and founded Advo-Care in 1993.

You've had a remarkable past ten years.

When we started Omnitrition, the first thing that I did was spend about ninety days developing the basic principles of the company. It was always principle number one to honor God through our faith, our family, and our friends.

Isn't that still an important principle for AdvoCare?

We've never wavered from that. So it's very important that we live that out, not just write it on some parchment and hang it on the wall. It's got to be who we become and who we are. If you have to go back and refer to your guiding principles, then you're not writing them from your heart. You're not writing what you believe. I believe your belief system is the most important thing governing any type of relationship.

How has that number one founding principle manifested itself with AdvoCare?

We have attracted like people; we've attracted like kind. We have basically had no problems with AdvoCare. In an industry where regulatory problems are common, where dissension among the field ranks is common, where there is a lot of jealousy between organizations, it's very difficult to manage and make one of these companies successful. We've never had those difficulties here. We did have one small episode, and that person is no longer with us. But we have drawn people who believe in the same value system. And for the most part, in our organization of very spiritually minded people, I'd like to tell you they're all committed born-again Christians, but I don't know their hearts, and there are a hundred thousand of them. For the most part, though, they are very committed.

We have three major events a year we call success schools. These are three-day forums where we bring people together. We'll have four thousand people at each one of them. And that's the capacity; we don't have room for any more than that. The highlight will almost always be our chapel service on Sunday morning. In February 2001 we had Richard Jackson speak. We bring evangelical gospel messages, we have an altar call, and people go to rooms for counsel. We'll normally have about forty or fifty people accept Christ at these things. We have had a tremendous amount of opportunity to share the gospel at Advo-Care, and it's because the principles of AdvoCare bring the right environment. We couldn't do it if our principles were different.

But let me add that AdvoCare is not a Christian company per se. I am a Christian. I believe in living my faith and running my company with Christian principles. We do make opportunities available for people to accept Christ. But the company is not a platform for trying to change others' beliefs. Let me put it this way. People of all faiths are welcome at AdvoCare.

Do your Christian principles apply to how you set up contracts and how you deal with people in the distribution and supply chains?

We have partnerships with people, basically. Our goal every day is to live our faith and to represent the Lord. That's what we feel we're here for. I'm on assignment; I'm an ambassador for Christ. People see Jesus, hopefully, through a relationship with this company or through a relationship with me.

269

How many distributors and partners do you have?

We have one hundred thousand distributors, and we have a very high participation rate. By that I mean we do not have huge numbers of inactive distributors. We have about a 40 percent activity rate. That's extremely high in our industry. We have about a 30–35 percent renewal rate, and that's also very high.

How many staff people do you have in Dallas?

About 125. Gil Stricklin of Marketplace Ministries has always been part of AdvoCare; we started that in the very beginning. I met Gil at Omnitrition and got to know him. When we founded AdvoCare, we wanted to have that type of relationship. We give people permission for Bible study and that type of thing.

Has holding fast to Christian principles posed any problems?

No. People know who we are. Our industry is based on people. If you can't get along with people, it's very difficult to be in this industry. You have a lot of charming people who are leaders within the industry, but their spiritual condition is not obvious. And you have various companies out there doing a tremendous job. For example, take Home Interiors. Mary Crowley was one of the finest Christian ladies that's ever been. Don Carter is a good Christian gentleman. Likewise, at the Amway Corporation, Rich DeVos and Jay Van Andel are fine Christian men and have given millions to Christian causes—as has Mary Crowley. That environment has been established by some of the leading companies in the field. So it's very easy in the direct-selling industry to live the Christian life. There's not a persecution thing.

If I were in a different field, manufacturing or something like that, it might be a challenge. But here we find it is very easy. It's who we are. It's what we do. We have our own little world here.

You are also involved in producing your product. Has there been difficulty maintaining your faith in that arena?

The challenge is always this, we don't cut corners. In building our products, we live our principles. That's been the strength of the AdvoCare product line. It's because you can believe in what we tell you about it. It is the finest product on the market, based on the highest science, and that's not just conversation, or publicity, or a marketing pitch. That is a reality. Over the years, we've never deviated from that. If we find that there is a way to improve the product manufacturing process, we do it. If it costs us money, that's just what we do. And we don't adjust the price.

We're committed to making the products the best. We tell our distributors and our customers that when science dictates that we make changes in the products, we do it without fanfare. It's not a marketing thing with us to update our products and make them better. If we find a new ingredient we could add to a product and reformulate that product so that it is better, we do it. It's just who we are. It's just what we do. So our products are in a constant cycle of reevaluation to make them the best. That job is really never done because science is ever emerging.

Unfortunately the history of the industry is to make it as cheap as you can and charge as much as possible.

What advice would you have for someone as they start to build their own career and their own company?

Commit your ways to the Lord, and he'll direct your path. If you work unto the Lord, he becomes your partner. The first thing that you have to do, I believe, is to develop your value system. If people don't know why they do what they do—and what's important to them in life—then they are very nonspecific, and they are very easily swayed by whatever current business book happens to be out or by whatever current thing is being talked about by the seminar crowd. It's very easy to change your thinking if you have no value system.

But if you have a value system that's based on the highest truth, and that truth is the Holy Scriptures, and you have made Jesus Christ the Lord of your life and you've made that commitment, and you're going to live by that commitment, then decisions become a lot easier. So first, you have to develop that value system and that principle in your life.

The second thing you have to do is know exactly and precisely what you want. I believe God gives you tremendous latitude to apply the skills that he's given you. But you have to discover where your strengths are and what you can do best. Then you work on that. You figure out what you want and go to work on that. Then you set a definite time limit for its achievement. Everything has to work with a sense of urgency.

In life, no one has a guarantee. We have to accept that life is risky. We live in a fallen world. Things are ever changing. Just because we say we're a Christian, we don't get a free pass. Many times it's more difficult for us because God is trying to work in us a conformity to Christ. And sometimes, if we have rough edges, we need to go through some different things in order to get the rough edges off. To learn that Jesus really is Lord and that he's not just someone we read about in the Gospels in the New Testament, that's what is vitally important.

The next thing would be to know where you are weak. If you do not have strength in some areas, surround yourself with people of like mind who have strength in that area. That's been one of the great things I have been able to do, surround myself with fully committed, born-again Christian people that are extremely talented, that make up for all the weaknesses that I possess. They lift me up, very similar to how Aaron helped Moses.

What if they struggle with your very first premise? How do they discern what their life's work will be?

I struggled with that for a long, long time. My advice to anyone would be to do something you love to do, something you would love to get up every morning and do. Find something where you love to be around the people. Find a career where you have just an endless amount of energy and devotion. If you don't like to get up in the morning and go to work, you're in trouble already. God says in his Scripture that he'll give you the desires of your heart. And your heart being your mind, whatever your mind is excited about, what gets you excited, I think God will equip you to get that job done. Of course, that's if it meets his values. We couldn't be involved in some type of activity God would not bless.

I could be selling books or I could be selling nutritional products. But I have a heart for nutrition. I've always had a heart for nutrition. As a young man, I always used those products. I always believed in nutritional products. This is not something I'm doing to earn money. This is something I'm doing because I love it. The direct-selling industry is the best way to sell nutritional products. That's why I'm in direct selling. If it were the Internet, I'd be doing the same thing but using the Internet as my marketing scheme.

But direct selling is the best and the reason is that we develop relationships. It's relationship selling. So if I want my products introduced to a person in the best fashion, I want it done by someone who uses those products, knows the products, and will follow up to guarantee success by the customer. That's why direct sales. You put all of that together, then you add to that a corporate culture of helping people. That's our whole goal here, to help people achieve what they want in life. We try to instill our value system as the principle by which we work, but each person brings their own value system as well.

Ultimately what we want to do is to strengthen the family. We want to provide opportunity for people to become debt free. We have a program within AdvoCare called Debt Busters. We use scriptural principles to help people become debt free. It's amazing how little money it takes to live once you owe no man anything but the loving. That's been a big thing for us.

What other principles are basic to AdvoCare?

We believe firmly in leadership. We've taken the leadership teachings of John Maxwell, whom we dearly love—we're big supporters. John is the author of *The Twenty-one Irrefutable*

273

Laws. He is a fabulous guy, and he has basically taken leadership as his cause. He's a pastor who has gone into the secular world. His leadership books have been instrumental in helping our company develop the thought of leadership within our distributor force. So we're also helping people become leaders. What we believe is this: Once we equip them with the opportunity to get a handle on their better health and their better wealth, if we can teach them to be leaders, they can be leaders within their church or their school or their community. They become people of influence. So the Christian businessman has an opportunity to get out there in his own community and tell others. Equipping the person to be a complete person is really what it's about.

That's one of the big attractions of AdvoCare. People get involved and they're used to these types of companies and the first thing they think about is a get-rich-quick scheme. It's not long before they learn that's not what we're about. The next thing they think, *Well, the products don't count*. They soon learn that's not it. Then they start looking a little deeper and say, "There's some substance here. And it's different than any company that's ever been in direct selling."

That's my goal.

Matthew K. Rose

President, CEO, and Director
Burlington Northern Santa Fe Corporation

I think Christians in the workplace often fall into the trap that says, "To really be a Christian, I have to leave the workplace and go to the mission field." And yet there is no better mission field than right here in American industry.

Matthew K. Rose

America moves on Burlington Northern Santa Fe's 33,500 track miles in twenty-eight states. Its nearly 40,000 employees ship chemicals, forest products, metals, minerals, consumer goods, and grains from coast to coast. And the man who makes Burlington Northern Santa Fe move is Matthew K. Rose. Rose, who majored in marketing and minored in logistics at the University of Missouri, is a natural for the railroad business. Despite his young age, he's been actively involved in the industry since 1981.

Rose joined Burlington Northern Santa Fe in 1993 and has moved on the corporate fast track to his current position where he now oversees one of the country's two hundred largest corporations.

Rose talks about his spiritual journey:

I grew up in a church all my life. But, as is so typical, when I went away to college, I kind of lost my faith. After I got married, however, I came back to know the Lord through Bible Study Fellowship. Bible Study Fellowship is a worldwide Bible study where you take a book of the Bible and study it for thirty-one weeks. I did it for eight years in my mid-twenties and through that became committed to Christ. My relationship with Christ really changed.

So you have been in touch with your faith throughout most of your working career?

At least the second half of my working career, I have. I've been working at my career for twenty years. The first five years of my career I was focused on nothing but promotion, success, and taking a very worldly view.

After I started really becoming in touch with Christ and my faith and turning everything over to him, my desire for promotions went way down. I had a real sense of contentment about nine years ago when we moved back to Fort Worth to work for the Burlington Northern. I came here with very much a sense of contentment that this is where God was calling me. I no longer had a personal need for promotion and things like that.

It's almost like a light switching on. When I finally got to that point, then all of a sudden my career took off. It really is so clear now. I started getting promoted every twelve to fourteen months. I was not looking for this at all.

About four years ago, the CEO of the railroad called me in his office and told me that I was going to be the next CEO of the company. At that time I was thirty-eight years old. I became president at the age of forty, CEO at the age of forty-one. From a chronological age standpoint, I am way ahead of my time and clearly the youngest CEO our company has ever had. It has been a unique opportunity.

That's one of those great mysteries of the Christian faith. To conquer death, you only have to die. To do well, you have to give up wanting to do well and give it over to the Lord.

I'm part of a Christian CEO forum, and Henry Blackaby is our sponsor. He always leads off with a devotional. About a year ago he was talking about Jabez's prayer, where he prays about "expanding your territory." At that time, I was still in an "I don't want my territory expanded any" mode. He convinced me that if this is God's calling, then this is what I need to do.

Are you saying that the prayer of Jabez implies that there are no cross-purposes between growing your company and a solid Christian walk?

When I didn't have a committed walk of faith, I used to think that there were two totally different lives. You had your life at work; you had your life at home and church. That was just so wrong! Through the study of the Word, I now believe that God has put me in this job.

I've really been touched by a couple of books. One of them is *Mission in the Marketplace* by Jeffrey Comment, the CEO of Helzberg Diamonds of Kansas City. It's a great book that really speaks to the fact that God has you in the workplace for a reason. You are to be the light in leadership, and that's exactly where God wants you. The other book was John Beckett's *Loving Monday*. It's another tremendous book about God calling us to the marketplace. It's amazing how God has touched my life by my being a Christian in the workplace today.

You are with a publicly held company. You're under very different constraints from someone who owns his own company.

We as a company have a company mission statement, we have a company vision statement, and we have company values. Our management team went to the Aspen Institute several years ago and developed these statements. If you look at the values that we as a company espouse, they are all what I would call Judeo-Christian values. The way we look at it, the way this country was formed and the covenants that the fathers of our country all agreed to, the way American industry is set up from a responsibility standpoint, the basis of all of these concepts are rooted in Judeo-Christian values.

277

I see it as an easy extension in terms of making sure that I have a beacon that, as long as I can understand what the Bible commands, I can apply those values to the corporation. I have never really had any conflict with that.

My public expression may be a little more inhibited, but I've found that even there people are yearning to see their leaders express their Christian faith.

Can you give us an example?

Late last summer, when I was going to be announced CEO of Burlington Northern Santa Fe, I was on a train trip with a number of reporters. They interviewed me and a lot of them were interested in my age or interested in this or that. But one of the reporters, who was from the local paper in Fort Worth, really honed in on my Christian faith and my beliefs.

Afterward, he wrote a business front-page article about that interview in the *Fort Worth Star Telegram*. His teaser line on Friday for the article on the following Monday read, "You'll find out what makes Matt Rose tick—and you'll be surprised."

I spent the whole weekend wondering what the reporter was going to say with, quite frankly, some apprehension. When Monday finally arrived and I read the article, the reporter was very appropriate in the way he wrote about my faith, and it glorified God. I got calls from literally all over the country from regular people, other business and civic leaders in the city, and pastors, all saying, "We appreciate your expressing your faith." It is just such a telling contrast to the world we live in. People don't generally do that. I did very little, yet people want to hear it. When I'm able to express my faith, I, hopefully, will always glorify God.

To whom are you accountable?

I have a couple of different accountability groups. First, I'm part of this Christian CEO forum. We get together once a month and we talk about what is going on in our lives. I also have accountability with several members of my church. A couple of them actually work within our company. They are people that I ask for pretty direct feedback. I want to make sure that they will tell me if they see or hear of me doing something that is not consistent.

And third, I've got a couple of people who are not in the business and who are not from the church but are just real solid Christian leaders in the U.S. I have developed mentoring relationships with some of them—I'm the mentee and they're the mentors. It's not unusual at all for them to call me during the middle of the day, and we'll pray about something that's going on in our businesses. If they see something in the newspaper that looks like a difficult situation, they'll write me a note of encouragement or prayer.

That's my accountability base from a couple of different angles. But at the end of the day, it's going to come back to the Scriptures. And as long as I'm reading the Scriptures, that's the best accountability I can have. It's hard to read the Bible on a consistent basis and not be consistent with your faith.

Have there been particular verses or a passage that has been meaningful to you?

First, the book about Jabez's prayer and expanding your territories has been really interesting. There is an awful lot in the Book of Exodus that I go back to as well. In Exodus 18, it talks about leadership and to rely on God. The Bible is filled with illustrations of Jesus setting the example. I've really enjoyed a couple of books on that topic, including *Jesus, CEO* [by Laurie Beth Jones], books that illustrate leadership qualities that are based on Jesus Christ.

What are the qualities that you would hope that a Christian businessman would exhibit?

Initially, you have the "moral fabric" issues that are probably in every company's vision or value statements. But at the end of the day, it's all about how you treat people. It's all about doing unto others as you would want them to do unto you. It's

279

also all about understanding that while we're all here on earth for a certain period of time and we have these things we call jobs and careers that we spend a lot of time on, this is *not* eternity. I look at the workplace as a place that God has called me to be right now. The place that I have to, through leadership, make sure that I am reaching out to people, trying to understand what is going on in people's lives.

What I always pray at the end of the day is that, hopefully, through my actions, people will look at my daily walk, and, if they're not believers, that they will question themselves and ask, *What is it that makes Matt Rose tick?* That might be a seed that's planted. That's not how you bring people salvation, but maybe that's a seed that spurs them to something else. That's the leadership of always trying to be consistent in the way you treat people and how people look at you doing a business deal. They see whether or not you apply integrity and values.

Do you think your vendors and suppliers and your forty thousand-plus employees know that you are a Christian?

I know a lot of them do because I get a lot of calls from employees. I get a lot of calls from suppliers and customers. And I know a lot of them don't know. We have a big territory, but I want people to know that. You do have a responsibility to not be overly pushy, and I don't want people to know that I'm a Christian and feel they *have* to adopt that. I want people to see in my actions that there is something in my life that leads me. Seeing that will be the seed. Then they've got to figure it out themselves. I do know a lot of people that I work with and deal with regularly know that I am a committed believer and, quite frankly, that creates a lot of the self-accountability.

You mean you are held to a higher level of accountability and scrutiny by people because you've made your Christian faith known?

Without a doubt, I think we are held to a higher standard, and we should be. I'm fine with that. I think, again, that's self-accountability. And quite frankly, the more people that know what my beliefs are, the more accountability there is. I just think that is the nature of the job. I'm in a very public job with the railroad.

There is tremendous opportunity here, whether I have an interview in the paper and I want to talk about my faith or when I want to be a part of the National Day of Prayer in the local community. Someone called me the other day and said, "We'd like to have a big deal at the National Day of Prayer out in the front courtyard. Do you have a problem with it?"

I said, "Not at all. I'd be there if I wasn't out of town." That's a blessing. And we have Bible studies within the building. If another faith wanted to use our building to study their faith, I'd allow that too. God puts us in jobs so that we have these opportunities.

Somebody comes to you and says they're thinking about business as a career. What advice would you as a Christian businessman have for them?

You have to understand that you don't separate your faith and your business career. I made a mistake for a long time doing that. Early on they will have to look at people and mentors and they will have to establish what values they aspire to in business. And at the end of the day, if they will just apply the values and the commandments in the Bible and stick to them, they'll be fine in business. There will always be tests along the line. But I think that the biggest confusion people have is when they think, *This is business; this isn't about my faith.* And that's just wrong.

As CEO, president, and director of Burlington Northern, do they still let you play with the engines?

Yes, every once in a while.

Is it still fun?

It really is. Last week, I took my management team of about 130 people and their spouses on a steam engine we had in town.

We hooked the steam engine to a bunch of passenger cars, took off for the afternoon, and spent about five hours on the railroad. We went through rural America. Everywhere we went, people came by and took pictures. And it's there that we really see what our railroad does, how it impacts people's lives, whether it is in the goods we transport, including the coal that heats and cools people's houses and the grain that gets to the market. When you get outside of the big cities and you get to see it firsthand again, now *that's* a lot of fun.

Horst H. Schulze

Vice Chairman
Ritz-Carlton Hotel Company, L.L.C.

God is watching everything you do. So do the right thing. Do exceptional things. Don't sit on the couch. Create and be active, whether it is in business or with your family or even in sports.

Horst H. Schulze

Horst H. Schulze knows hotels. Since arriving from Europe (where he worked in world-class hotels in Switzerland, France, England, and his native Germany), Schulze's name has become synonymous with excellence in the industry.

After various positions in the Hyatt Hotels chain, Schulze joined The Ritz-Carlton Company in 1983 as vice president for operations. In 1987 Schulze was appointed executive vice president and was later promoted to president and chief operating officer in February 1988. In this capacity Schulze was responsible for the two-billion-dollar Ritz-Carlton operations worldwide. In February 2001 Schulze was named vice chairman of the company.

During his watch, the Ritz-Carlton Hotel Company was awarded two Malcolm Baldrige National Quality Awards (1992 and 1999) for his efforts in melding old-world beauty and charm with contemporary efficiency. *Hotels* magazine recently named Schulze "Corporate Hotelier of the World," and he has received the prestigious Ishikawa medal for his personal contributions to the quality movement.

The man with the lilting accent, who began his career as a waiter-apprentice in Germany at age fourteen, has also forged a second career for himself as a motivational speaker. Schulze speaks mov-

ingly on a number of topics dear to his heart, including strategic planning, leadership, quality management, service management, and customer satisfaction. And undergirding it all is his Christian faith.

I'm Lutheran and so I went to a confirmation Bible class as
a kid. The tradition is that when you finish with your confirmation class, the pastor—who has been with you for two or
three years of Bible class—gives you a guiding word from the
Bible. Mine is from Psalm 9:14 [NASB]—"He will cover you with
His pinons, and under His wings you may seek refuge. His faith-
fulness is a shield and bulwark." That was given to me and it
was a presence in my mind and subconscious mind—I was
never without it. I used it when I was experiencing difficulties.
The belief was there, however superficial. It was based on the
institutional belief system. But Christ was not in me. There was
an amount of belief, but Christ was not in me.

Was there a time that Christ became more real to you?

Yes. When I married for the second time, my wife, Sheri, and
I moved in 1981 to Chicago. Sheri said, "It's time that we look
for a church." I was not a denominational person, even though
I'm still a Lutheran. I'm not denominationally oriented, so I
don't have to go to a Lutheran church or anything like that. So
we searched for a church. We went from church to church. And
frankly I was unhappier in each one.

In '83 I accepted a new job to form the Ritz-Carlton Hotel
Company—though we didn't have that name at the time. It was
my dream to create something special, so I accepted the job in
Atlanta. Since my wife was pregnant, I was here alone at first.
Sheri said, "Since you are there by yourself, why don't you take
the time and find a church that pleases you, since you are the
one who always complains about it?"

So I visited a number of churches. One day I walked into a
church and I felt that there was a presence I'd never felt before.
I called Sheri and said, "I tell you what. I actually was happy in
a church today. It was a big church, but I forgot the name of it."

She said, "What denomination was it?"

I said, "Gee, I don't know. It's close to my apartment, so I just walked in. It's some guy by the name of Stanley or something like that."

She said, "Charles Stanley?"

I said, "Yes! How did you know?"

"Well, he *is* pretty well-known."

In June Sheri moved to Atlanta and we went to Dr. Stanley's church. We wanted to join, but we learned that we would have to get baptized. I didn't want to do it because, after all, I'm already baptized in the Lutheran church. But soon we became very active and met a young pastor with whom we became friends. At the time, I was still traditional and stubborn and heavily learned in my institutional Christianity. And I thought, perhaps a little bit, that the Baptists were a cult. I was scared of it, and the whole born-again thing, I had heard, was something really terrible. "Born agains" must be really crazy people who run around and jump on tables or whatever they do.

Fortunately this young pastor slowly, patiently explained what it means. I was not reachable by just saying, "Hey, this is just relying on Christ." I was not reachable because I was scared. I was suspicious—super-suspicious—of anything else because of my background. When I finally understood, it was so easy and I accepted Christ. That was late 1983. I joined a Bible class that meets every Friday.

Could you tell a difference in your management style from before 1983 and after 1983? Did it make a difference in how you did business?

Yes. But in my case it was truly a slow walk. It was not that Christ walked into my life and I was a different person the next day. Before, I had never really started to question and ask Jesus what he thought was right: "Is this the right direction?" And suddenly, all the values that I had now had different and multiple meanings. In everything I started to question myself, *Is this of value to us? And is this serving Christ?*

For example, before, when something pertained to Ritz-Carlton, I would have said, "Does it make money?" I still ask that question because I'm in business. But now, in addition, I always say, "Is it honorable? Does this have value?"

Christian values became a part of my decision-making process. For example, at that time the in-room movie business was becoming more and more dominant in hotels. I didn't accept X-rated movies in my hotel, even though I was pressured and told by many owners, "Wait a minute. This makes much more money." Even though there is big money in X-rated movies, I don't care. We're not in the porno business. We're in the hotel business. I took all dirty magazines, all nudie magazines, even *Playboy*, out of the gift shops.

That came from asking, *What business am I in?* And the answer was, *You're in the hotel business.* So I combined the business decisions with good morals.

What it gave me in turn was that suddenly I had the business of great organizations that look at and respect those kinds of things in a positive way. So, it gave me *more* business.

Ever since I was a little kid, I learned that I'm in the service business, but not a servant. We, in the business, are not servants. We are ladies and gentlemen offering fine professional service. But after my conversion, it became much, much deeper to me. And I said, *As a Christian, I also have to look at it as serving my employees.* Now I treat them with new respect and, accordingly, involve them in all the decisions and values of the organization. My decisions have become more weighted, more questioning. I ask, *Where is God in this? Where is God in what I'm doing here?* And, of course, I don't undertake anything without carefully saying, *Is this of value for* all *concerned? But, first of all, is the value also what God would accept?* I don't make decisions without praying on it and questioning myself.

Could you talk a little bit more about how your faith has had an impact on your dealings with your employees?

As I said, let's take this matter of ladies and gentlemen. Before, I always said, "I expect you to behave like ladies and gentlemen. If you do it well, then you *are* ladies and gentlemen." But it went from there to saying to my managers, "We have made a promise here to our employees and management at the same time. We have made a promise that they will be treated like ladies and gentlemen, that they will be respected as valuable human beings. That's part of the organization. They are not here to fulfill functions only, but they are ladies and gentlemen and they are part of the company." We created a whole system of informing them, of making them part of the organization, of telling them the values of the organization, of respecting and caring for them. We've tried to create a promise to the customers that they are a respected part of the organization, and to the employees as well.

In the meantime, the Ritz-Carlton organization became worldwide. I certainly couldn't mandate Christian values, but I could let them know that I am a Christian, that my values come from a Christian viewpoint. I didn't say that my values are Christian—that would not be possible in the Middle East and in Asia—but I let them know that I am a Christian and consequently the values exhibited came from a Christian viewpoint and these are the values of the organization.

How does your faith enter into other areas of your life?

Something happened to change the course of my life. In 1994 it was discovered that I had cancer. I was told that it was a very, very serious cancer. I had an operation the next day. Initially chemo was recommended, but I did not heed this advice. After several similar and unassociated incidents directed by God, it became clear to me that I should go on a certain diet, which I did. With God's love and this diet that was put before me, I came out of the cancer. It became so ultimately clear to me that I have always been driven by specific goals and accomplishments. I also recognized in my own ego that, all of a sudden, I'm not in charge. It also became clear that I needed God—just as anybody else would recognize this fact.

And then I was able to go back to my employees afterward. I had received five thousand cards and letters from them. I went back before them and said, "During a moment like that, you see that you need three things. You need your family, you need friends, and very definitely you need God. I share this with you," I told them, "to give you something. Not at all to overpower you—as the president of the company, I have no right to do that—but I think I have an obligation to share with you what I know is very important because everybody will face a moment in life where they need those things." So I was able to share this and have been able to share many times since.

You once quoted a sign you'd seen in a friend's office that said, "God is watching. Give him a good job." What does that mean to you?

That means that you, in every moment, in whatever you do, you have to be conscious that you are in the presence of the ultimate Creator of everything. The most important person in the world is sitting in the stands watching exactly what you do. God is watching everything you do. So do the right thing. Do exceptional things. Don't sit on the couch. Create and be active, whether it is in business or with your family or even in your sports. Do this, then turn around and look at this statement and ask, "Are you pleased?"

Mind you, I don't want to be deep here. That is a dangerous thing. He is not looking for the deed; he is looking for my faith. I'm very aware of him, but nevertheless, once you have that faith and know that he is there, you should do things that please him.

It seems that at the Ritz-Carlton, you've created the pursuit of excellence as if it is a ministry in itself.

With this philosophy—give them a good show—you don't go to work to fulfill functions. You go to work to create excellence. I think we have that obligation in life, and in whatever it may be that we are doing. If I'm a dishwasher, I don't think I should go to work to wash dishes. I believe I should go to create excellence in that particular area. And if I'm in that particular area creating excellence with Christian values and God in mind, then God clearly would be pleased just as much as if I'm the CEO of the largest company in the world and creating excellence there. For him, there is no difference.

So for me, the reason for going to work is the reason to create excellence. You create excellence because of your relationship with the Creator and all those that have entrusted money to you (i.e., investors). In the parable of the talents, God wasn't pleased with the one that buried the money. He was pleased with the one that exhibited excellence in creating profit. Excellence in creating money for those that have entrusted money to me, the investors; excellence for the employees; excellence for the customers; and excellence for the community—that's my purpose of going to work.

I want to create the ability and work environment for all employees to have a purpose and value when going to work.

I know you have begun a new venture. What is that?

I am not active with the Ritz-Carlton Hotel Company any longer. Currently I am in the process of creating a new company. I have been talking with people that may join me in this endeavor, even though I don't know exactly what I'm going to do, mind you. But I told them, "If you join me, if my direction is where I think it goes, I will give you ownership in my company. I will give you a good salary. But I am insisting from the beginning that, from the ownership returns, I will take 10 percent out, as I want to be an organization, a company, that tithes. As an individual with a salary, I will tithe. And as a company, I am going to tithe. I have shared that with anyone who joins me. If they get money out of ownership proceeds, meaning profit distribution, I will keep 10 percent and sit down with them and decide where it goes. I have formed this company with my personal goal to make a major contribution to—and maybe even eventually create—my own service management school, where in order to join the school, the first course of the curriculum is Christian values.

I think it is values that are missing. Values are still known, but they are not lived anymore. We have explained away so many of these values. Now we say, "It's okay to do certain things." Values have not disappeared. If you do things wrong, that's a sin. Values have gone down if we believe that doing wrong is okay.

What has the response been as you've approached people with this concept?

It was fully accepted. But obviously the first people that I talked to were friends of mine with similar values.

As a Christian, what advice would you have for a young person going into the business world now?

My strongest advice is that you do not look at work as work. Know that in some fashion, you have been directed there to be creative. Consequently your work is creating. Believe that you clearly know you have been directed, you have come to do this work through some guidance, through some involvement with God. So, if you can allow your mind to say, *I'm here. Direct me,* then you will automatically, I believe, create excellence, not just work. If you look at it as work, I believe that you are probably being told that you are in the wrong place. Work has to be done to create excellence. If the assignment is only work and a paycheck, then excellence cannot be achieved.

With every hotel I opened, I did the initial training in the hotels around the world. At first, when I did the orientation, I told our new employees who we were as a company. On the second day, I sat down with a group from each different department and I asked, "What do you want to do? What do you want to accomplish here?" If they said, "excellence," I'd write on a flip chart "excellence." And I said finally, "This is the reason why you go to work."

One day somebody behind me said, "I'm going to work to make money." I turned around and said to him, "You answer me: Who makes more money—the one that accomplishes excellence or the one that just works?" The answer is simple. And it's never excellence unless there are sincere values involved in it. So go out and understand your values and create excellence.

That's what I can recommend.

J. O. Stewart Jr.

Founder, El Paso Disposal
Owner, President, and CEO,
Stewart Holdings

Entrepreneurs are unusual people. They generally have some degree of vision, little fear, a limited grasp of the facts, great energy, great imagination, and limited accounting and management skills. More often than not, they fail, not from a lack of business success but from too much success. They outrun either their financial capacity or their own organizational, managerial, and administrative ability.

I am an entrepreneur. Most of the above applied to me. Fortunately the Lord provided very talented people to teach, guide, and help me. Also, fortunately, I was able to get out of their way most of the time.

J. O. Stewart

It takes a visionary to see the future. But J. O. Stewart Jr. saw something few others saw and built one of the largest waste disposal companies in America. That's impressive enough. But what is of even more lasting value is how J. O.—along with lifelong partner, Marlene— managed to maintain an active Christian presence in one of the most rough and tumble industries in the world.

The Stewarts began as a husband and wife musical team, working with a Billy Graham–type organization for young people. They attended graduate school together at the University of Southern California and tried to make a living singing about the Lord. In 1969 the young couple, with their one-year-old son, James, in tow, moved to El Paso.

"I realized I was never going to make any money in the music business, so we packed up our meager possessions, gave our old car away, and came home to El Paso," Stewart recalled.

The young couple started El Paso Disposal in May of 1970 with a rented garbage truck, five thousand dollars, some steel to make garbage containers, and a tiny office. "I was really ignorant of what it took to start a business," Stewart now admits, "so I didn't know it couldn't be done that way. We just did it." Within a few months, the growing garbage business demanded all their time.

Eventually El Paso Disposal had 350 employees and reached from Texas to New Mexico to southern Colorado and into Mexico.

Despite the demands on their time, the Stewarts have remained extraordinarily active in their community and church. And, with the recent sale of El Paso Disposal and related companies, they have been able to fulfill a lifelong dream of establishing Stewart Holdings, a private foundation and investment company committed to enacting Christian principles in a tangible way.

Stewart Holdings's mandate reads this way: "It is our purpose to invest these funds in the work of the Kingdom of God. To that end, we are seeking godly counsel from qualified experts who are believers in critical, life-changing Christian ministries worldwide."

There are periodic events in our personal and/or business life that are difficult to explain in strictly human or rational-mind parameters. For those of us who are followers of Jesus Christ as Savior and Lord, there is the distinct possibility/probability that these events often reflect the supernatural intervention by the Lord. Certainly there are such events that we don't recognize as such and thus fail to give thanks and recognition to our heavenly Father. And then there are events we would clarify as "negative occurrences" that are, in fact, part of God's plan in our lives to accomplish his will and purposes in us. We generally don't recognize these negative events as from God nor do we give thanks "in all things."

Certain major events dramatically impacted the direction of our business activity beyond any rational-mind explanation. These were miraculous divine interventions and provisions.

The following six defining events are special occurrences that we feel were ordered of the Lord in allowing us to continue owning, operating, and growing the company. We believe that Jesus is Lord of all our affairs to the degree we allow him to be.

First, in 1972 after our first year of operation, the opportunity for growth was significantly exceeding the financial capabilities of the company. I had no personal assets or funds. The original partners had exceeded their ability as guarantors due to the first twelve months of growth and resultant borrowing. My family, who had money, was sure I was too big for my pants.

A very wealthy older businessman, Dale Resler of El Paso, volunteered, without solicitation, to loan the company up to five hundred thousand dollars until such time as the company was bankable. No personal guarantees, pledging of stock, or control was required—only my personal commitment to tell Mr. Resler everything I planned to do and not to spend any money on assets he did not approve.

Mr. Resler was a sophisticated businessman, longtime bank board member and prominent El Paso citizen. Without his help, we would have lost control of the company. *The Lord provided even before we asked.*

Second, in 1975 we were growing fast. We were hungry. As a result, we made our competitor mad, real mad. He made a deal with the richest man in El Paso. They would start a third company and put the squeeze on this new upstart—me. They knew I didn't have much money. They did it. I was in trouble. I began to pray.

Driving my Volkswagen home one afternoon, I was praying out loud, urgently asking the Lord to help. As I prayed, the words "Isaiah 7" came into my mind. I ignored that random thought and kept praying. A second time, "Isaiah 7," a third time "Isaiah 7." Finally, I said, "Thank you, Lord, for Isaiah 7." When I got home, I asked my wife to read Isaiah 7. She asked me why. "I don't know. It seemed to be an answer to my prayer today." Indeed it was. Isaiah 7, verses 1 through 9, was God's answer. Two years later, the new company closed up and we bought our *mad* competitor at a bargain price. *I stood in faith, and God gave us the victory.*

293

Third, in the trash business, the key to profits and protection from competitors is owning your own landfill. It's like owning your own bank. In 1987 a very large multibillion-dollar international garbage company—I'll call them "Big Garbage"—was gobbling up everyone. You either sold to them at their dictated price *or else*. The deepest pocket wins. I wouldn't sell; therefore, they moved into El Paso.

For the previous seven years, I had tried to buy 160 acres of desert land west of El Paso. There was a small community dump on the property. It was a great location for a major landfill. Every year, I would walk around the property claiming it in the name of Jesus. The owners wouldn't sell it to me. Now I *had* to have it!

A Christian friend named Clinton Wolf told me one day that he could buy it for me. He did so.

One month after Big Garbage came to town, I opened the landfill. Overnight, we converted a 750,000-dollar-per-year expense—our fees paid to the city landfills—into a 750,000-dollar-per-year income center, most of which was profit. *God's supply system was just in time.*

Fourth, in 1989 it was really getting tough. Big Garbage was eating our lunch. In just eight months, our profits moved from 50,000-dollars-per-month positive to 50,000-dollars-per-month negative. Even with the landfill, we couldn't survive long.

On August 1 we got a telephone call from the Texaco Refinery in El Paso. "Could we accept refinery petroleum sludge?" Texas wouldn't allow the El Paso city landfill to accept such sludge. But our landfill was right over the state line in New Mexico. New Mexico said we could accept the material. But how much sludge was there? Would it bail us out?

In the ensuing three months, the refinery sent us 750,000 dollars worth of material and they paid immediately. Our cost of handling was less than 10 percent of gross. It happened again. We learned once again that God was our source, our banker, our provider.

Fifth, in 1989, when I needed him most, God sent me the greatest street warrior of all time, Oscar O'Bryant. Oscar was tall, outgoing, cheerful, entertaining, warm, congenial, and friendly. He was sixty-seven years old. He had the energy of a thirty year old. And underneath the sweet surface was a tough, street-smart fighting machine.

He had worked for the M & M Company marketing candies. He was the best. He went to work for Big Garbage in the early 1980s. He knew all their tricks. But Oscar always walked on the edge. He pushed the envelope to the max. Because of his age, Big Garbage let him go.

And you picked him up?

Well, I needed help. Big Garbage was still after me. The battle was in the streets—going company to company, store to store, to secure contracts to haul the trash. It was a fight—bribes, threats, immoral acts, manipulation. It was corporate America at its worst. I didn't know how to fight on their level.

I called Oscar. "Can you help me? Can you come? Now?"

His answer was yes, and he came. He took our eight outside sales reps and began to teach them, train them, help them, threaten them, lead them in the streets of El Paso to fight to save our company. We met at 6:30 A.M. each morning for one hour of sales training—how to sell, how to save an account, how to take an account back. Then at 8 A.M., he led us all out into the streets of El Paso. If someone had a tough customer, they'd call Oscar and he would meet them at the customer's office. He took the hardest cases himself. He worked twelve to fourteen hours per day, six days a week.

Did this work? How did it sit with your employees?

We hated him; we loved him; he was great; he was unbearable; he was honest; he was a crook; he was a warrior. Not one of our people quit. They became warriors.

One year later, Oscar came into my office. It was 2 P.M. on a Thursday. Big Garbage had given up. We had not only survived, we had won! Our whole industry nationwide knew it. Oscar's big shoulders shook as we wept together like children. We were spent. We were physically and emotionally exhausted. God provided a champion. He was our Samson. His hair was still long. His strength remained. We both gave thanks to God.

And sixth, in 1996 a new challenge arose. He was a billionaire named Wayne Huizenga. He started Waste Management and made a fortune. He bought Blockbuster Video, built it, and sold it several years later for a multibillion-dollar profit. He was Wall Street's darling.

Now he was starting a new garbage company, Republic Industries. He went public. He was buying garbage companies fast at very high multiples, paying one hundred million dollars for companies that six months before were only valued at fifty million dollars.

Were you tempted to sell?

We were in Las Vegas for the 1996 annual garbage convention. It's a big deal in our industry—twenty thousand people, all members, all major and minor companies. It was a feeding frenzy. Republic Industries' stock was hot.

We were at dinner at Caesar's Palace. We were the guests of five major garbage company owner/operators and their wives who had all sold their companies in the previous four months. They were ecstatic, crazy with excitement. All had new airplanes, new diamonds, new everything. They had each sold their sixty-million-dollar companies for one hundred and twenty million dollars of Republic stock and in four months the stock had increased in value by 50 percent. Man, what a celebration!

What was I to do? My partners said sell; my advisors said sell; my bankers were friendlier than hungry dogs. I took immediate action. I left Las Vegas and went home. I needed space. I needed to pray. I needed godly wisdom.

And you received that wisdom?

Four nights after I'd gotten back, I had a dream early one morning. Now I've never had a dream that I thought had a spiritual implication, so this was new to me. In the dream, I was walking down a hallway and Marlene was walking behind me, but quite a ways behind me. And I walked into this room where a very voluptuous woman made herself available. I looked back for Marlene, and Marlene had turned into another room. I looked back to the woman and, suddenly, the dream was over.

Then immediately I had the interpretation of the dream. This is not a thing I had time to think about. I was just barely waking up. Immediately the thought came that the woman represented the lust for money, while Marlene represented the will of God. It didn't tell me *not* to sell the business. It told me not to lust for money in seeking the decision. I took this definitely as a sign from the Lord that I was to seek counsel and God's wisdom in what I should do.

Over several months, I made the decision not to sell. That decision went against my immediate advisors and my partner, who was absolutely going crazy to sell. But in the days that followed, Republic Industries' stock fell by two-thirds. And everybody who had sold out, except maybe a couple of the very first buyers, had taken the stock. When the time came later to sell my company, I ended up selling it for 20 percent more and got the full dollar.

So you made the right decision.

Ultimately I think the issue was that I could have done that and still have lost the money. I don't conclude that just doing well financially indicated I did the right thing. Intellectually, I don't think that's necessarily correct. But I did do what I felt like I was supposed to do, counter to a lot of circumstantial evidence.

How does a Christian maintain a Christian presence in a company that's got to be run like any other company? Employees may still steal; employees may still have to be fired; competitors may still do illegal things against you.

I think that employees *are* going to steal. Employees *are* going to do things they should not do. Therefore, you need to create as effective a security system as possible, without it becoming a prison, to make it very difficult. That just comes with good accounting methods, good inventory methods, good responsible reporting methods, and good supervisors. If you expect all employees to be honest, all employees are not going to be honest. If you give them the opportunity to steal, some are going to do it and you're going to have to fire them. And you're going to lose good people.

That reflects a lot of us. A lot of us will stumble and make serious mistakes if given the opportunity. That's how I approach that. I did my very best to give employees an opportunity to succeed, do well, and be highly accountable.

El Paso Disposal is not a Christian company. There are people in the company who are Christians, but you never advertised yourselves as a religious organization.

We thought that would be an improper thing to do. We worked aggressively to hire leadership and executive leadership who were believers. We were not looking for Methodist, Baptist, Pentecostal, charismatic. Instead, we were looking for those who were Christians, whether they were Catholic or Methodist or Presbyterian or Pentecostal, who had a concept of the lordship of Christ and an ability to work within this context.

Did you have corporate guidelines or a mission statement to reinforce that concept?

It was strictly by example and association, even more than verbal. We did, on occasion, with our executives have times that we would pray. But we were careful not to spiritualize everything. We would try to operate within good business principles.

Another thing, about ten years ago, I was complaining to a very, very successful executive friend of mine, who was not a Christian, about the work and all the work I was having. He really got a little impatient and said, "J. O., why don't you go hire the very best people that you can find, people that are smarter than you are, and let them do what they do well? And then quit complaining."

I did. I brought aboard the very best people I could find. They were far stronger than I was and I gave them responsibility and authority. The results were outstanding.

Now, how do we run a company on Christian principles? First of all, marketing your products is a matter of finding the very best product available, or creating the very best service, and taking it to people and getting them to buy from you. It's not trying to create a product and deceive anybody. That's a misunderstanding of marketing. You want to sell people what they really need and you want to bring the best possible product and you want to ask them to buy it from you.

Number two, in negotiations with competitors or the people who are buying your products—your customers—you want a situation where everybody wins. Our philosophy toward our customers was this: If the customer wins, we can never lose. So we did our best to make sure the customer won. In dealing with our competitors or dealing with our vendors or dealing with the people that wanted to buy our service, we wanted them to be treated properly and do well. You *can* do that and stay within a Christian context. We did avoid payoffs and money under the table, because that is poor business and it always comes back to bite you. We got somewhat involved in politics as well, but it was always aboveboard. We would give services and give money to those we supported, but it was always above the table and it was always a matter of record. And we never were embarrassed by doing so.

Tell us about Stewart Holdings.

We're involved with investments through investment advisors and we're involved in real estate investments that have developed all the way from Florida to Idaho to Arizona. They're fascinating and interesting projects that have taken time to come about, but they are all very interesting projects.

But the most interesting project we're doing is a project to develop affordable housing in Central and South America and in the Dominican Republic. We're looking at a project that involves ten to twenty thousand homes in the Dominican Republic and also developing homes in Mexico. We've also had contacts from Paraguay and Belize and other Central American countries, but we're not ready for that yet.

The concept is to build communities of one thousand to twelve hundred homes with a town square, a cultural center, day care for children, schools, and some commercial space. Building a community does not create community. Therefore, we are developing a training program to equip the residents to become a functioning community. There is a great deal of research going to develop this model. It's not necessarily a Christian structure as much as a biblical structure.

Stewart Holdings is a straightforwardly Christian project. Is that by design?

Yes, absolutely. There are three elements of Stewart Holdings—the J. O. and Marlene Stewart Foundation, the charitable remainder trust, and the investment company. It's our intent to give it *all* away over time. We want to give away all the earnings, except those earnings that support the team and support Marlene and myself. We created a smaller foundation with a larger investment company because we felt like we had greater liberty with the investment company to create an enhancement of the corpus that would allow us to give more money away in the future.

In our first year, we gave away only five hundred thousand dollars. I told the staff last week that we had to do better than that. Now this year, let's challenge ourselves to give away one million dollars and seek to double that each of the next two years.

As a Christian who is a businessman, what advice do you have for that young person who's thinking of going into business?

First of all, you surround yourself with qualified people that have strength where you have weakness. And they ought to be people of like mind and like concept.

Second, you need to have a vision and dream for the future, and you need to understand the difference between vision and dreams and reality. Sometimes you can see a vision and a dream, but you have to measure that by an aspect of reality and know the difference between the two in trying to bring something to fulfillment.

Third, do that work that is meaningful and fulfilling to you. Take advice, but in the end, listen to that inner voice and commit yourself to your dream.

Finally, failure is not a disgrace or a tragedy. It's a learning experience and the foundation of a new beginning.

Resources

For more information on Christians in the marketplace, please contact:

Marketplace Ministries
12900 Preston Road, Suite 1215
Dallas, TX 75230-1328
972-385-7657
mmihq@marketplaceministries.com

Christian Business Men's Committee
4505 Fitch Avenue
Baltimore, MD 21236
410-661-5665
plantz@cbmc.com

Executive Books
206 West Allen Street
Mechanicsburg, PA 17055
717-766-9499
www.ExecutiveBooks.com
cetjones@aol.com

Robert Darden is the author of twenty books and worked as the gospel music editor for *Billboard* magazine for more than ten years. For the past fourteen years he has served as senior editor of the nationally distributed magazine *The Door*. A popular speaker for seminars, symposiums, and conferences, he is currently an assistant professor of English at Baylor University. His next project is a history of Black gospel music.

P. J. Richardson is the founder of Tanglewood Holdings Inc. and The Reeves Group, where he serves as chairman and CEO. A well-known and successful East Coast businessman, he collaborated with Robert Darden on two other books.